Sir Walter Scott: Landscape and Locality

Sir Walter Scott:
Landscape and Locality

JAMES REED

THE ATHLONE PRESS
LONDON

First published 1980 by The Athlone Press
at 90–91 Great Russell Street, London WC1B 3PY

The Athlone Press is an imprint of Bemrose UK Limited

Distributor in U.S.A. and Canada
Humanities Press Inc
New Jersey

British Library Cataloguing in Publication Data

Reed, James,
Sir Walter Scott: Landscape and Locality
1. Scott, *Sir* Walter, bart. –
Criticism and interpretation
2. Landscape in literature
828'.7'09   PR5343.L3

ISBN 0 485 11197 7

Printed in Great Britain by
Western Printing Services Ltd, Bristol

To the Memory of
M.E.T., H.A.B., F.F.C., R.E.J.

To abstract the mind from all local emotion would be impossible, if it were endeavoured, and would be foolish, if it were possible. Whatever withdraws us from the power of our senses; whatever makes the past, the distant, or the future predominate over the present, advances us in the dignity of thinking beings. Far from me and from my friends, be such frigid philosophy as may conduct us indifferent and unmoved over any ground which has been dignified by wisdom, bravery or virtue. That man is little to be envied, whose patriotism would not gain force upon the plain of *Marathon*, or whose piety would not grow warmer among the ruins of Iona!

Dr Johnson, A *Journey to the Western Islands*

The minds of men are formed by their habitations.

Scott, *Tales of a Grandfather*

Acknowledgements

Both friends and institutions have helped me generously, and often unwittingly, in the preparation of this book. I owe a special debt, however, to Alan Hindle whose capacity for total literary recall and whose roving bibliographical eye have been a constant stimulus to me.

I am also grateful to Mrs Mary Moorman who has kindly allowed me to use her lithograph of *Wordsworth and Scott at Newark Tower*, and to John MacLeod of MacLeod for permission to reproduce Allan Ramsay's portrait of *Norman, 22nd Chief of MacLeod*, from the Dunvegan Castle collection.

I wish also to thank the Trustees of the National Library of Scotland and the British Library Board for permission to reproduce photographs as follows (National Library of Scotland: Plates 2, 3, 4, 7; British Library: Plates 5, 6).

J.R.

Contents

Plates

Introduction

This book is an attempt to read Scott's poems and novels more fully by taking account of his literary exploitation of landscape and locality. It is not a Guide to the Scott Country, nor is it a work of topographical annotation. I do not believe my approach can be profitably made to all of Scott's works, not even in any illuminating sense to all of his Scottish novels, and I have excluded from detailed consideration all works in which I felt that environmental factors did not play a major part. My concern throughout is with the whole landscape: people, history, architecture, traditions, insofar as they enrich the tale being told. I have not concerned myself except incidentally with Scott's powers of description on those occasions when he is simply looking at the view, and this, I hope, will explain the scant attention I give to *Old Mortality*, arguably the finest of the Waverley Novels, as well as to *Rob Roy*, *The Fair Maid of Perth*, and the great *novellen The Two Drovers* and *The Highland Widow*.

For over a century, with varying emphasis, Scott's fame as a writer has grown from his distinction both as a historical novelist and as a man of wholesome morals. His reputation has, moreover, been distorted south of the Tweed by a general belief that though Scott was good for the young (Carlyle strongly approved of his 'general *healthiness* of mind') his Scottish dialogue was too difficult, and as a result generations of schoolchildren (some to this day nursing nostalgic, middle-aged resentments) have been morally fortified in English by the medieval heroics of *Ivanhoe*, *The Talisman*, or the Elizabethan romance of *Kenilworth*, and left in ignorance of *The Bride of Lammermoor*, *The Heart of Midlothian* and *Old Mortality*. 'One of the great religious teachers of Scottish Christendom', Dean Stanley called him,[1] and Walter Bagehot in a fine critique of The Waverley Novels in 1858, wrote,

> You can scarcely lay down any novel of his without a strong feeling that the world in which the fiction has been laid, and in which your imagination has been moving, is one subject to laws of retribution which, though not apparent on a superficial glance, are yet in steady and consistent operation, and will be quite sure to work their due effect, if time is only given to them.[2]

But other laws operate in Scott's work, too, and we see their effect in the formation of his characters. These 'laws' in a very loose sense, arise from the interaction of time (history), environment and locality; that is to say, they exert their forces in a total landscape, one which includes, as well as the view, an assemblage of men and women, animals, dwellings, language, and the temporal operations which brought them into being and subject them to change. Such a context makes one immediately aware of past and present, and, as Dr Johnson well perceived, of the active presence of the past.

Scottish writers have always been more responsive to the literary potential of their own tongue in a familiar locality than their English counterparts, an attitude expressed with some feeling by Allan Ramsay in his Preface to his collection of old songs, *The Ever Green* (1724):

> When these good old *Bards* wrote, we had not yet made Use of imported trimming upon our Cloaths, nor of foreign Embroidery in our Writings. Their *Poetry* is the Product of their own Country, not pilfered and spoiled in the transportation from abroad. Their *Images* are native, and their Landskips domestick; copied from those Fields and Meadows we every Day behold.
>
> The *Morning* rises (in the Poets Description) as she does in the *Scottish* horizon. We are not carried to *Greece* or *Italy* for a Shade, a Stream or a Breeze. The *Groves* rise in our own Valleys; the *Rivers* flow from our own Fountains, and the *Winds* blow upon our own Hills. I find not Fault with those Things, as they are in *Greece* or *Italy*: but with a *Northern Poet* for fetching his Materials from these Places, in a Poem, of which his own Country is the Scene, as our *Hymners* to the *Spring* and *Makers of Pastorals* frequently do.

To answer literary affectation with the claims of realistic local observation is a substantial movement in the direction of Robert Fergusson, Robert Burns and Walter Scott, and it is worth recalling that Ramsay's *Tea Table Miscellany* and *The Ever Green* exercised a very early influence on Scott,[3] who shared this view almost to excess, and found himself in an embarrassed dilemma. With all his heart, he loved the Scottish past, where he found a romantic feudalism by whose pattern he himself tried to live while eschewing the brutality, suffering and ignorance of the actuality. We hear Scott the feudal laird speaking in the voice of Lord Huntinglen, in *The Fortunes of Nigel* (1821):

> 'When you attain possession of your inheritance. . . . I trust you will not add one to the idle followers of the Court, but reside on your patrimonial estate, cherish your ancient tenants, relieve and assist your poor kinsmen, protect the poor against subaltern oppression, and

do what our fathers used to do, with fewer lights and with less means than we have.' (Ch. X)

On the other hand, he believed with all his mind that the turbulent, heroic history of an independent, noble, if primitive Scotland had been rendered obsolete when the flame of Jacobitism was quenched in the middle of the eighteenth century. The note is caught with some passion by Wordsworth in a relatively undistinguished collection of poems published a year before Scott's death:

> The pibroch's note, discountenanced or mute;
> The Roman kilt degraded to a toy
> Of quaint apparel for a half-spoilt boy;
> The target mouldering like ungathered fruit;
> The smoking steam-boat eager in pursuit,
> As eagerly pursued; the umbrella spread
> To weather-fend the Celtic herdsman's head—
> All speak of manners withering to the root,
> And of old honours, too, and passions high. . . [4]

With his realistic eye, Scott saw that the future of Scotland lay in strengthening the union with England, and that the Scot would have to learn to accommodate a twin loyalty, to become a supporter of the House of Hanover without at the same time betraying ideals which were inextricably bound up with the royal House of Stuart. It was an impossible necessity to which he submitted with a nostalgic dignity and sincerity, but not without fear; what he understood by the word 'democracy' and the trend of political events in the early nineteenth century threatened to erase all that he revered in what he saw as the Scottish national character, and in ordinary human relationships, as he expresses them through the mouth of Huntinglen. In his *Journal* for 14 March 1826, he records:

They are gradually destroying what remains of nationality and making the country *tabula rasa* for doctrines of bold innovation. Their loosening and grinding down all those peculiarities which distinguished us as Scotsmen will throw the country into a state in which it will be universally turned to democracy, and instead of canny Saunders they will have a very dangerous North British neighbourhood.

This attitude arose, I believe, from his conviction that a man becomes what he does become, not by the exercise of reason or reflection, or by any conscious choice of direction on his own part, but almost entirely by heredity and, in a very wide sense, by the influence of environment, a sense which includes language, profession, and domestic manners as well as containing landscape with its own, often emotionally interpreted, history.

Other uses of landscape in literature are more commonly recognisable. Edward Garnett, for example, writing of Joseph Conrad's use of location in *Nostromo* (1904) said:

> Mr Conrad has a special poetic sense for the *psychology of scene*, by which the human drama brought before us is seen in its just relation to the whole enveloping drama of Nature around, forming both the immediate environment and the distant background.[5]

This landscape, where the scene symbolises, or mirrors or echoes by its mood or appearance the human situation within it, is emphatically not Scott's approach. Nor does this comment of T. S. Eliot on Thomas Hardy represent a function of Scott's landscapes:

> In consequence of his self-absorption, he makes a great deal of landscape; for landscape is a passive creature which lends itself to an author's mood. Landscape is fitted too for the purposes of an author who is interested not at all in men's minds, but only in their emotions; and perhaps only in men as vehicles for emotions.[6]

Scott's defence against this is that his landscapes are almost always defined or qualified by the conditions of locality; that is, by the spirit of a particular place with its identifying associations. At his best, Scott uses a precise knowledge of both the topographical and historical significance of places, as I hope the following chapters will demonstrate. This approach to landscape was not entirely new, but Scott was the first to exploit its fictional possibilities, as R. L. Stevenson perceived:

> The character of a place is often not perfectly expressed in its associations. An event strikes root and grows into a legend, when it has happened among congenial surroundings. Ugly actions, above all in ugly places, have the true romantic quality, and become an undying property of their scene. To a man like Scott, the different appearances of nature seemed each to contain its own legend ready-made, which it was his to call forth; in such or such a place, only such or such events ought with propriety to happen; and in this spirit he made the *Lady of the Lake* for Ben Venue, the *Heart of Midlothian* for Edinburgh, and the *Pirate*, so indifferently written but so romantically conceived, for the desolate islands and roaring tideways of the North.[7]

No one, however, can write of Scott without an uneasy feeling of impudence; be like a little dog following a brass band, or like Rose

Flammock in *The Bethrothed* dragging forward her father, where we see, like the figures in an ancient monument, 'a small cherub, singularly inadequate to the task...hoisting upward towards the empyrean the fleshly bulk of some ponderous tenant of the tomb'. I am not able to assist Scott any further in that direction, but I hope that some of the ideas in this book may enable his readers to converse with relevance when they overtake him.

CHAPTER I

Scott: Landscape, Nature and Locality

From the beginning it was the *power* and not the appearance of locality and landscape that obsessed Scott. Nurtured in a region rich in tradition and legend, a country tragically endowed with battlefields (where else could one find tourist maps that mark *Massacres*?), whose terrain was an irresistible invitation to the historian and antiquary, Scott became, like Tennyson's Ulysses, a part of all that he met; to the end of his days he shared with the world his delight in these things, his communication touched always with illuminating perceptions and humane understanding. 'His local attachments', Dorothy Wordsworth wrote in 1805, 'are more strong than those of any person I ever saw.'[1] Virtually the originator of the historical novel, he was the first British novelist to see landscape as a literary medium as well as a pictorial one (though he did not invariably use it so); and his landscapes are real territories. Whatever fictional gloss may be applied, when he is writing of Scotland, and especially of his own Border region, Scott is recording, not inventing; his vision grows out of an objective world, a place of time and the senses. Before Scott, that is to say before 1805 when *The Lay of the Last Minstrel* appeared, landscape rarely appeared as an organic element in prose fiction. Smollett's *Humphry Clinker* (1771) is exceptional in both the extent and the fidelity of its topographical element, but the emphasis remains documentary rather than novelistic. Matthew Bramble, the central character in this epistolary work, records and comments faithfully, but stands apart. Locality, in the eighteenth-century novel, is largely unidentified or neutral; landscape little more than painted scenery, applied to the events from the outside and bearing no significant relationship to them. Between the allegorical territories of Bunyan and the precisely delineated localities of Scott, most of the action in novels is played out in a topographical vacuum, conventionally contained by Town and Country.

In poetry, on the other hand, nature and landscape have always been expressive of more than their mere appearance, their roles varied by the dictates of changing taste but operating before the time of Scott and Wordsworth broadly speaking in three ways. The classically derived pastorals of the sixteenth and seventeenth centuries present landscape as the idyllic habitat of unspoilt, natural man, seen in contrast to his cultivated and unhappy urban brother. During this period, too, the garden, a symbol of man controlling nature, has a twofold function: to some it means progress and enlightenment, to others, a defiling, a violation of innocence. It is a strain which virtually comes to an end in the work of Andrew Marvell:

> Luxurious Man, to bring his Vice in use,
> Did after him the World seduce;
> And from the fields the Flow'rs and Plants allure,
> Where Nature was most plain and pure.
> (*The Mower against Gardens*)

The subjugation of wild nature is seen here in terms of sexual corruption, echoing the loss of Eden.

In the eighteenth century, the balance shifted. Capability Brown tamed nature, and tired city dwellers sought escape in the safe tranquillity of a selectively contemplated (but not necessarily observed) landscape, whose features bore no more than a formal, stylised relation to the reality.

> O taste corrupt! that luxury and pomp,
> In specious names of polish'd manners veil'd,
> Should proudly banish Nature's simple charms!
> All-beauteous Nature! by thy boundless charms
> Oppress'd O where shall I begin thy praise,
> Where turn th'ecstatick eye, how ease my breast
> That pants with wild astonishment and love!

So writes Joseph Warton in *The Enthusiast: or the Lover of Nature*, in 1744, conveniently providing us a few lines later with an inventory of these simple and boundless charms: lowing ox, playful lamb, distant waterfall, pastoral reed, choral birds and neighing steed, which

> all, all conspire
> To raise, to soothe, to harmonise the mind.

The third function arose from nature's copious provision of material for moral analogues: 'Thus', wrote John Dyer in *Grongar Hill* (1726)

> Thus is Nature's Vesture wrought
> To instruct our wand'ring Thought,

an approach which F. N. C. Munday's *Needwood Forest* (1776) makes quite explicit:

B

Those thorns protect the forest's hopes;
That tree the slender ivy props;
Thus rise the mighty on the mean!
Thus on the strong the feeble lean!

Throughout the eighteenth century external nature, however moralised, remains firmly in the world outside; only later, and particularly in the writing of Wordsworth and Coleridge, is fact adequately translated into symbol, does object become image, so that the poet may be

well pleased to recognise
In nature and the language of the sense
The anchor of my purest thoughts, the nurse
The guide, the guardian of my heart, and soul
Of all my moral being.[2]

This is one of the more profitable developments of the eighteenth century preoccupation with Personification which so easily degenerated into a merely conventional rhetoric; but Scott chose a different starting point, and travelled a different route. He remained almost wholly untouched by either the moralising or the Wordsworthian views of nature, and neither his poetry nor his prose takes recognisable colour from such themes, though one does find occasional examples. In any discussion of this kind, it is essential to try to place Scott's approach to nature and landscape as closely as possible in its true literary-historical context; that is, in an emotional and intellectual climate of pre-Wordsworthian consciousness. His immediate predecessors as we have seen, had regarded man's natural environment as a state quite different from, and often antagonistic to, the environment which man had created for himself. Theirs was an urban view, cultivated by an urban literary élite for whom nature existed as a series of objects.

At the same time, curiously enough, literary antiquarians such as Bishop Percy were collecting material which was rich in landscape material, but seen as locality rather than as nature. In the Border Ballads, which so powerfully influenced Scott from his childhood onwards, we find recorded (though the eighteenth-century enthusiasts did not appreciate this fully) the sorrow, joy, humour and conflict of a remote and tenuously surviving society contained in a natural landscape which appears not as a source of philosophical reflection, nor as a quarry for moral analogues, nor as a spiritual power; more than a mere backdrop, Ballad landscape provides an organic context for action, both in its moulding of the characters who belong, and in the way it enables us to interpret their lives. 'The Twa Corbies' are a far cry from Warton's 'choral birds'.

For Wordsworth, nature and man are different but related components of one larger whole; components which interact physically, morally, and spiritually. In the long run, Wordsworth's view superseded that of his eighteenth-century forebears, but it might have been different if Scott's commitment to poetry had been stronger than his devotion to history and Scotland. What he does is see man, and the works of man, in a total landscape: land, buildings, people, manners, history, fused by time. Like the ballad makers, he uses his own idiom from the region he knows best, but the approach is transferable. Scott's man leaves in his wake ruined towers, decaying abbeys, flints, spearheads, broken helmets, bones; legacies of a feudal faith and a romantic chivalry. Every walk or ride with Scott was a History Trail imbued, like his writing, with the anecdotal, reminiscent richness of the experienced and informed observer. Only now is the Wordsworthian outlook losing some of its tyranny; only now are we beginning to return more frequently to see man in his landscape, rather than the landscape alone; now we may be inclined to renounce our next Highland, Alpine or Lakeland holiday for an exploration of our nineteenth-century industrial heritage in the wilder regions, say, of West Yorkshire, where woollen mills quietly decay in the valley bottoms, and where violent tales of coining and machine-breaking whisper to us from the old stone of Hebden Bridge and Heptonstall. The idioms of Scott, and those of, say Norman Nicholson, Ted Hughes, Edwin Morgan and R. S. Thomas are very different but they see and use landscape in a way that he would appreciate and Wordsworth would not.

In Scott's work nature is seldom an independent transcendental force; commonly, it forms part of a landscape which he sees primarily not as poet or philosopher but as countryman, predator, historian, soldier; and though he often presents landscape as beautiful or aweful, it is more frequently territory to be excavated, hunted or fought over, or in some way subdued. His literary exploitation of locality and landscape opened the way, however, indirectly followed, for Dickens's London, Emily Brontë's Haworth, Hardy's Wessex, Conrad's Eastern archipelagos, and the supremely topographical nuances of Joyce's Dublin.

But it is clear that Scott's interests and insights are much more than parochial or touristic; the dangers of seeing the environment of creative works in such a narrow way are well exemplified by an edition of *The Lady of the Lake*, published in 1904, with a topographical commentary by the then Astronomer Royal;[3] this almost entirely misses the point, since interpretation is obscured by the simple process of identifying, measuring and equating places and distances. Scott's concern in his best work is first of all with human beings, specific in time and place; as he sets them in a landscape conditioned by history and time, so are we increasingly able to understand them; when landscape and character are divorced, Scott becomes no more than a tourist, a painter of brilliant scenery, and whether one admires his skill in this, or scorns his turgidity, the matter makes little contribution to literary understanding. It was the *immediacy* of place which most affected Scott. Much has been written about his powers as a 'descriptive writer', but for him, the event, not the panorama, was what counted. 'His sense of the beauties of nature, and power of describing them, are carefully *kept down*', he wrote approvingly of Henry Mackenzie.[4] Scott's own response to the power of place is evident throughout his life: 'To me', he wrote of his early years, 'the wandering over the field of Bannockburn was the source of more exquisite pleasure than gazing upon the celebrated landscape from the battlements of Stirling Castle.'[5] Coleridge provides an interesting corollary:

> Dear Sir Walter Scott and myself were exact, but harmonious opposites in this;- that every old ruin, hill, river or tree called up in his mind a host of historical or biographical associations. . . .whereas, for myself, notwithstanding Dr. Johnson, I believe I should walk over the plain of Marathon without taking more interest in it than in any other plain of similar features.[6]

We shall do well, in reading Scott, to accept his own distinction between the celebrated 'prospect' and the peopled landscape even if, as in the case of Bannockburn, the people are ghosts. As he wrote in 1804:

> Tradition depends on locality. The scene of a celebrated battle, the ruins of an ancient tower, the 'historic stone' over the grave of a hero, the hill and the valley inhabited of old by a particular tribe, remind posterity of events which are sometimes recorded in their very names. Even a race of strangers, when the lapse of years has induced them no longer to account themselves such, welcome any fiction by which they can associate their ancestors with the scenes in which they themselves live, as transplanted trees push forth every fibre that may connect them with the soil to which they are transferred.[7]

To the end, place remained uppermost in his consciousness; Lockhart recalls Scott on his last journey to Abbotsford, torpid and dying: 'as we descended the vale of Gala, he began to gaze about him, and by degrees it was obvious that he was recognising the features of that familiar landscape. Presently he murmured a name or two—"Gala Water, surely—Buckholm—Torwoodlee!" '.[8]

Of course, one tends to think of Scott as a novelist, and therefore to see his eye for landscape in this context; but the truth is more extended:

he was 32 when his *Minstrelsy of the Scottish Border* was completed in 1803; by 1810 his reputation as a poet was secure after *The Lay of the Last Minstrel, Marmion,* and *The Lady of the Lake,* and though he had tentatively begun *Waverley* in 1805, he did not resume it for nearly a decade, and published it anonymously in 1814 at the age of 43. It is as a historian and traveller that his feeling for land and people first becomes apparent and explicit, in his long and meticulous Introduction to the *Minstrelsy;* here was the first channelling of that obsession of which he had spoken a dozen years before to his friend and fellow law student, William Clerk. From Langleeford, under Cheviot in Northumberland, where he spent his twentieth birthday in 1791, he wrote:

> To add to my satisfaction, we are amidst places renowned by feats of former days; each hill is crowned with a tower, or camp, or cairn, and in no such situation can you be near more fields of battle: Flodden, Otterburn, Chevy Chase, Ford Castle, Chillingham Castle, Copland Castle, and many other scenes of blood, are within the compass of a forenoon's ride.[9]

The following year he took his finals as advocate, committed at last to what he later described as 'the dry and barren wilderness of forms and conveyances',[10] and wrote again to Clerk from his uncle's house, Rosebank near Kelso, about another expedition into Northumberland:

> There are several lakes among the mountains above Hexham, well worth going many miles to see . . . They are surrounded by old towers and castles, in situations most savagely romantic; what would I have given to have been able to take effect-pieces from some of them! Upon the Tyne, about Hexham, the country has a different aspect presenting much of the beautiful, though less of the sublime.[11]

The vogue words 'beautiful' and 'sublime' call for brief comment here, since they indicate ways of looking at the environment, both current and influential in Scott's time, which have no small bearing on an understanding of his own methods. In 1756, Edmund Burke had published a lengthy treatise, *A Philosophical Inquiry into the Origin of Our Ideas of the Sublime and Beautiful,* one of many disquisitions of the period on Taste. The *Sublime,* he argues, is effected by whatever is capable of exciting ideas of pain, danger and terror; it produces the strongest emotions of which the mind is capable: astonishment, admiration, reverence, respect. The *Beautiful,* on the other hand, is that which causes love; beautiful things are small, smooth, of varied parts, delicate, and of clear, bright but not glaring colour. Both give, in curious ways, delight, the beautiful through its smoothness, the sublime through its roughness; this is the distinction Scott makes in the passage just quoted between the different appeals of North and South Tynedales. Burke's was an influential document, presenting clearly and precisely ideas which had long been current in more nebulous forms. Thirty years earlier, for instance, James Thomson, author of *The Seasons* (and a Borderer) wrote to David Mallet, a friend and fellow poet:

> My idea of your poem is a description of the grand works of Nature raised and animated by moral and sublime reflections: therefore before you quit this earth you ought to leave no great scene unvisited. Eruptions, earthquakes, the sea wrought into a horrible tempest, the abyss amidst whose amazing prospects, how pleasing must that be of a deep valley, covered with all the tender profusion of the spring. Here, if you could insert a sketch of the deluge, what more affecting and noble? Sublimity must be the characteristic of your piece.[12]

Discussion of the subject was dominated in the later eighteenth century by the works of William Gilpin and Sir Uvedale Price who are concerned principally with an idea which Burke does not use, but which arises from the sublime and the beautiful: the *Picturesque*.

> Among all the objects of art, the picturesque eye is perhaps most inquisitive after the elegant relics of ancient architecture; the ruined tower, the Gothic arch, the remains of castles and abbeys. These are the richest legacies of art. They are consecrated by time, and almost deserve the veneration we pay to the works of nature itself.[13]

Attitudes like Gilpin's show a concern only with the pleasing *arrangement* of objects; like museum pieces, they remain dead, fossilised history. The theory of the picturesque offers no life, and its central absurdities appear in the kind of joke to which its more extreme disciples gave rise: 'The rector's horse is *beautiful*, the curate's is picturesque.'[14] Price tells the story of an enthusiast whose wife humbly suggested that two of their three cows would be adequate to their needs; 'Lord, my dear', he replied, 'two cows, you know, can never group.'[15] Gilpin himself was firm about cattle, but in the end found them unsatisfactory; two are inadequate, but 'with three you are sure of a good group, except indeed they all stand in the same attitude and at equal distances'.[16]

A touching example comes from Scott's own household, in the words of Tom Purdie, the poacher whom Scott took into his service as shepherd:

> 'When I came here first', said Tom to the factor's wife, 'I was little better than a beast, and knew nae mair than a cow what was pretty

ORKNEY
ISLANDS

SHETLAND
ISLANDS

The Pirate

ORKNEY
ISLANDS

HEBRIDES

SKYE

LOCH NAN UAMH

MULL

Oban

Inverary

Inverness

Aberdeen

Waverley

Waverley
Fair Maid of Perth

Antiquary

Arbroath

*Legend of
Montrose*

Perth

*Fair Maid
of Perth*
Abbot

*Legend of
Montrose*

*Lady of the
Lake*

Waverley

FIRTH OF FORTH

Rob Roy

Stirling

Marmion

*Heart of
Midlothian*

*Bridge of
Lammermoor*

*Fast
Castle*

The Abbot

Glasgow
Rob Roy
Old Mortality

Edinburgh
Waverley

Marmion
Rob Roy

Ashestiel

*St Ronans
Well*

Lay of Last Minstrel

*Castle
Dangerous Black*
Dwarf

Abbotsford

Melrose

Monastery
The Abbot

Ayr

*Old
Mortality*

Dumfries

Redgauntlet

Guy Mannering

SOLWAY FIRTH

Carlisle

Allonby

IRELAND

ENGLAND

Guy Mannering

THE PLATES

1. WORDSWORTH AND SCOTT AT NEWARK TOWER, 1831, from a painting by George Cattermole. Wordsworth recorded the occasion in 'Yarrow Revisited'. (*The Lay of the Last Minstrel*)

2. FAST CASTLE, Berwickshire. Engraved from a painting done specially for Scott and given to him by the artist, the Rev. J. Thompson of Duddingston, in 1823 (see Lockhart, iv, 78). 'Like the nest of some sea-eagle.' (*The Bride of Lammermoor*)

3. PLAIDED HIGHLANDERS c.1730, wearing belted plaids (precursors of the kilt) and trews. These latter were close fitting, and cut on the cross to give elasticity. They were obsolete by about 1800, having given way to tartan trousers, still called trews. (*Waverley*)

4. NORMAN, 22nd CHIEF OF MACLEOD, by Allan Ramsay, 1748. Note that this picture was made during the proscription of Highland dress. (*Waverley*)

5. EDINBURGH: BRITISH SOLDIERS, by Paul Sandby, 1 March 1750. Sandby was official draughtsman to a detailed army survey of Scotland ordered by the English government, 1744–55. (*Waverley*)

6. EDINBURGH: LIFE IN THE HIGH STREET, by Paul Sandby, 1 March 1750. (*Guy Mannering, The Heart of Midlothian, Waverley*)

7. EDINBURGH: WEST BOW, by T. Allom. 'The steep and crooked street called the Bow, by which the fatal procession was to descend from the High Street', for the execution of Porteous in the Grassmarket. (*The Heart of Midlothian*)

Cover: CRICHTON CASTLE, by J. M. W. Turner. 'The castle of Ravenswood, occupying, and in some measure commanding, a pass betwixt Berwickshire and the Lothians.' (*The Bride of Lammermoor*)

1 (*above*). Wordsworth and Scott at Newark Castle   2 (*below*). Fast Castle

3. Highlanders

4. Norman, 22nd Chief
of MacLeod

5. Edinburgh: British Soldiers

6. Edinburgh: Life in the High Street

7. Edinburgh: West Bow

and what was ugly. I was cuif enough to think that the bonniest thing in a countryside was a corn-field enclosed in four stane dykes; but now I ken the difference. Look this way, Mrs. Laidlaw, and I'll show you what the gentlefolks likes. See ye there now the sun glinting on Melrose Abbey? It's no aw bright, nor it's no aw shadows neither, but just a bit screed o' light—and a bit daud o' dark yonder like, and that's what they ca' picturesque; and indeed, it maun be confessed it is unco bonnie to look at.'[17]

The cult was satirised in Combe and Rowlandson's *Dr. Syntax in Search of the Picturesque* (1809) where, of birds, Combe writes:

> But still, whate'er their form or feather,
> You cannot make them group together;
> For let them swim or let them fly
> The picturesque they all defy . . .

and later . . .

> To the fine steed you sportsmen bow
> But picturesque prefers a cow.
>
> (Canto XIV)

It is interesting to find that Gilpin also commented on the Tyne valley, but his eyes, in the same year as Scott wrote to Clerk about Hexham, saw a very different prospect:

> . . . . even scenes the most barren of beauty, will furnish amusement. Perhaps no part of England comes more under this description than that tract of barren country, through which the great military road passes from Newcastle to Carlisle.[18] It is a waste, with little interruption, through a space of forty miles. But even here, we have always something to amuse the eye. The interchangeable patches of heath, and greensward make an agreeable variety. Often too on these vast tracts of intersecting grounds we see beautiful lights, softening off along the sides of the hills: and often we see them adorned with cattle, flocks of sheep, heathcocks, grouse, plover and flights of other wildfowl. A group of cattle, standing in the shade on the edge of a dark hill, and relieved by a lighter distance beyond them, will often make a complete picture without any other accompaniment.[19]

The effect of this approximation to landscape painting is apparent in much of the poetry of the eighteenth century, though it is often coexistent with Burke or Gilpin, rather than a result of their teaching: everything stops while the poet invites us to admire the view and its composition. As usual, the tendency is most pronounced in minor verse. John Scott of Amwell writes:

> How various is yon view! delicious hills
> Bounding smooth vales, smooth vales by winding streams
> Divided, that here glide thro grassy banks
> In open sun, there wander under shade
> Of aspen tall, or ancient elm, whose boughs
> O'erhang grey castles, and romantic farms . . .
> How picturesque the view![20]

Castles and farms here are not places where men and women live or work or fight; they are shapely objects of sentimental reflection. Thirty years later, in 1805, Wordsworth (who, like Scott, saw in man 'an object of delight/Of pure imagination and of love') was reproaching himself for having indulged the vogue:

> Oh! Soul of Nature! that dost overflow
> With passion and with life, what feeble men
> Walk on this earth! how feeble have I been
> When thou wert in thy strength! Nor this through stroke
> Of human suffering, such as justifies
> Remissness and inaptitude of mind,
> But through presumption, even in pleasure pleased
> Unworthily, disliking here, and there,
> Liking, by rules of mimic art transferred
> To things above all art. But more, for this,
> Although a strong infection of the age,
> Was never much my habit, giving way
> To a comparison of scene with scene,
> Bent overmuch on superficial things,
> Pampering myself with meagre novelties
> Of colour and proportion, to the moods
> Of time and season, to the moral power
> The affections, and the spirit of the place,
> Less sensible.[21]

Scott's interest, however, is not a philosophical one, but purely, even severely, practical; passive adoration is not enough, because for him a view is a context, not a canvas; it is a world of action, not an object of contemplation; it is an environment with all the associations of history, heredity and legend. Writing of *Annan Water* in 1801, he said, 'I wish it had possessed more of that locality which I account among the highest graces of which the old Ballad is susceptible';[22] and a year later he was discussing the word 'locality' in a letter to Anna Seward:

A very commonplace and obvious epithet, when applied to a scene which we have been accustomed to view with pleasure, recalls to us not merely the local scenery, but a thousand little nameless associations which we are unable to separate or to define. In some verses of that eccentric but admirable poet, Coleridge, he talks of

> An old rude tale that suited well
> The ruins wild and hoary.

I think there are few who have not been in some degree touched with this local sympathy.... We are often charmed by the effect of local description, and sometimes impute that effect to the poet, which is produced by the recollections and associations which his verses excite ... I fear our poetical taste is in general much more linked with our prejudices of birth, of education, and of habitual thinking, than our vanity will allow us to suppose.[23]

The feeling behind the passage is Burke intensified:

Besides such things as affect us in various manners, according to their natural powers, there are associations made at that early season which we find it very hard afterwards to distinguish from natural effects.[24]

The theorists of the Sublime, the Beautiful, and the Picturesque affected Scott in another way too, as their reflections influenced the practice of landscape gardening. As a practitioner himself, Scott inevitably felt antagonistic towards the more precious followers of Lancelot Brown; 'capability men' he called them contemptuously, but his attitude arises not from philosophical or even agricultural principles, but from a conservationist's caution about sweeping away irreplaceable objects, natural or manmade, to make way for fashionable, ephemeral perspectives whose main purpose was to flatter a proprietor's self-esteem. His supreme example of the insensitive and blind folly of this 'school of spade and mattock' is the anecdote of one, Robertson, a pupil of Capability Brown's, who was commissioned to lay out the grounds of Duddingston House, near Edinburgh. He refused to incorporate in the view the nearby ruins of Craigmillar Castle on the grounds that 'seen all over the country [it] was a common prostitute', excluded Duddingston Loch (now ironically a bird sanctuary) because it did not fall within his lordship's property, and retained the 800 foot Arthur's Seat only because it was too bulky to be kept out of sight.[25] Scott wrote of this in

1828, when he was the grand old man, but fifteen years earlier he had expressed a similar point of view in an entertainingly anachronistic passage in *The Bridal of Triermain*, where he put the following lines into the mouth of Lyulph, a medieval minstrel:

> Thus in the garden's narrow bound,
> Flank'd by some castle's Gothic round,
> Fain would the artist's skill provide,
> The limits of his realms to hide.
> The walks in labyrinths he twines,
> Shade after shade with skill combines,
> With many a varied flowing knot,
> And copse, and arbour, decks the spot,
> Tempting the hasty foot to stay,
> And linger on the lovely way—
> Vain art! vain hope! 'tis fruitless all!
> At length we reach the bounding wall,
> And, sick of flower and trim-dress'd tree,
> Long for rough glades and forest free.
>
> (Canto II.5)

This is not to say that Scott was either uninterested in or blind to the value of contemporary views on the aesthetic use of land; it is simply to emphasise his sense of proportion, and his own opinion of what was important in a landscape. In the process of turning Cartley Hole into Abbotsford he put current ideas into practice, but commented ironically to Lady Abercorn: 'I have been studying Price with all my eyes and am not without hopes of converting an old gravel-pit into a bower and an exhausted quarry into a bathing house. So you see my dear Madam how deeply I am bit with the madness of the picturesque and if your Ladyship hears that I have caught a rheumatic fever in the gravel-pit or have been drowned in the quarry I trust you will give me credit for dying a martyr to taste.'[26]

The best landscape passages in Scott's poetry and novels reproduce an organic and vital context for human activity; frequently he represents a power not subject in the same way as his characters to the forces of time and change, and consequently one which appears as a counter by which man's own passing may be reckoned. The theme is a recurrent one, but an early example occurs in *The Lady of the Lake*. We are on an ancient battlefield:

> Where scatter'd lay the bones of men,
> In some forgotten battle slain,
> All bleach'd by drifting wind and rain.

It might have tam'd a warrior's heart,
To view such mockery of his art!
The knot-grass fetter'd there the hand,
Which once could burst an iron band;
Beneath the broad and ample bone,
That buckler's heart to fear unknown,
A feeble and a timorous guest,
The field-fare fram'd her lowly nest,
There the slow blind-worm left his slime,
On the fleet limbs that mock'd at time;
And there, too, lay the leader's skull,
Still wreathed with chaplet, flush'd and full,
For heath-bell with her purple bloom
Supplied the bonnet and the plume.
(Canto III.5)

Scott was impatient of the Metaphysical poets,[27] but his knot-grass manacle here has something of the force of Donne's 'bracelet of bright hair about the bone'. It is perhaps worth reinforcing the point finally with an example of the literature of instant decay, or ruins without history, present without past.

Happy art thou if thou canst call thine own
Such scenes as these: where Nature and where Time
Have work'd congenial; where a scatter'd host
Of antique oaks darken thy sidelong hills;
While, rushing thro' their branches, rifted cliffs
Dart their white heads, and glitter thro' the gloom.
More happy still, if one superior rock
Bear on its brow the shiver'd fragment huge
Of some old Norman fortress; happier far,
Ah, then most happy, if thy vale below
Wash, with the crystal coolness of its rills,
Some mould'ring abbey's ivy-vested wall.[28]

Landscapes are integral to Scott's work, a means of evocative communication bearing within it all that the author can possibly give of the spirit of the place, held and controlled by the richness of tradition and legend released by proper names.

It is important, too, that our appreciation of Scott's literary landscapes should reflect some knowledge of Scott and his contemporaries as travellers and tourists; only so shall we discover the near uniqueness of his vision, and learn something of how we came to look as we do at our own environment.

The literature of tourism in Britain is very old, but its examples appear only sporadically before 1770, when Arthur Young produced *A Six Months Tour through the North of England*. After this, similar, and often very inferior publications proliferated at such a rate as the century closed, that Dr Syntax's Bookseller could exclaim when the worthy parson tried to sell him his book ('In short, goodman, it is a Tour'):

> A Tour, indeed! I've had enough
> Of Tours, and such-like flimsy stuff.
> What a fool's errand you have made
> (I speak the language of the trade,)
> To travel all the country o'er,
> And write what has been writ before!
> We can get Tours—don't make wry faces,
> From those who never saw the places.
> (*Dr Syntax in Search of the Picturesque*, c. XXII)

I have indicated something of what painters, art critics, land 'improvers' and gardeners saw in landscape, and the more absurd extremes to which those were led whose vision was even narrower than their fashionable illusions. Scott's use of landscape, however, requires another sighting point if one is to achieve a true perspective of it, and none is better than Dorothy Wordsworth's *Recollections of a Tour Made in Scotland*, in 1803. This is an important work, indeed probably the last literary record of Scotland before the irreversible changes which came about as a result of the direct influence of Scott's writing on the Scottish tourist trade. After the publication of *The Lady of the Lake* in 1810, it became impossible for anyone to see Scotland again as Dorothy and William saw it. Only seven years earlier, Dorothy remembered the amusement of the highland farmhands on the shores of Loch Katrine: 'A laugh was on every face when Wm. said we were come to see the Trossachs'.[29]

Throughout the *Recollections*, she shows herself much concerned with landscape, and with the human environment, both as beautiful and useful; she misses the trees and hedgerows of her own country, but shows a perceptive appreciation of the peopled solitudes whose inhabitants are a natural and inevitable part of the countryside, linked by their labours, bound by its yield, in farming, fishing or mining. She is conscious, too, of ways of looking, and of the artificiality of simply viewing a prospect. The freedom of vision she seeks makes her rebellious at the idea of having her sight directed, especially by interference with natural contours and flora. Like her brother, she insists that what is natural is beautiful, and that all intrusions upon the land by man must be governed by the natural character of the place. 'Going in search of scenery' she regards as new-fangled and worthy only her scorn, while her contempt for the picturesque is quietly eloquent: their boatman on Loch Katrine 'would often say, after he had compassed the turning of a point, "This is a bonny part", and he always chose the bonniest, with greater skill than our prospect-hunters and "picturesque travellers"; places screened from the winds—that was the first point; the rest followed of course,—richer growing trees, rocks and banks, and curves which the eye delights in'.[30] Unlike Scott, she rarely sees or feels history; she seems only mildly aware of the ambience of the past; castles, ruined and preferably unrestored, form an interesting part of the view, but do little to rouse her to extended comment. This in itself is an interesting example of how her own theories are realised; the ancient ruins of abbey or tower having become almost totally absorbed into the surrounding land, continue their existence as natural objects rather than as historic monuments, and call for no deeper or richer response than rocks and stones and trees.

It is no small relief to come to such a quiet, sensitive observation of *what is there*, after the picturesque posturings of the prospect-hunters. Dorothy's eye sees, her imagination records, in an unsophisticated sequence.

For the Wordsworths, and especially for William, landscape was a multifarious manifestation of nature, comprising many elements, including the observer, and exercising the most profound spiritual and moral power over man; this view is precisely presented in the closing lines of the passage quoted earlier where Wordsworth regrets his earlier insensitivity to

> the moods
> Of time and season, to the moral power
> The affections, and the spirit of the place,

This attitude to external nature, with all the ramifications to which it gave rise, has long been known, understood and accepted; it is the view which has ultimately directed our own eyes and minds in the twentieth century, with country holidays, climbing and walking, YHA, National Trust, and an unabated desire to find in nature some truth, some repose, some eventual quietude or spiritual comfort, a promise of faith.

Scott's approach, equally valid, has been slower to mature possibly because the responses he requires are specific, or arise from specific localities (not necessarily his own) whereas Wordsworth's are more nebulous; where he speaks of Man and Nature, Scott gives us Men and Places. Scott's grasp of the past reveals a comprehensive hold on history, not in all its bookish bloodlessness but as a vital and revitalising force, available to all who care to draw it from tradition, song, legend and landscape, as well as from original documentary sources. For Scott, the very stones cried out of an antiquity which lay about him from his infancy, felt in the blood and felt along the heart.

His most convincing, most enduring characters are simply not conceivable apart from the world they inhabit (which is why the Scottish novels are so much superior to those located in England or Europe); and this is at the same time a world their identities create for us. We would be unwise, however, to see them only in the broad features of a Scottish landscape, its surface broken intermittently, conveniently and even picturesquely by battlefields, pele towers and rusty accoutrements, amid which characters appear as a quaintly articulate peasantry singing their way through nostalgic balladry in the innocence of an idyllic feudalism. At their best, Scott's people and places knit together in time, as do Wolf's Crag and Caleb Balderstone in *The Bride of Lammermoor,* Newark Tower and the minstrel in *The Lay,* Solway Firth and Darsie Latimer in *Redgauntlet.* And in his careful contextual placing in history and locality of such figures as Wandering Willie, Meg Merrilies, Madge Wildfire and the Mucklebackits, Scott so manipulates his material as to allow each to contribute to our understanding of moral man. In the novels for which he is likely to be longest remembered, Scott's view narrows from open fell to domestic hearth, from battlefield heroics to the individual dilemma, from inflated, artificial rhetoric to the hysteria of fear; and from the acres which embody all that remains of traditional Scotland before 1745, to the individual edifice swept away by 'improvement' or nourished by vanity and sentiment. Local influences have always produced their own loyalties and conflicting moral pressures, and Scott, himself a victim, is a most sensitive, if not always wholly successful writer on the theme. The hero of *Waverley,* for example, must learn to live in a world where personal friendships and political allegiances clash, and where, in the debris of their collision, he discovers himself. For some time, young Edward Waverley, having separated both from his father, and from the uncle who has brought him up (both men politically antagonistic), finds himself morally suspended between the genial hospitality and pedantic Jacobitism of the Baron Bradwardine, the fierce and practical prosecution of the same cause by Flora MacIvor and her brother, Fergus, and his native, though purely theoretical, loyalty to the Hanoverian monarchy. Scott shows the pressures on Waverley's mind and conscience by his use of environment rather than by argument, and through all the hero's adventures from his childhood at Waverley-Honour to the Highland refuge of MacIvor, and on the battlefields of Prestonpans and Clifton Moor, locality appears as a context of moral issues, not merely as an attractive scene of action, meditation or soliloquy. It is the known place and the historic date which concentrate the argument.

In adolescence, Mirkwood Mere in the park of Waverley-Honour feeds Waverley's romantic dreams, rooted in the legendary past; later, the landscape, dress and speech of the Highlanders infect him with a fierce Jacobite fervour, and it is only on the field of Prestonpans that he seriously feels a loss of integrity. Confronted with the reality of having to kill not only his own countrymen, but men of his former regiment, he is shocked into a recognition of the state into which he has drifted. Here, it is through dialect and dress that Scott makes his moral point.

> The English cavalry approached so near, that Waverley could plainly recognise the standard of the troops he had formerly commanded, and hear the trumpets and kettle-drums sound the signal of advance, which he had so often obeyed. He could hear, too, the well-known word given in the English dialect, by the equally well-distinguished voice of the commanding officer, for whom he had once felt so much respect. It was at that instant, that, looking around him, he saw the wild dress and appearance of his Highland associates, heard their whispers in an uncouth and unknown language, looked upon his own dress, so unlike that which he had worn from his infancy, and wished to awake from what seemed at the moment a dream, strange, horrible, and unnatural.   (Ch. 46)

This is a far cry from Waverley's first vision of the Highlands, where, in the retreat of Donald Bean Lean he 'prepared himself to meet a stern, gigantic, ferocious figure, such as Salvator would have chosen to be the central object of a group of banditti' (Ch. 17).

Once Waverley has admitted his dilemma to himself, one expects a decision; but the young man is no moral philosopher: he is influenced by forces of the moment, and in this instance the day ends with a double blow to scatter his doubts. As the two friends lie down to sleep, Waverley makes a melancholy comment on the fighting which will begin on the morrow, and Fergus replies:

> 'You must only think of your sword, and by whom it was given. All other reflections are now TOO LATE.'
>
> With the opiate contained in this undeniable remark, Edward endeavoured to lull the tumult of his conflicting feelings. The Chieftain and he, combining their plaids, made a comfortable and warm couch. Callum, sitting down at their head (for it was his duty, to watch upon the immediate person of the Chief), began a long mournful song in Gaelic, to a low and uniform tune, which, like the sound of the wind at a distance, soon lulled them to sleep.   (Ch. 46)

C

Waverley had been given the sword by Prince Charles; 'A prince to live and die under,' he had said enthusiastically after their first meeting. Fergus's reference to the weapon here recalls Waverley's first, uncritical allegiance to Charles, while the Gaelic chant of Callum Beg offers a vivid symbol of the romantic subjugation of his moral scruples. In this context, the notion of the two men 'combining their plaids' takes on an unintentional irony.

The interplay of character and place which Scott began here was a significant innovation in English fiction, and has remained a curiously neglected aspect of Scott's work. In his hands, the drawing together of events has more than a melodramatic coincidental quality of the kind one may be inclined to question in Dickens or Hardy. One feels, with Scott, that place and time—*this* place at *this* time—exert such power on the characters moving within them that, however coincidental a particular event may appear to be—Latimer's first meeting with Redgauntlet, for example, or the recognition scene in *Guy Mannering* when Harry Bertram hears the flageolet at Ellangowan, or the story of Elspeth of the Craigburnfoot in *The Antiquary*—such a character at such a place and time would be inescapably subject to such forces. 'These things', John Buchan remarked of such episodes, 'are great drama, for they proceed from the clash of character, but they are also epic, for they show the conflicts of history sublimated and focussed by a triumphant imagination.'[31]

Scott occupied himself seriously and successfully with the literary possibilities of landscape, locality, and environments both domestic and national; he was a man absorbed by the nature of the moral power, as well as the history, of a changing Scotland, regretting with a resigned strength the passing of a small world of moral certainties, a world where he discovered for himself that

> No longer can we learn our good
> From chances of a neighbourhood.[32]

CHAPTER II

The Poems

The wide acclaim and phenomenal commercial success which greeted the publication of Scott's early poems is not easy to understand; today they have few readers, and those academic critics who notice them at all tend to do so with a barely tolerant condescension. Yet in 1813, Byron could write,

> He is undoubtedly the Monarch of Parnassus, and the most *English* of bards. I should place Rogers next in the living list (I value him more as the last of the *best* school—Moore and Campbell both third—Southey and Wordsworth and Coleridge—the rest—thus:

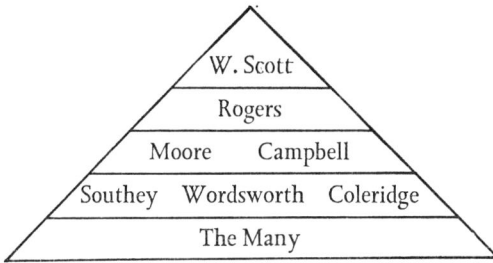

> ——I have ranked the names upon my triangle more upon what I believe popular opinion, than any decided opinion of my own.[1]

For much of his writing life Byron, like Scott, regarded himself as an entertainer rather than as a teacher, prophet or moralist. He 'scribbled' to please, but never felt for long that Byron the poet was a more significant being than Byron the rebel or politician. It is consequently the last sentence in this *Journal* entry that lends force to his remarks: his assessment of popular opinion in making out the class list of his contemporaries. For us, social and literary idioms are very different and have almost totally inverted Byron's parnassian pyramid, but one feature of Scott's poetry remains, if anything, more acceptable today than it was in his own time: the evocation of specific localities in a literary style which goes deeper than mere description, adding a rich social and historical depth to mere narrative. We can now see Scott more clearly, and perhaps more generously, as the pioneer in a kind of poetry which sets individuals in the organic context—social, historical, and geographical—which has helped to form their identities; a poetry which seeks through the exploration of these elements to enrich the reader's understanding by placing before him man in a recognisable frame, not exclusively or unintelligibly local, but sufficiently so defined as to be both realistic and relevant. In Scott's time, apart from Wordsworth (who had a poor opinion of Scott as a poet), both John Clare and George Crabbe exploited locality in their different ways but neither had the local scholarship nor the sense of history that seems to have motivated Scott throughout his life, and that enabled him to universalise episodes and emotions which in other circumstances would never have been considered south of Kelso.

I do not wish to exaggerate the value either of the poetry in itself, or of its importance to Scott ('I was never fond of my own poetry', he wrote later, 'and am now much out of conceit with it').[2] He was no innovator either of form or (in his verse) of language; but in his use of locality and environment he presented a new dimension which, though it proved barren (if exciting) in his verse, was abundantly fruitful in his prose fiction. Taken on its own terms, Scott's poetry is effective insofar as it uses the natural physical environment and its associations to increase the reader's awareness not only of, say, the medieval Borders, but of the rich potential of his own locality. This clearly does not result in the deep moral and introspective tones of philosophical verse such as Wordsworth's but it has its place as one approach to recording and reflecting on the human condition. Scott, too, heard and understood the still, sad music of humanity. He did not hesitate, however, to renounce a medium in which, despite his commercial success, he always worked uncomfortably, as soon as he recognised the rightness of prose for what he had to say. The process of finding the right voice is after all a familiar one in literary history and it seems reasonable to suggest that Scott was misled into poetry by his interest in ballads and romance. From childhood he was the convivial raconteur and the memoirs and letters of his numerous friends and visitors give generous testimony of his success. Verse composition would seem a natural development for the editor of Sir Tristrem and The Minstrelsy of the Scottish Border, but it proved, in Scott's case, a literary dead end.

For us, a century and a half later, the three major narrative poems provide a valuable introduction to the understanding of Scott the novelist: that is, as a novelist of Scotland.

In this chapter, my main concern is with The Lay of the Last Minstrel (1805), Marmion (1808), and The Lady of the Lake (1810). Though Scott continued to write poetry for some years after this, it was with wavering motives and waning interest. The stress on character which he attempts in *Rokeby* (1812) shows his attention attracted to themes more appropriate to the novel and in his 1830 Introduction to this poem he explains its comparative failure and, incidentally, acknowledges his own limitations. His style has had many imitators, he argues, the bad bringing him into disrepute, the good revealing his inadequacies. Moreover, at the time he was acutely aware of the shadow of Byron (with whom he tended to be bracketed by his contemporaries as the greatest of living poets), whose superiority he unhesitatingly recognised. 'There would have been little wisdom in measuring my force with so formidable an antagonist; and I was as likely to tire of playing the second fiddle in the concert as my audience of hearing me.' Scott's commitment was to Scotland, not to poetry. By the end of the first decade of the nineteenth century he had worked out the mine of romantic narrative verse and was no longer prepared, or even equipped, to prospect further in this field. It is worth recalling, however, that from the date of his verse translations from the German of Bürger, in 1796 when he was 25, until about 1812, Scott's literary interests were almost exclusively poetic. During these sixteen years he reviewed numerous collections of verse, as well as producing major and definitive editions of *The Minstrelsy of the Scottish Border* (1802–3), *Sir Tristrem*, a medieval romance (1804), and the *Life and Works of John Dryden,* in eighteen volumes (1808). The three long poems he wrote during this time had by the end of 1810 sold 57,000 copies.

Though he was unashamedly pleased by this popular success (and he never rated himself higher than a popular writer) it also worried him. He grew afraid of overproducing as a poet; of wearing out his welcome with an enthusiastic reading public by presenting them with one work too many. Invariably cool about his own literary merit, he told Matthew Hartsonge, who had sent him some very indifferent poems for comment, that his poetry was 'perhaps deficient in some of the more gaudy and dashing requisites which at present attract immediate and extensive popularity'.[3] Once he felt this recipe losing its power, he turned irrevocably to prose fiction, changing the medium, but not the message. This he summarises neatly in an explanation of his 'Notes and Occasional Dissertations' in the *Minstrelsy*: 'By such efforts, feeble as they are, I may contribute somewhat to the history of my native country, the peculiar features of whose manners and character are daily melting and dissolving into those of our sister and ally.'[4] Here Scott is speaking with the ventriloquial voice that permeates his work; the speaker is the loyal subject of the House of Hanover; the voice that of a Jacobite sympathiser, in whose tones reverberates the melancholy resignation not simply of a lost cause but of a world in which the manner and traditions of ancient Scotland are being fast eroded by a new, abrasive English culture.

The change to prose was not, of course, committed overnight. Scott had begun *Waverley* as early as 1805 but set it aside, discouraged. On its publication in 1814, he sent a copy to his friend John Morritt of Rokeby Hall, near Barnard Castle in Durham county, describing it, in words which closely echo the *Minstrelsy* statements, as 'a very old attempt of mine to embody some traits of those characters and manners peculiar to Scotland, the last remnants of which vanished during my own youth, so that few or no traces now remain'.[5] As a boy, apprenticed to his father's law business, Scott had met old men who had been 'out' in the risings of 1715 and 1745; the vigorous Stewart of Invernahyle impressed him unforgettably in this respect, putting the young man in living touch with history, helping him to make it part of himself. This was the history he was to embody so successfully in his Scottish fiction, but not before he had drained off in verse the medieval romantic turbulence within him.

Before examining the three main works, I wish to glance briefly at *The Bridal of Triermain*. This is a trifling pseudo-fairytale, alien to tradition; full of marvels, yet almost void of imagination; studded with small jewels of poetry whose lustre is often dimmed by the sombre wing of the Stuffed Owl. An obvious and easy target for critical ridicule, it is nevertheless useful as a polarising agent, in which we may see Scott's best and worst closely juxtaposed: faults and virtues which, once appreciated, may help to clear the approach to his other works.

The poem consists of three Cantos, each in three parts: the eighteenth-century courtship of Arthur and Lucy, in the process of which the former plays the merry minstrel and tells her the tale of the twelfth-century Roland de Vaux of Triermain, which in turn includes Lyulph's Tale, the Bard's Arthurian story. Absurdity is never far away at any point, and in a variety of forms, for example, doggerel:

> And the frank-hearted Monarch full little did wot
> That she smiled, in his absence, on brave Lancelot.
>
> (I. xi)

silliness which time has only confirmed:

> Each Maiden's short barbaric vest
> Left all unclosed the knee and breast
> And limbs of shapely jet.   (III.xx)

and a trivialised landscape such as we find in the remarks of Arthur to Lucy after he has won her:

> But, Lucy, turn thee now, to view
>   Up the fair glen, our destined way:
> The fairy path that we pursue,
> Distinguished but by greener hue,
>   Winds round the purple brae,
> While Alpine flowers of varied dye
> For carpet serve or tapestry . . .
>
> . . .
> 'Tis true that mortals cannot tell
> What waits them in the distant dell;
> But be it hap, or be it harm
> We tread the pathway arm in arm.
>   (III, Intro. iii)

The slackness of thought here, the poverty of language, the enervation of the lines, need no critical elaboration; but in the same poem, when Scott is working on material which he not only understands but feels, we find a very different style, energetic, confident and effective, quite unlike the flaccid vapourings of Arthur.

> Bewcastle now must keep the Hold,
>   Speir-Adam's steeds must bide in stall,
> Of Hartley-burn the bowmen bold
>   Must only shoot from battled wall;
> And Liddesdale may buckle spur,
>   And Teviot now may belt the brand,
> Tarras and Ewes keep nightly stir,
>   And Eskdale foray Cumberland.   (III.i)

In these lines, place and action are welded in heat. Because Roland de Vaux is absent, the English Borderers remain helpless in their peles while their Scottish counterparts foray at will. Scott adopts the Border usage of place-name, usually that of a valley or a stronghold, to denote persons, both leaders and their followers, and so a poetic intensity and economy directly derived from the Ballads are felt through such names as 'Bewcastle', 'Speir-Adam', 'Liddesdale', 'Teviot'. This language is heavy with association in Ballad and history: Bewcastle Waste, for example, is in Cumberland, west of the River Irthing (Dandie Dinmont was attacked by marauders here in *Guy Mannering*), and most of the action of the Ballad of *Hobbie Noble* is played out on this broad stretch of barren fell stretching north to the border, including in its expanse the shattered shell of Bewcastle castle, Speir-Adam (later Spadeadam) and a number of ruined pele towers. Triermain Castle lies a little south of the Waste, near Gilsland where in 1797 Scott met Charlotte Carpenter whom he married that December. Liddesdale was Armstrong country just north of the border in the west, most feared and most ruthless region of Border reivers until the seventeenth century.

> Of Liddisdaill the commoun theifis
> Sae peartly steillis now and reifis,
> That nane may keip
> Horse, nolt, nor scheip,
> Nor yett dar sleip
> For their mischeifis.[6]

In this region, every name in the list contributes its tale of family, raid or feud without further explanation if one has the Ballads in mind. Out of the Ballads and romances which he knew so well, and the territory in which he lived, worked, studied and played, Scott forged a narrative style and structure of some ephemeral interest which in *Triermain* we see in its decline. *Rokeby* is a more considerable achievement than its contemporary, though sharing many of its faults in a milder degree. A tale set during the Civil War, it barely glances at the issues of rebellion, concentrating almost wholly on the romantic story. It is the last poem of any significance that Scott wrote and in spite of, or even because of the care he took in getting the environment right, it has a detached and studied air which kills with a scrupulous correctness of detail the quick spirit which animates his earlier works. Hereafter, almost all of his verse appeared as incidental lyrics in the novels.

In the early poems, whatever their faults, placename, family and land-scape dominate the narrative with a localising power which, rightly understood, not only enhances them but helps to redress the balance of those features which no longer appeal to the twentieth-century reader. This is nowhere more completely accomplished than in the poem that Scott looked upon as his first original work,[7] *The Lay of the Last Minstrel*.

Initially, Scott undertook to write an Imitation Ballad, to be included in Part III of *The Minstrelsy*. He was unhappy, however, about the ballad quatrain as a satisfactory medium for popular poetry. Odd as it seems now, Scott believed it to be a restriction on syntax and style and in any case a form out of favour with the public. This is just another indication that, outside a small circle of antiquarian enthusiasts over the previous half century, the ballad form had not yet become fully acceptable as anything other than a crude medium for crude material, while the literary ballads, especially those of Coleridge and Wordsworth (*Lyrical Ballads* appeared in 1798), had not yet exerted the influence that was later to be so powerful. Scott inclined to the octosyllabic couplet, but in order to avoid its temptations to 'a habit of slovenly composition', he cast about for some way of modifying its mechanism. This he found when he recalled hearing Sir John Stoddart recite from memory fragments of Coleridge's then unpublished *Christabel*, which seemed to provide a firm verse structure with the flexible irregularities he sought: 'It was in *Christabel* that I first found [this measure] used in serious poetry, and it is to Mr. Coleridge that I am bound to make the acknowledgement due from the pupil to his master.'[8] But this debt appeared in another light at the time, to those who knew both poems. At this distance of years, apart from the line, 'Jesu, Maria, shield us well', the similarities between the poems are not glaring, but they worried William and Dorothy Wordsworth when they were with Scott in Jedburgh during their visit to him in 1803 at the end of their Scottish tour. One would give much to have been present that night when, as Wordsworth told Lockhart much later, Scott 'partly read, partly recited, sometimes in an enthusiastic style of chant, the first four cantos of *The Lay of the Last Minstrel*; and the novelty of the manners, the clear picturesque descriptions, and the easy glowing energy of much of the verse, greatly delighted me'.[9] At the time, however, he felt guilty at not having pointed out what he felt was patent, if unconscious plagiarism.[10]

Ironically, it was Coleridge (no mean plagiarist) who feared charges of plagiarism, since he delayed publication until 1816, as he explains in his Preface to the poem. More important, however, is his description of the underlying principle of his verse form (one can see it now as a forerunner of Hopkins's sprung Rhythm) which probably never occurred to Scott. 'The metre of *Christabel*', Coleridge writes, 'is not, properly speaking, irregular, though it may seem so from its being founded on a new principle: namely that of counting in each line the accents not the syllables', and the variation of the number of syllables 'is not introduced wantonly, or for the mere ends of convenience, but in correspondence with some transition, in the nature of the imagery or passion.'

Scott's note to Wordsworth is probably a sufficient summary of the circumstances of the poem's origin: it 'has the merit of being written with heart and goodwill and for no other reason than to discharge my mind of ideas which from infancy have rushed upon it'.[11] His search for a style in a medium which he later rejected altogether is not without its interest. However, the completed proportions of the poem made it unsuitable for inclusion in the *Minstrelsy*, and in the end it appeared in the first week of January, 1805.

The Lay subjects us to fewer fine flourishes and merely decorative digressions than were later to become common with Scott, and though it still lacks the true Ballad economy it derives similar force from its use of locality and the exploitation of the connotations of place, personality and family. Like the Ballad singers, Scott is speaking to an audience who specifically understand these terms and hence their values in the poem; so, while the morality of his work is universal, it is commonplace, even naïve, whereas the locality is unique, without being exclusive. Education and sophisticated methods of communication have long robbed us of the excuses for ignorance which Scott's contemporaries could offer, and Jeffrey's stricture in his review of the poem that 'The locality of the subject is likely to obstruct its popularity', has lost much of its force. Now, more easily than ever before, Scott readers may walk where Scott characters and their maker once trod, in paths whose topographical charm is vividly reinforced by Guides to the Scott Country and memories of television dramatisations of the novels. The appreciation of environment as a literary medium begins here.

What *The Lay* offers, read in the light of locality, is a brief insight into the life of the Border as it was from the middle ages to the seventeenth century; it is an insight whose acute vividness is sufficient to subdue, if not dispel, the occasional absurdities. In many ways it functions as a Ballad, tempering Border violence with Border scholarship. Jeffrey scorned the intrusion of Scott's antiquarian passions into the narrative but, as families increasingly disperse, losing their sense of place, as dialects decay, and as the buildings made by organic communities vanish for ever beneath the towering monuments of Approved Architecture, are these passions so irrelevant now, and in literature?

The whims and digressions of the story barely concern us here. Fundamentally Scott tells of two lovers, Margaret of Buccleuch and young Lord Cranstoun, separated by a long-standing feud between their families, the Scotts and the Kerrs, and their eventual reconciliation. It is a curious tale, marred in the telling by sheer anecdotal ebullience; what follows is not a detailed critical appraisal of the poem; rather an attempt to show the nature of a genre, environmental literature, of which Scott himself never seems to have recognised the full potential, and never developed.

Scott presents the Minstrel, outside his Lay, in the Introduction, and in the short coda which concludes each Canto. We first see him in a context of Time, Landscape, and Manners, the three features which predominate in Scott's fictional world, as indeed, in his own real one. The singer is the *last* Minstrel because we are in the late seventeenth century and the day of the bard is by:

> Old times were changed, old manners gone;
> A stranger filled the Stuarts' throne;
> The bigots of the iron time
> Had called his harmless art a crime.

The first two lines directly voice Scott's own sympathies; he has already isolated the aged Minstrel in cold and loneliness and so the old manners of feudal hospitality can be practised by the Duchess, a theme very close to the heart of the generous laird of Abbotsford. In place

> He pass'd where Newark's stately tower
> Looks out from Yarrow's birchen bower.

Even such simple lines lock time with place, locating a late seventeenth-century event within a region richly steeped in earlier Ballad and tradition; the river and the tower carry the Minstrel and his tale into the present, both Scott's and ours. Newark stands above the Yarrow Water just before it meets Ettrick Water, runs past Selkirk and into the Tweed. The hold of Newark stands today, foursquare, overlooking the valley near the small cottage where the explorer Mungo Park, Scott's friend and neighbour, was born. It was the scene of more than one English siege, and in spite of its strength was burnt in 1549, being later renovated at intervals until it was unroofed in the eighteenth century and left to decay. The river, of course, conjures up all the violence, love and yearning of those most tragic of all Ballads, *The Dowie Dens of Yarrow*, *The Douglas Tragedy*, *Rare Willie's Drowned in Yarrow*; taken with tower and Minstrel, Yarrow is a literary indicator, much more than a mere proper noun. Even the Lady is a Border Widow; she had married the Duke of Monmouth, son to Charles II, who was executed in 1685 for rebellion against James II, and she might well have lamented with the Widow of the Ballad,

> There came a man by middle day
> He spied his sport and went away;
> And brought the king that very night,
> Who brake my bower and slew my knight.

Such unobtrusive and probably unconscious resemblances bring the Ballad world very close. Echoes of other Border songs haunt the poem: William of Deloraine is 'good at need' like the Cranstanes of *The Raid of the Reidswire*; the Goblin, Gilpin Horner, like Carl Hood in *Earl Brand*, is 'always for ill and never for good'; the Lady of Buccleuch asks why the English Wardens ride over the border 'against the truce of Border tide', a subtle counterpointing of the lines in *Kinmont Willie* (which may, indeed, be Scott's own) where Buccleuch, Keeper of Liddesdale, asks

> 'And have they ta'en him, Kinmont Willie,
> Against the truce of Border tide?'

Stanzas vi and vii also capture the high tension beneath the conviviality of certain Border meetings, such as one finds again in the *Reidswire* Ballad.

The Minstrel is welcomed to Newark, warmed, fed and invited to entertain the company. Before he begins his tale, Scott offers us a slight but touchingly humane passage on the tremulous old man's failure to tune his harp; lines which convey briefly but generously the sympathy and tact of true hospitality,

> The pitying Duchess praised its chime
> And gave him heart, and gave him time,

and so the lay begins. The codas to each Canto add little, concentrating with quiet melancholy on themes of youth, age and the sense of loss.

The plot is slight but some passages reward critical attention, especially if we bear in mind two of Jeffrey's objections: that 'there is a great deal of gratuitous and digressive description', and that 'the reader will meet with very heavy passages and with a variety of details which are not likely to interest anyone but a Borderer or an antiquary'. After a century and a half, these remain current views of Scott's work, as would most of Jeffrey's meticulous and just review; but our own eyes and minds, having been educated to no small degree by Scott and Wordsworth, see differently, and need no longer accept judgements given with, in this sense, untutored vision.

Easter Deloraine and Wester Deloraine lie in the Ettrick Valley midway between the towers of Kirkhope and Tushielaw, land long in the possession of the Scotts. William of Deloraine, the Lady's messenger from Branksome to Melrose (on, it must be admitted, a successful but totally pointless quest for an enchanted book) is identified and characterised on his first appearance almost entirely in terms of his relationship to his environment.

> A stark moss-trooping Scott was he,
> As e'er couch'd Border lance by knee;
> Through Solway Sands, through Tarras Moss,
> Blindfold, he knew the paths to cross;
> By wily turns, by desperate bounds,
> Had baffled Percy's best bloodhounds;
> In Eske or Liddel, fords were none
> But he would ride them one by one;
> Alike to him was time or tide,
> December's snow or July's pride;
> Alike to him was tide or time,
> Moonless midnight or matin prime;

Steady of heart, and stout of hand,
As ever drove prey from Cumberland;
Five times outlawed had he been,
By England's King, and Scotland's Queen.

(I.xxi)

'Moss-trooping Scott' establishes both occupation, nationality (though Borderer first) and family, each implying the other; a moss-trooper was a Borderer who, living largely on the theft of cattle indifferently either side of the border, made his predatory raids in small companies (as a rule) and retired, especially when pursued, into the mosses and hags of the low-lying parts of the Border, especially those, like the Tarras Moss, about the Solway Firth. Robert Carey, Warden of the West March, gives a lively and personal account of an encounter with moss-troopers in 1601, when he led a punitive expedition against them:[12]

> The chief outlaws at our coming, fled their houses where they dwelt, and betook themselves to a large and great forest (with all their goods) which was called the Tarras. It was of that strength, and so surrounded with bogs and marsh grounds, and thick bushes and shrubs as they feared not the force nor power of England nor Scotland so long as they were there. They sent me word that I was like the first puff of a haggis, hottest at the first, and bade me stay there as long as the weather would give me leave; they would stay in the Tarras wood, till I was weary of lying in the waste.

The moss-trooper paid his allegiance to family and chief, rather than to country and crown, but this was generally true throughout the Borders.

The place-names here also carry clear overtones of danger and depredation. The Tarras Water flows into the River Esk a mile or two north of Gilnockie, home of the Armstrong family whose exploits are celebrated in some of the most famous of the Riding Ballads, like *Kinmont Willie*, and *Johnnie Armstrong*. Further south, the Esk joins the Liddel Water in Liddesdale, whose fearsome reputation I have already mentioned.

Deloraine's intimate knowledge of the paths and fords of the region is characteristic of the experienced Border reiver; essential to survival in a land where all thieves' routes were watched and patrolled. Hobbie Noble, in the Ballad, was such a knowledgeable guide (banished to Liddesdale from Bewcastle) even in the dark:

'But will ye stay till the day gae down,
    Until the night come o'er the grund,

> And I'd be a guide worth any twa
> That may in Liddesdale be found.'

The implications of the characterisation are neatly concluded in the final couplet—Deloraine has been repeatedly outlawed by both realms. Even his disregard for season is telling, since major reiving forays were seasonal, made at a time of year when cattle were strong enough to drive well after they had been stolen, when guards at the crossings were slack or suborned, indeed whenever the hope of stealing cattle without fear of capture was strongest.

> Such men will never lightly steal before Lammas [Aug. 1,] for fear of the assises, but beeing once past, they return to their former trade: and unless in such yeares as they cannot ride upon the wastes by reason of stormes and snowes, the last moneths in the yeare are theyr chiefe tyme of stealing: for then are the nightes longest, theyr horse hard at meate, and will ride best, cattell strong, and will drive furthest: after Candlemas [Feb. 2] the nightes grow shorter, all cattell grow weaker, and oates growing dearer, they feed their horses worst, and quickly turne them to grasse.[13]

Deloraine's eighteen-mile ride from Branksome to Melrose is a precisely routed journey and though its cliché-bound stanzas rarely rise above the 'light horse' level the movement of the whole is enriched by substantial, and integral topographical-historical allusion. Mere annotation here would simply deaden the fire and pace of the episode, but some comment may help the reader to an appreciation of Scott's achievement.

The gallop begins at stanza xxv, and the knights arrival at Melrose Abbey concludes Canto First. Scott punctuates his way by drawing our attention to three special features of the landscape: pele towers, ancient remains, local anecdotes and associations; features, Scott implies, which are not only present to the eye, but relevant to the narrative in its exact placing of the events. His stress is not on the arrangement of the view, nor on its power to arouse moral reflection, but on the insights it offers into human history, regional life, and the passage of time.

> Soon in his saddle sate he fast,
> And soon the steep descent he past,
> Soon cross'd the sounding barbican,
> And soon the Teviot side he won.
> Eastward the wooded path he rode,—
> Green hazels o'er his bonnet nod;
> He pass'd the Peel of Goldiland,
> And cross'd old Borthwick's roaring strand;

> Dimly he view'd the moat-hill's mound,
> Where Druid shades still flitted round;
> In Hawick twinkled many a light;
> Behind him soon they set in night;
> And soon he spurr'd his courser keen
> Beneath the tower of Hazeldean.   (I.xxv)

In all, between Branksome and Melrose the rider passes five pele towers, each a significant pointer to the history of the area and the way of life of Border families. The mention of six towers in a journey of only eighteen miles is in itself a succinct indication of the unsettled nature of the region and of the economy of a people who found it necessary to inhabit relatively small dwellings, with single rooms disposed one above the other over a vaulted basement and with stone walls up to twelve feet thick. The purpose of Scott's emphasis in the opening stanzas on armed readiness at Branksome is made incidentally clearer by the implication that it is no more than a routine element of life in the Borders, though the stress is on the danger of attack from England rather than on the threat from mosstroopers:

> They watch against Southern force and guile,
>   Lest Scroop, or Howard, or Percy's powers,
> Threaten Branksome's lordly towers,
>   From Warkworth, or Naworth or merry Carlisle.
>   (I.vi)

Branksome, where, in the old Ballad, Jamie Telfer appealed for help when his own tower was attacked, is an ancient Scott stronghold on the River Teviot, and Jamie did not plead in vain:

> 'Gar warn the water, braid and wide,
>   Gar warn it sune and hastily!
> They that winna ride for Telfer's kye,
>   Let them never look in the face o' me!
>
> 'Warn Wat o' Harden, and his sons,
>   Wi' them will Borthwick water ride;
> Warn Gaudilands, and Allanhaugh,
>   And Gilmanscleugh, and Commonside.'

So responded the old Laird of Buccleuch.

Downstream, nearer Hawick and where the Borthwick Water meets Teviot, Goldielands Tower ('Gaudilands' in the Ballad) looks out north-west towards Ettrick; another Scott pele, it was once known from its site as the watch tower of Branksome. After this, Deloraine moves northward, away from Teviot, to Hazeldean (Hassendean) yet another hold of the Scotts, and Horsliehill, an Elliot possession, from where William Elliot rode out in 1564 to murder Scott of Hassendean. Though Deloraine's journey to Melrose is much more direct than Marmion's to Edinburgh, Scott allows him one poetic detour to Minto Crags, a piece of sheer romantic self-indulgence.

> A moment now he slack'd his speed,
> A moment breathed his panting steed;
> Drew saddle-girth and corslet band,
> And loosen'd in the sheath his brand.
> On Minto-crags the moonbeams glint,
> Where Barnhill hew'd his bed of flint;
> Who flung his outlaw'd limbs to rest,
> Where falcons hang their giddy nest.
>
> (xxvii)

This is the site of Fatlips Castle, once the property of Turnbull of Barnhills, a notorious freebooter. Deloraine moves back on course, however, passing Halidon (Holydean) Castle which belonged to the Kerrs of Cessford. It is long demolished but perhaps the traveller glimpsed in the moonlight an inscription on the lintel: 'Feer God. Flee from sin. Mak for the lyfe everlasting to the end. Dem Isobel Ker, 1530.'

This last tower returns us directly to the theme of the lay, and the Minstrel recalls the origin of the Scott feud with the Carrs upon which the romance of the story mainly rests. In the summer of 1526, the 14-year-old James V sought the help of Buccleuch to rescue him from the tyranny and ambition of his guardian, the Earl of Angus. The King's party, with Hume, Kerr of Cessford, and Ferniehurst, returning to Edinburgh from a judicial visit to the Borders, was waylaid by the Scotts, supported by the Elliots. Buccleuch was defeated, but in the flight James Elliot slew the Laird of Cessford and the long feud began as

> gallant Cessford's heart-blood dear
> Reek'd on dark Elliot's Border spear.

After applause and refreshment, the Minstrel resumes with the widely quoted lines of Canto Second,

> If thou wouldst view fair Melrose aright,
> Go visit it by the pale moonlight . . .

What follows is no more than a competent piece of gothic chiaroscuro, effective in its way but unoriginal, using the tried and approved eighteenth-century recipe which called for ruins, moonlight, owls and the attendant Melancholy. Scott does localise, with Melrose, Tweed, St David, and our reading of Canto First helps us to place the abbey in a wider topographical context, but this is a relatively slight development of such conventional views and responses as we find for example in Thomas Warton's lines:

> Beneath yon ruin'd Abbey's moss-grown piles
> Oft let me sit, at twilight hour of Eve,
> Where thro' some western window the pale moon
> Pours her long-levell'd rule of streaming light;
> While sullen sacred silence reigns around,
> Save the lone screech-owl's note who builds his bow'r
> Amid the mould'ring caverns dark and damp.[14]

Scott clings effortlessly and thoughtlessly to the eighteenth-century convention and we learn without surprise that he had himself never visited the Abbey by moonlight, often as he had stayed in Melrose. Many years later he was asked to transcribe, as a form of autograph, this Melrose passage. He obliged, confessing 'that I had been guilty of sending persons a bat-hunting to see the ruins of Melrose by moonlight which I never saw myself', and he altered the closing lines:

> Then go—and meditate with awe
> On scenes the author never saw
> Who never wander'd by the moon
> To see what could be seen by noon.[15]

Romantic landscape appears much more successfully in Canto Third (XXIV–XXVII). Evening draws in, and the lovely Margaret in a Ballad pose 'On the high turret sitting lone', thinks of her forbidden lover. As she looks over the Border landscape from Branksome we see her view in terms of pastoral stereotypes: western star rising over the hill: 'the hour of silence and of rest'; rock, wood and water. But these turn out not to be scenery at all; the star is really a warning beacon, the hill a look-out point, and the rest of the landscape an amplifier of the noises of battle. For Margaret, when she interprets the scene

> Scarce could she draw her tighten'd breath,
> For well she knew the fire of death.

And the nature image is neatly inverted when

> Spears in wild disorder shook,
> Like reeds beside a frozen brook.

D

Then, as the battle approaches, the landscape suddenly draws tight in a
poetic slip-knot:

> 'On Penchryst glows a bale of fire,
> And three are kindling on Priesthaughswire;
>   Ride out, ride out
>   The foe to scout!
> Mount, mount for Branksome, every man!
> Thou, Todrig, warn the Johnstone clan,
>   That ever are true and stout—
> Ye need not send to Liddesdale;
> For when they see the blazing bale
> Elliots and Armstrongs never fail . . .'
>
> (III.xxvii)

What appeared to be a star and was a beacon now multiplies around in
summons and response, silently reinforcing the call to family and dale in
stanza 27:

> And soon a score of fires I ween,
> From height, and hill, and cliff, were seen;
> Each with warlike tidings fraught;
> Each from each the signal caught . . .
>   . . .
> They gleamed on many a dusky tarn,
> On many a cairn's grey pyramid,
> Where urns of mighty chiefs lie hid;
> Till high Dunedin blazes saw
> From Soltra and Dumpender Law.
>
> (III.xxix)

In the opening lines of Canto Fourth, the landscape again mediates
past and present, as the Minstrel reflects before continuing the tale:

> Sweet Teviot! on thy silver tide
>   The glaring bale-fires blaze no more;
> No longer steel-clad warriors ride
>   Along thy wild and willow'd shore;
> Where'er thou wind'st, by dale or hill,
> All, all is peaceful, all is still,
>   As if thy waves, since Time was born,
> Since first they roll'd upon the Tweed,
> Had only heard the shepherd's reed,
>   Nor started at the bugle-horn.

The passage barely requires glossing, but it is worth reinforcing the point that here again Scott, like the Ballad men, is making certain assumptions about Border consciousness, an appreciation of which renders more acute our awareness of the old and dormant violence now tranquillised and romanticised in mossy ruins.

Probably the best known lines in the whole of Scott open Canto Sixth; often they are quoted incompletely and thus misunderstood. The first words,

> Breathes there the man with soul so dead
> Who never to himself hath said,
> This is my own, my native land!

are followed by thirteen lines of severe and stirring patriotic rhetoric; he who knows not love of country shall go down

> To the vile dust from whence he sprung,
> Unwept, unhonour'd, and unsung.

But this is no abstract national patriotism, and the sentiment, in a different oratorical key, modulates to lucidity in the next stanza:

> O Caledonia, stern and wild,
> Meet nurse for a poetic child!
> Land of brown heath and shaggy wood,
> Land of the mountain and the flood,
> Land of my sires! what mortal hand
> Can e'er untie the filial band,
> That knits me to thy rugged strand! . . .
> . . .
> By Yarrow's streams still let me stray,
> Though none should guide my feeble way;
> Still feel the breeze down Ettrick break,
> Although it chill my wither'd cheek;
> Still lay my head by Teviot Stone . . .
>
> (VI.i,ii)

Apart from this being a hint to the Lady that he would like to remain at Newark (a hint she generously takes), it is noticeable that Minstrel/ Scott is not here celebrating, as one might patriotically expect, the martial exploits of his sires, but the external face of the land, in such a way that the unspecific mountain and flood are made concrete in the names of Yarrow, Ettrick, Teviot; names which confirm the regional quality of the tale as well as bearing in such a setting all the violent and tragic weight of Border balladry and strife.

Unlike the typical Ballad, however, *The Lay* concludes in romantic serenity Scott's sop to his public rather than fidelity to the Border. In the tale, the feuding families are reconciled by the marriage of the lovers, and the Minstrel ends his days at Newark Tower, the deserving dependent of lordly benevolence, while

> summer smiled on sweet Bowhill,
> And July's eve, with balmy breath,
> Waved the blue-bells on Newark heath;
> When throstles sung in Harehead Shaw
> And corn was green on Carterhaugh.

The faults of *The Lay*—its digressions, structural incoherence, pointless incidents, narrative weakness—are too well known for repetition. I have tried to demonstrate the literary skill with which Scott handles environmental material; his ultimate failure as a poet arises, I believe, directly from his unwillingness or inability to reconcile this expertise to a sustaining structure with tauter plot, more penetrating characterisation, and hence to develop its considerable potential. What could have formed the basis of a new and serious literary method we see only intermittently exploited in *The Lay*; in the two narrative poems that follow it, Scott's unawareness of his originality becomes even more clear.

Landscape in *Marmion* is for the most part utilitarian, adequately containing and directing the narrative topographically, but nowhere providing the kind of literary enrichment by local connotation that appears in *The Lay*. The plot is indeed a gothic melodrama of trumpery treachery, coincidence and improbability. As an adventure story it is poor; as a 'Tale of Flodden Field' it is negligible, since it deals neither with the truth nor the tragedy of that memorable battle. Nevertheless, its place in literary history, precisely because of the irrepressible localisations, is important enough to warrant consideration of certain passages. The description of Holy Island, for example, in Canto Second, moves from the fairly simple verse topography of stanza 9 to a description of the twelfth-century priory which compares curiously with that of Melrose Abbey in *The Lay*.

This description is the culmination of a series of views of the Northumbrian coast as a party of nuns (which includes the Lady Clare) approaches Holy Island by sea. We are first impressed by its strength. Scott gives 'The Castle with its battled walls' a passing mention in stanza 9, but the renovated fortress which now stands on Beblowe Crag was not built until the middle of the sixteenth century, and then from stones of the Priory, dissolved in 1537. It is likely, however, that the crag held a small look-out, and a small fort surmounted the Heugh, a ridge to the south. Throughout stanzas 9 and 10 Scott's description is rich in its apprehension of time and the works of man, as well as faithful in mood to the atmosphere of this haunted place; he magnifies the dimensions of the castle without distorting the truth, and he wisely invents nothing. The manufactured gothic splendours of moonlit Melrose have no place in this picture of the bleak, exposed, repeatedly ravaged island of Lindisfarne. During its flourishing years, the Priory incorporated its own defensive features in the massive, romanesque structure; and it is the bulk and weight of this frame that Scott emphasises, with some chronological freedom. No trace remains of the original seventh-century monastery, so severely and repeatedly attacked by Danes during the eighth century. The existing ruins are those of a building begun in the late eleventh century.

> In Saxon strength that abbey frown'd
> With massive arches broad and round,
> > That rose alternate, row and row,
> > On ponderous columns, short and low,
> > > Built ere the art was known,
> > By pointed aisle and shafted stalk,
> > The arcades of an alley'd walk
> > > To emulate in stone.
> > On the deep walls, the heathen Dane
> > Had pour'd his impious rage in vain;
> > And needful was such strength to these,
> > Exposed to the tempestuous seas,
> > Scourg'd by the winds' eternal sway
> > Open to rovers fierce as they,
> > Which could twelve hundred years withstand
> > Winds, waves, and northern pirates' hand.
> > Not but that portions of the pile,
> > Rebuilded in a later style,
> > Show'd where the spoiler's hand had been;
> > Not but the wasting sea-breeze keen
> > Had worn the pillar's carving quaint,
> > And moulder'd in his niche the saint,
> > And rounded with consuming power,
> > The pointed angles of each tower;
> > Yet still entire the abbey stood,
> > Like veteran, worn, but unsubdued.   (II.x)

The Priory is at once church and fortress, strong both against the hand of man and the withering power of the elements. Unlike the moonlit Melrose Abbey, this place stands for Time, not Mood, a symbol of continuity, of human endurance, of man's inhumanity, and of his dedication.

Marmion begins his journey from Norham to Edinburgh in Canto Third, pursuing a route circuitous enough to cast grave doubts on the qualifications of his supposed guide, but he suspects nothing. 'Why', Scott was once asked, 'did ever mortal coming from England to Edinburgh go by Gifford, Crichton Castle, Borthwick[16] Castle, and over the top of Blackford Hill?' Scott thought the objection irrelevant: 'It was my good pleasure to bring Marmion by that route, for the purpose of describing the places you have mentioned, and the view from Blackford Hill— it was his business to find the road and pick his steps the best way he could.' However, he later recanted.[17] I do not think Scott's attitude here is merely frivolous. He is claiming the right to use the environment as a *poet*, not as a geographer. His liberties with route and landscape enrich his theme without significant distortion, as a painter may move a tree or demolish a building to capture the spirit of the place. Marmion must move through a landscape which makes clear his situation as an enemy alien, traversing localities whose history has made his present.

The party reaches Gifford in the evening, to find the tower closed against them: 'To Scotland's camp the Lord was gane'. This is the first clear indication of the Scots' preparations for war, though at that hour, and in the absence of the lord, any tower would have remained closed to Scot or Englishman indifferently. Nevertheless, the lack or refusal of genuine hospitality, for whatever reason, always in Scott carries strong overtones of bleak rejection. We remember Norham. In spite of its military readiness and strict routine, it is a place of gaiety and colourful hospitality. Marmion arrives in splendour at a yet peaceful castle, is ceremoniously welcomed and lavishly entertained. (Jeffrey took exception to this. There was, he complained, 'a debasing lowness and vulgarity in some passages, which we think must be offensive to every reader of delicacy ... The venison pasties, we think, are of this description'.) Now, Marmion and his train spend the night at the local inn and, after a nocturnal adventure not to the present purpose, a jaded knight resumes his progress in a south-westerly direction to Crichton Castle, a thirteenth-century hold some ten miles south-east of the capital, on the Midlothian Tyne. It had long been a favourite haunt of Scott's (he was to draw on it again ten years later as the basis for Ravenswood Castle in *The Heart of Midlothian*), and he lingers fondly here, turning aside from his narrative to reflect on the presence of the past—his own as well as Crichton's.

> Crichtoun! though now thy miry court
>   But pens the lazy steer and sheep,
>   Thy turrets rude and totter'd keep
> Have been the minstrel's lov'd resort . . .
>
>   . . .
>
> Still rises unimpair'd below,
> The courtyard's graceful portico;
> Above its cornice, row and row
>   Of fair hewn facets richly show
>   Their pointed diamond form,
>   Though there but houseless cattle go
>   To shield them from the storm.

(IV.xi)

Conscious of the departed glory, Scott recreates it in Marmion's welcome, though now, as at Gifford, hospitality is qualified by preparations for war. Marmion is greeted by Sir David Lindesay of the Mount, the King's representative who, with all courtesy, sees that he is watched as an enemy emissary. The Lord of Crichton, Adam Hepburn, shortly to die at Flodden, has already gone to join the Scottish force and the visitor is received with only 'melancholy state'. The presence of Lindesay provides an impressive testimonial to the importance of Marmion's mission though, as Scott admits, it is historically impossible; Lindesay was at the time on a diplomatic visit to France, virtually threatening Henry VIII there with a Scottish invasion if he did not return to redress their grievances.

One can appreciate now the function of the reciprocating elements of splendour and tension; as the one diminishes, the other increases. Hospitality everywhere, even at Norham, is in some way moderated by the threat of arms, but Scott, up to the point at which Marmion reaches Edinburgh, achieves his tension obliquely through traditional entertainment or its absence rather than by descriptions of rearmament or the mustering of forces. Indeed, as the towers have been temporarily abandoned by their owners, the accumulating sense of desertion and dispersal reinforces the power of an assembly at Edinburgh when we eventually reach it in stanza 25. The towers remain in the hands of lonely women, 'sorrowing' and 'cautious', whose role it will soon be to lament when 'the flowers of the forest are a' wede away'. Scott, the soldier manqué because of his lameness, saw the profession of arms as a noble and romantic activity, but both as a historian and as one who had close contacts with troops, he was not unaware of its dehumanising power.

After two nights at Crichton, Marmion and his men travel the last stage to Edinburgh, where their approach again allows Scott a nostalgic glance at his own past; a glance over time again, marked on this occasion by his own sense not only of loss, but of change on the face of the land where on Blackford Hill,

> Now, from the summit to the plain
> Waves all the hill with yellow grain
>   And o'er the landscape as I look
> Nought do I see unchanged remain,
>   Save the rude cliffs and chiming brook.
> To me they make a heavy moan,
> Of early friendships past and gone.

The opening quatrain here echoes the ambiguity, the paradox of Scott's attitude to time and to Scotland; while seeing fair evidence of the eighteenth-century improvements in Scottish husbandry in a hillside covered with grain, he nevertheless mourns the passing within his own lifetime of Blackford's uncultivated wilderness where he had played as a boy.[18] Only cliff and brook abide, as the many change and pass. Moreover, this is no mere portrait of the Poet in Rêverie; it is the culminating point of a threefold figure of some force, Gifford, Crichton, Blackford, binding the fictional/historical past to the present. Scottish national pride and the Stuart cause did not mildly pass away after the Jacobite rising of 1745; and James IV's doomed preparations for war in the summer of 1513 are not without echoes of Charles Edward's gathering of the clans in Glenfinnan for the early victories and later disaster of his bid for the throne, a theme treated with depth and insight in Waverley. Scott's description of the Edinburgh preparations as Marmion saw them is rich in colour, place-name, tribe and clan; the episode is a long one, occupying ten stanzas in Canto Fourth and six in the following Canto before Marmion reaches Holyrood. What Jeffrey rejected as 'a redundancy of minute description' is truly a patient accumulation of material in a mounting wave which ultimately crashes down on Flodden and vanishes. After the battle, Scott's language degenerates into helpless cliché, hopelessly inadequate to convey a nation's grief; survivors ride from the field

> To town and tower, to town and dale,
> To tell red Flodden's dismal tale,
> And raise the universal wail.
> Tradition, legend, tune, and song,
> Shall many an age that wail prolong.

Once more we have a poem demonstrating Scott's strength, and his failure to develop it, partly because he did not see his opportunity, partly because he was simply careless and completed the work hurriedly; his personal affairs came first and the income *Marmion* would bring was too urgently needed for him to delay with postponement and polish.

As soon as Scott moves away from the Borders, in *The Lady of the Lake*, environment ceases to play a significant part and landscape, presented in geographical or tourist phrase, appears only as scenery; no real locality is established in terms of terrain, tradition and manners. An enduring admiration for Scott's powers of description has blurred the fact that in this work his set pieces are descriptive only, quite without penetration, lacking any place in time which characterises the environment of the first two poems; the historical period, supposedly the reign of James V, has little bearing on the narrative or the action. Walter Bagehot called the poem 'a sort of *boudoir* ballad'.

The point Scott had reached after some six years of verse composition can scarcely be described as development. His vigorous descriptions of Highland scenery and activity; the hunt, the summoning of the clans, the Trossachs, brilliant as they often are, remain tourist pieces, lacking the incisive and informative economy which carries his Border themes. Names here are no more than map references; they identify peaks, rivers and lochs without giving them any literary value, and in the end one is much inclined to accept Coleridge's assessment:

> In short, what I felt in *Marmion*, I feel still more in *The Lady of the Lake*—viz. that a man accustomed to cast words in metre, and familiar with descriptive Poets and Tourists, himself a Picturesque Tourist, must be troubled with a mental strangury, if he could not lift up his leg six times at six different Corners, and each time p— a canto.[19]

The King and Roderick Dhu go from Loch Katrine to Stirling, a messenger summons the clans, we see a Highland wedding and a Highland funeral; but for all their energy, the characters remain mere figures before a backcloth, not men and women moving through time and history. The absence of a convincing environment in the story of human events is made more conspicuous by the abrupt eruption of realism in Canto Fifth. James V (the supposed hunter, Fitzjames) meets Roderick Dhu and accuses him of lawless depredation in the south:

> 'Winning mean prey by causeless strife,
> Wrenching from ruin'd Lowland swain
> His herds and harvest rear'd in vain.—
> Methinks a soul, like thine, should scorn
> The spoils from such foul foray borne.'

and Roderick, the Gael, replies:

'Saxon, from yonder mountain high,
I mark'd thee send delighted eye,
Far to the south and east, where lay,
Extended in succession gay,
Deep waving fields and pastures green,
With gentle slopes and groves between:-
These fertile plains, that soften'd vale,
Were once the birthright of the Gael;
The stranger came with iron hand,
And from our fathers reft the land . . .

. . .

Pent in this fortress of the North,
Think'st thou we will not sally forth,
To spoil the spoiler as we may,
And from the robber rend the prey?'

    The matter here had to wait for prose: clan against Crown, Gael against Saxon, Highlander against Lowlander. They were old themes, arising from that cultural and racial clash first described by the historian John Fordun in 1380:

> The people of the coast are of domestic and civilised habits, trusty, patient and urbane, decent in their attire, affable and peaceful, devout in Divine worship yet always prone to resist a wrong at the hand of their enemies. The highlanders and people of the islands, on the other hand, are a savage and untamed nation, rude and independent, given to rapine, easy-living, of a docile and warm disposition, comely in person but unsightly in dress, hostile to the English people and language and owing to diversity of speech even to their own nation, and exceedingly cruel.[20]

It is a subject on which Scott the historian was very well informed, but clearly one to which he does not respond with the intensity that Border themes aroused; and so the history of a people where environment and manners play so distinguishing a part is subdued by an inchoate romantic fervour which Scott felt appropriate to verse. In spite of its success (25,000 copies sold in eight months) the whole work is marked by an uncertainty of touch more pronounced than in the aberrations of *The Lay* and *Marmion*.

    One fine passage I have already considered in Chapter I (pp. 16–17); this seems to me the only point in *The Lady of the Lake* where Scott succeeds in placing his characters in a context of time and tradition, and thereby breathing into them historical life; but the story of Brian the Hermit which occupies four stanzas in Canto Third has no counterpart elsewhere in this work, and his function as a character is more picturesque than anything else.

Scott's abandonment of poetry was inevitable. In spite of phenomenal popularity and soaring sales, his verse between 1805 and 1813 demonstrates a diminution rather than a development of his technical skill and structural ingenuity, showing only an increasing rigidity of form and cadence. Some of the contributory causes of the decline were evident from the beginning and Scott became acutely aware of them as time went on; his avowedly casual approach to verse writing, his haste and general carelessness, his concern with money, and his adopted pose of aiming low, of being a mere entertainer. The necessary cause, however, I believe to be more fundamental; Scott chose to write in the language of an alien, that is to say an English, literary tradition, though his themes in *The Lay*, *Marmion*, and *The Lady of the Lake* were quintessentially Scots. This imposed strains which ultimately dislocated the language, matter and style of his poetry, inducing a condition which time and fame only aggravated, for the Scots literary tradition was old, indigenous and strong.

In the fifteenth century, Scottish vernacular literature had a stature and significance of European proportions, especially in the writing of Robert Henryson, William Dunbar and Gavin Douglas. Within a hundred years, and largely it would appear as a result of the peculiarly oppressive nature of the Reformation in Scotland, the medieval glories were shrunk to a little measure; ancient centres of worship were destroyed, folk dance and drama were proscribed, and the written language rapidly became anglicised. Scots endured as a spoken but not as a literary tongue, and in the world of letters until the middle of the eighteenth century its influence was little felt. When Dr Johnson visited Edinburgh in 1773, he commented that 'the great, the learned, the ambitious and the vain all cultivate the English phrases and the English pronunciation'. A 'Society for Promoting the Reading and Speaking of the English Language' was formed; the prospectus, one historian comments, was not encouraging:

> As the intercourse between this part of Great Britain and the capital daily increases, gentlemen have long been sensible of the disadvantage under which they labour from their imperfect knowledge of the English language and the impropriety with which they speak it ... Experience hath convinced Scotsmen that it is not impossible for persons born and educated in this country to acquire such as to write it with considerable purity. But with regard to speaking with propriety it has generally been taken for granted that there was no prospect of attempting anything with any prospect of success.[21]

The folk tradition, however, did not die out entirely and, kept alive largely by oral transmission and by its colloquial currency in rural areas, re-emerged into literature in the later eighteenth century in the work of Robert Burns, directly influenced by the poetry of Robert Fergusson, and stimulated indirectly by the new interest in ballad collecting by such men as Allan Ramsay and David Herd.

One of the most cogent and impassioned comments on the problem of the language of Scots literature was made in 1808 by Francis Jeffrey in an article on Burns's poetry written for *The Edinburgh Review*. It deserves full quotation:

> . . . we must take leave to apprise our Southern readers that all his best pieces are written in Scotch; and that it is impossible for them to form any adequate judgment of their merits, without a pretty long residence among those who still use that language. To be able to translate the words is but a small part of the knowledge that is necessary. The whole genius and idiom of the language must be familiar; and the characters, and habits, and associations of those who speak it. We beg leave, too, in passing, to observe, that this Scotch is not to be considered as a provincial dialect, the vehicle only of rustic vulgarity and rude local humour. It is the language of a whole country, long an independent kingdom, and still separate in laws, character and manners. It is by no means peculiar to the vulgar; but it is the common speech of the whole nation in early life, and, with many of its exalted and accomplished individuals, throughout their whole existence; and though it be true that, in later times, it has been, in some measure, laid aside by the more ambitious and aspiring of the present generation, it is still recollected, even by them, as the familiar language of their childhood, and of those who were the earliest objects of their love and veneration. It is connected, in their imagination, not only with that olden time which is uniformly conceived as more pure, lofty, and simple than the present, but also with all the soft and bright colours of remembered childhood and domestic affection. All its phrases conjure up images of schoolday innocence, and sports, and friendships which have no pattern in succeeding years. And to all this, that it is the language of a great body of poetry with which almost all Scotchmen are familiar; and, in particular, of a great multitude of songs, written with more tenderness, nature, and feeling, than any other lyric compositions that are extant, and we may perhaps be allowed to say that the Scotch is, in reality, a highly poetical language; and that it is an ignorant as well as an illiberal prejudice, which would seek to confound it with the barbarous dialects of Yorkshire or Devon.[22]

The language of English neo-classicism held little that could enrich

Scott's themes, but when he turned his mind to the novel the precise and controlled manipulation of the two resulted in his greatest work.

After *Rokeby*, he began to express in what Walter Bagehot called 'more pliable prose' all the themes, and more, which had in vain dredged for depth in the poetry. It was as if this medium had dammed a flow whose pressure at last, in *Waverley*, burst it apart. Years before *The Lay* appeared, Wordsworth had commented scathingly on the state of contemporary letters; great literature, he complained, was neglected in favour of 'frantic novels, sickly and stupid German tragedies, and deluges of idle and extravagant stories in verse'.[23] In the decade that followed, verse found new directions without help from Scott but his influence on the novel was impressive. Contemporaries were struck by the extended realism of his writing; by the masterly interweaving of those features which, as Balzac later remarked in his preface to *La Comédie Humaine*, had become the very basis of nineteenth-century fiction: Drama, Character, Landscape, Description.

CHAPTER III

Waverley (1814)

Of some twenty-five novels by Scott, fourteen are concerned entirely with Scotland, and of these, ten with Scotland in the eighteenth century.[1] As history, the events portrayed are near-contemporary for Scott; certainly near enough in most cases for him to have associated from childhood with those who saw them happen. During the impressionable years from his convalescence at Sandyknowe after the attack of poliomyelitis which lamed him for life, to the period of his travels in the Highlands as his father's representative, he was in constant and vivid contact with old warriors; men who had been 'out' in the Jacobite risings of 1715 and 1745, old Scots who fed his restless romantic imagination with copious anecdotes and reminiscence. At the age of six, he was exploring the battlefield of Prestonpans where the Scots, under Charles Edward Stuart, routed the English army in 1745, and by the time he was Writer's Apprentice to his father he had 'penetrated into the Highlands, and formed those friendships among the surviving heroes of 1745 which laid the foundation for one great class of his works'.[2]

Scott repeated these Highland visits for several years, and the experiences he underwent, the tales he heard, and the men and women he met provided rich material for the Waverley Novels. As the outstanding pioneer of the historical novel, the man who went furthest ahead and opened up the widest field, Scott's prime advantage lay in his dealing with living history. This is essentially why his Scottish novels, and especially those set in the eighteenth century, are infinitely superior to the mainly medieval English tales. The scattered gems of the latter never quite compensate for their bookishness; they embody no vivifying spirit which can sustain, or even excuse their *longueurs*; the former are immediate in their impact on us, as the events were when they impressed Scott. 'The minds of men', he wrote for his grandson in 1827, 'are formed by their habitations.'[3] When Apprentice Scott visited those habitations, both in the Borders and in the Highlands, the breath of those who lived and died there in the Scottish troubles after 1688 was still warm upon them. This is the factor, Scott's direct apprehension of the life of his characters, in their world, not his, that allows Lukács to comment: 'Historical authenticity means for [Scott] the quality of the inner life, the morality, heroism, capacity for sacrifice, steadfastness etc., peculiar to a given age. This is the important, imperishable and—for the history of literature—epoch-making thing about Scott's historical authenticity . . .',[4] though the substance of such authenticity lies, I would submit, in the Scottish novels and not elsewhere.

Waverley is a significant work, not only because it is the first historical novel, but because it is where we see the beginning of Scott as a novelist, engaging with themes which obsessed him for most of his life; themes personal as well as historic and romantic; themes, indeed, where one sees in the medium of romantic fiction a means of interpreting the history of a people, of analysing human nature, and, through both of these, a process of self-discovery, self-knowledge. Deep in Scott, inescapable in all his dealings with the present as well as with the past, lay the uneasiness of the anglicised Scot, the contradiction of Jacobite sympathies and Hanoverian loyalties, the paradox of the realist who recognises the economic advantages of union with England, and the nationalist whose whole being cries out in shame at the betrayal of his traditions and his culture. In 1806, for example, Scott spoke long and eloquently at a debate of the Faculty of Advocates on the importance of preserving Scotland's most valuable institutions, especially the courts of law and the administration of justice, against government attempts to abolish them. After the meeting, he was complimented by his friends, who treated the whole matter somewhat lightheartedly. But for Scott, this had been no mere academic, rhetorical exercise: ' "No, no—'tis no laughing matter; little by little, whatever your wishes may be, you will destroy and undermine, until nothing of what makes Scotland Scotland shall remain." And so saying, he turned round to conceal his agitation—but not until Mr Jeffrey saw tears gushing down his cheek.'[5]

This is a concern which, in one way or another, informs almost all of the Scottish novels, and is particularly acute in *Waverley, Guy Mannering*, and *Redgauntlet*, where economic, military, cultural and political contexts are employed to give psychological depth to the dilemmas of an anxious, alienated hero.

From his earliest years, Edward Waverley's life is marked by divided loyalties. He is brought up to young manhood between the neglect or indifference of his father, Richard Waverley, dissatisfied younger brother, and the indolent indulgence of his uncle, Sir Everard, of Waverley-Honour; between the wavering Whig allegiance of his place-seeking father, and the Tory, High Church prejudices of his uncle; between the insincerities of an ostensibly Hanoverian supporter, and the sincere but inactive Jacobite sympathies of an English country gentleman.

Apart from an introductory account of Edward's childhood and youth, the entire action of Waverley takes place just before and during the Jacobite rising of 1745, up to the point where the movement was crushed for ever at the battle of Culloden in 1746 (though Scott returns to its later stirrings in Redgauntlet). Some understanding, therefore, of this phase of Scottish history is fundamental to an appreciation of the colours it took in Scott's eyes and his attempted analysis of the problem of loyalties. 'Seriously,' he wrote shortly before the publication of this first novel, 'I am very glad I did not live in 1745, for though as a lawyer I could not have pleaded Charles's right, and as a clergyman I could not have prayed for him, yet as a soldier I would, I am sure, against the conviction of my better reason, have fought for him even to the bottom of the gallows.'[6]

The Royal Scottish House of Stuart began directly to influence English affairs when James VI of Scotland became also James I of England on the death of Queen Elizabeth I in 1603, and the crowns of the two countries, though not the parliaments, became one. James was succeeded by his son, Charles I (beheaded in 1649), but the Stuart line continued after the Commonwealth with the restoration of Charles II in 1660. Their Roman Catholic allegiances, however, led to much disaffection, which culminated in 1688 in the expulsion of James II, Charles's brother and successor. He was succeeded by his son-in-law, William of Orange, a good Protestant, and the Stuart line came to an end with Anne, William's sister-in-law, daughter of James II. She died in 1714. The Union of the two parliaments was achieved during her reign, in 1707.

It was the exiled branch of the Stuart line that gave rise to the Jacobite movement (Jacobus is Latin for James), which so much affected Scottish attitudes in the eighteenth century and had so little political or practical impact. The expelled James II or VII spent the rest of his life in France, where Louis XIV used him and his following as a permanent but ultimately barren threat to Britain. It is with his son, James Francis Edward, the Chevalier de St George, that Stuart attempts to regain the throne begin, activated largely by the accession to the British throne on Anne's death of George I of Hanover, a prince with little knowledge of England, but a Protestant, and a collateral descendant of Charles I. The alternative was the Catholic James Francis Edward, widely recognised by his supporters as James III of England and VIII of Scotland, bred in exile, but nourished in the hope that the throne would be his.

His attempts to gain it, the most notable in 1715, failed, but the Jacobite torch was handed to his son, Charles Edward Stuart, romantically, and sadly, known as Bonnie Prince Charlie. By now, the thread which connected the Stuarts with the British throne was stretched very fine indeed. Political winds changed, James was no longer welcome in France and went to Rome, where Charles Edward was born in 1720 and brought up in the Catholic faith (his only brother and possible successor, Henry, Duke of York, became a Cardinal), and in the belief that he was heir to the united kingdoms. His first sight of them, in his twenty-fifth year, was from the deck of a French light frigate of eighteen guns, the *Du Teillay* (later known as the *Doutelle*) in July, 1745. He had come from France, with very dubious French support, and landed with only a few companions on the tiny Hebridean island of Eriskay, between Barra and South Uist. France was fickle, the English Jacobites diminishing both in numbers and conviction, but from this moment Charles Edward set out to conquer a kingdom. All he had was youth, a winning personality and romantic ambition. Not much. Yet, as Sir Charles Petrie remarks, 'had there been a Charles Edward in the field [in 1715] the Stuart cause must have triumphed'.[7]

The young Prince set foot on the Scottish mainland at a point on the northern shore of Loch-nan-Uamh, a sea loch driving in from the Sound of Arisaig. From here, he moved inland, virtually alone, accumulating Highland support on his way; most followed him under the influence of an abstract Stuart loyalty rather than a cool, practical appraisal of the state of the kingdom. By August 19 he was unfurling the royal standard in Glenfinnan at the head of Loch Shiel, fifteen miles east from his landing, proclaiming himself king, and marching towards Perth with near 2000 Highlanders.

During the march south, he had to contend with hostility or indifference in the districts he traversed, intrigue and contention among his leaders, and the traditional conduct of Highlanders after fighting, when they tended to disperse to take home their loot. By the time he reached Derby, after a courageous and determined penetration south of the border, the odds were heavily against him. No help had come from France, and the practical backing of the English Jacobites was derisory. The English forces, in some disarray after their defeat at Prestonpans in September, were now closing in, and with an ill grace Charles accepted the advice of his commanders and turned north. He crossed the border on December 19 and, after sporadic campaigning in the early months of 1746, finally engaged the English at Culloden, a few miles east of Inverness, in mid-April. His army was mercilessly destroyed and, once more virtually alone as he had come, he retreated, constantly pursued, back through the Western Isles, to France. A cairn marks the spot on Loch-nan-Uamh where he embarked, not far from where he had landed fourteen months before.

The possibilities that Scott saw here for fiction were extensive in their

E

paradoxical complexity: his hero must resolve for himself, in the light of experience, not of books or reflection, conflicts between Catholic and Protestant, Stuart and Hanoverian, Scots and English, contemplation and action, romance and reality, love and war, selfishness and altruism, metropolitan and provincial cultures. With deceptive simplicity, he describes his approach in his prefatory *Postscript to Waverley*:

> Now for the purpose of preserving some idea of the ancient manners of which I have witnessed the almost total extinction, I have embodied in imaginary scenes, and ascribed to fictitious characters, a part of the incidents which I then in youth received from those who were actors in them ... It has been my object to describe these persons, not by a caricatured and exaggerated use of the national dialect, but by their habits, manners, and feelings ...

and he acknowledges his debt to Maria Edgeworth, whose Irish regional novels, and especially *Castle Rackrent* (1800) and *The Absentee* (1812), had impressed him, striking out as they did to open up new territory for fiction. It is likely that the direction he indicates in the *Postscript* was taken late; that is to say, not when he wrote the first six chapters in 1805, and set them aside, but in 1814 when he was well aware of the appeal of his own regional themes in verse. We find him writing to Matthew Hartsonge, when *Waverley* was almost finished, that he had 'been delighted by the new vol. of Miss Edgeworth's Fashionable Tales especially by that of the absentee'.[8] A few weeks later, he wrote again to Hartsonge (who, of course, was unaware of the identity of the author of *Waverley*) that 'the Author must have had your inimitable Miss Edgeworth strongly in his view, for the manner is palpably imitated while the pictures are original'.[9] Later, he was to become more confident, more independent in his exploitation of Scottish features, and more successfully adventurous in his use of dialect; no character in *Waverley*, for example, has the folk stature of later dialect speakers like Dandie Dinmont in *Guy Mannering*, Edie Ochiltree in *The Antiquary*, or Cuddie Headrigg in *Old Mortality*. One reason for this, apart from an understandable caution, may well be that Scott was not a Highlander, and most of the Scottish action of *Waverley* occurs either in the Highlands or in the society of Highlanders; they would, in any event, speak Gaelic. Scott's greatest achievements in the characterisation of Scots people are always men and women of the Lowlands and the Borders, folk of his own country. The characters of *Waverley* are, however endeared to him, foreign to his deepest affections, and hence lacking in the intense inclusive realism in the life of place and family with which he endowed those other creations. Scott exploits the literary possibilities of locality in depth in his Scottish novels (and not at all elsewhere) and one may see the germ of this development in *Waverley*, both in the first chapters of the work (where it cannot have been his conscious intention) and in Edward's experiences in Scotland among Highlanders of varying social status and in Prince Charles's army.

What we find in *Waverley* is a sequence of events which imposes a series of tests on the young hero; these, successfully endured, though not without some ethical equivocation, lead him from the time when, a cloistered romantic, he writes:

> So, on the idle dreams of youth,
> Breaks the loud trumpet-call of truth,
> Bids each fair vision pass away,
> Like landscape on the lake that lay,
> As fair, as fitting, and as frail,
> As that which fled the Autumn gale,
> For ever dead to fancy's eye,
> Be each gay form that glided by,
> While dreams of love and lady's charms
> Give place to honour and to arms!

to those days, after the retreating battle of Clifton Moor, when, a fugitive in hiding,

it was in many a winter walk by the shores of Ullswater that he acquired a more complete mastery of a spirit tamed by adversity, than his former experience had given him; and that he felt himself entitled to say firmly, though perhaps with a sigh, that the romance of his life was ended, and that its real history had commenced.   (Ch. LX)

The tests provide a way of assessing his reactions to new localities, new social groups, and their customs, and the state of total, and endangered, isolation. The action of the novel and the process of his self-discovery lead him to Scotland as an officer in the English army, and later back to England as an officer in the Scots army of young Charles Stuart. Between these two excursions he is the guest of the Baron Bradwardine in the Perthshire lowlands, a Jacobite of the old school and friend of Sir Everard; of Donald Bean Lean, Highland predator, and of Fergus MacIvor, a dedicated Highland supporter of Charles Edward, with whom Edward forms a deep friendship.

In this first novel, Scott shows us through the medium of locality the growth of a young man's mind but, as we shall see, not without involving himself in moral as well as vocational difficulties, from which he emerges a little tousled.

The first six chapters serve as a prologue to the main action of the tale, covering Edward Waverley's boyhood and youth up to the time in 1745 when he takes a commission in the English army. What is interesting about Scott's conception here is that the main influence on the youth's mind is (as in Scott's own case) bookish, not parental, and up to the age of adolescence the boy leads an increasingly isolated life of the imagination. The two most potent sources from which this is fed are the huge library of Waverley-Honour, the scene of his wholly undirected, voracious reading, and the traditional tales and family legends told him by his uncle Everard and Aunt Rachel, Everard's sister.

Caught between a guilty sense of duty to field sports (which he dislikes) and learning (to which he cannot apply himself in any organised fashion) Edward develops a habit of taking a book in his pocket and a gun and spaniel at his side, and escaping into the hunting forest of Waverley-Chase, a vast area traversed by long broad avenues, where he would seek out the remoter paths which led him not to a quiet refuge for study but to a remote, dark lake, Mirkwood Mere, beyond the cliffs of a heavily wooded pass; 'there stood in former times, a solitary tower upon a rock almost surrounded by water, which had acquired the name of the Strength of Waverley because, in perilous times, it had often been the refuge of the family' (Ch. IV). It is this, rather than literature or action, which really stimulates his imagination. Only here, in touch with the physical presence of the past, with the stones and landscape which bear mute witness to the history of his family, can he 'chew the cud of sweet and bitter fancy'.

These chapters offer us a detailed and sensitive portrait of an adolescent boy—not the most frequent theme in the fiction of the period—and much of the material is clearly drawn from the author's own youth. The writing is leisurely, the study sympathetic without solemnity or sermonising. Edward is always ill at ease in company, even with young men of his own age:

> A deep and increasing sensibility added to this dislike of society. The idea of having committed the slightest solecism in politeness, whether real or imaginary, was agony to him; for perhaps even guilt itself does not impose upon some minds so keen a sense of shame and remorse, as a modest, sensitive, and inexperienced youth feels from the consciousness of having neglected etiquette, or excited ridicule. (Ch. IV)

Unfortunately, Scott does not continue in this vein, and even allowing for his modest and waggish self-depreciation, the hero that grows out of these chapters is not entirely a fulfilment of them, but closer than is comfortable to Scott's later description of him as a 'sneaking piece of imbecility'.[10] Mirkwood Mere and its tower, in spite of their apparent effect on Edward's youthful spirit, have no literary place. They pass out of Edward's mind as they pass out of the reader's and leave barely a trace. The history which is to mould the hero is that of his own time, and though *Waverley* contains many and frequent references to the past, especially in the pedantic garrulity of Baron Bradwardine, one is not often conscious of its pressure on present events, a pressure which Scott so often applies in other novels through the medium of locality.

Edward's romantic dreams of gallantry are soon dispersed by chill reality. He finds himself first in the English army in Dundee, holding a captain's commission obtained through his father's influence; it is an opportunity that Sir Everard views with mixed feelings. Here, he discovers he has no taste for the technicalities of military leadership, nor for the kind of application and industry that their acquisition demands. In his first setting out for Scotland to join his unit in Dundee, abandoned, he feels, to his own guidance and direction, he is apprehensive and hopeful, entering upon a world where 'for a time, all was beautiful because all was new'; but just as the romantic boy was something of a misfit at Waverley-Honour, so here he proves a blundering recruit, finds military discipline little to his liking, and takes leave in Perthshire at the estate of his uncle's old friend, the Baron Bradwardine.

Again, he enters a new environment whose terms he must learn. Bradwardine has been 'out' in the '15 and is now, like others of his persuasion, disarmed and discredited, and a continuing object of suspicion to Edward's commanding officer. To Edward, he is indistinguishably friend and foe, host, protector, entertainer, and, by purist standards, a traitor to the crown. Edward's journey into Scotland, though it takes place long after the Union of Parliaments in 1707, is in fact, like Marmion's, an excursion into alien, potentially enemy, yet nominally allied territory. It turns out too to be a journey into his own mind. Host and guest are widely separated by both age and attitude, opposed especially in matters of politics and poetry, yet 'they met upon history as on a neutral ground' where an old Jacobitish pedant and a young Hanoverian romantic can co-exist. Here is a very early and casual statement of what was to form the somewhat inchoate but nevertheless substantial philosophy of human relationships in a political world which underlies Scott's fiction; what matters to Scott in the broad as well as the narrow view is not the hostility of opposing parties but their reciprocity. The first is negative, destructive; the second painful certainly, pregnant with loss, dishonour and grief, since on this view one must both destroy and mourn one's enemies, yet, in the end, a creative opposition of mutual regard, positive, tending in the long run to reconciliation rather than annihilation. It represents Scott's own search for a way through his own dilemma; a difficult and profound theme, probably inescapably tragic, involving as it must apparently irreparable divisions of loyalty and love on a personal as well as a political level. But Scott never wrote of these things (and possibly could not bear to contemplate them) in terms of tragedy. In *Waverley*, as we shall see, he has not yet learned to tread without harm the tightrope he has chosen both for himself and for his hero.

Edward Waverley spends six weeks at Tully-Veolan, drawing closer to the Bradwardines, incurring his commanding officer's diplomatic displeasure for associating with those who had declined to take the oath of allegiance, passing his days in tranquil retreat from the emotional and intellectual demands of the outside world. At Tully-Veolan, as at Waverley-Honour, it is still possible for his romantic imagination to obscure reality; for example, he fails to appreciate the unassuming domestic charm of Rose Bradwardine (the Baron's only child, whom he eventually marries) because he is still seeking an impossible romance. Rose was too frank, too confiding, too kind; amiable qualities, undoubtedly, but destructive of the marvellous with which a youth of imagination delights to address the empress of his affections' (Ch. XIV). It is only when he has become the victim of deceit and cruelty that his appreciation of Rose emerges, though she remains second best to Flora Mac-Ivor whom Edward loves throughout as the wild romantic heroine of his dreams. But here too his imagination deceives him, concealing from his conscious mind the other Flora, the dedicated and ruthless Jacobite, married to a political cause. In the end, Flora, like Redgauntlet, enduringly loyal to her defeated ideal, retires to a French nunnery, haunted by the guilty belief that it is her fierce devotion to the Stuarts that has led her brother Fergus to a traitor's scaffold. But Edward has much to endure before his last meeting with Flora in Carlisle, as she sits sewing her condemned brother's shroud.

When, however, in Chapter VIII, Waverley arrives at the Perthshire manor-house of Tully-Veolan, Scott allows the reader as well as the hero plenty of time to become absorbed into a new, Highland, culture, which will soon draw him out of his prejudices, drive him further into himself. We are not given a mere romantic description of the mountain view, but a brief panorama which Scott uses simply, yet, with an eye to what follows, richly, to establish a relationship in both actual and symbolic terms. 'Edward gradually approached the Highlands of Perthshire, which had at first appeared a blue outline in the horizon, but now swelled into huge gigantic masses, which frowned defiance over the more level country that lay beneath them' (Ch. VII). On the contrary, Scott's immediate concern is not with the broader landscape at all, but with the more intimate details of the Tully-Veolan *ménage*. Of the eight chapters he gives to events here before Waverley moves into the Highlands, two are taken up entirely with a close and sympathetic description of the house and its people.

It is important, incidentally, that we should discriminate (since Scott does not always do so) between those scenes and occurrences which affect Waverley's mind and those on which he *appears* to reflect but in which it is really Scott speaking and offering information as a kind of touristic documentation. For instance, when he first rides into the village of Tully-Veolan, Edward finds the squalor and poverty very different from 'the smiling neatness of English cottages'. Scott devotes several informative pages to this picture of an environment both economically and socially depressed, but the place remains functionally dead, external to the narrative for most of the novel. Unlike village and castle in *The Bride of Lammermoor*, the relationship in *Waverley* between the local community and the big house is negligible. When we read that 'it seemed, upon the whole, as if poverty, and indolence, its too frequent companion, were combining to depress the natural genius and acquired information of a hardy, intelligent, and reflecting peasantry', we recognise that we are looking into Scott's mind, not Waverley's.

For a short time we find action suspended. After his somewhat withdrawn, introspective youth at Waverley-Honour, followed by the unwelcome shock of military training, Edward first sees in Tully-Veolan a return to the tranquillity of his uncle's country house:

> The solitude and repose of the whole scene seemed almost monastic; and Waverley, who had given his horse to his servant on entering the first gate, walked slowly down the avenue, enjoying the grateful and cooling shade, and so much pleased with the placid ideas of rest and seclusion excited by this confined and quiet scene, that he forgot the misery and dirt of the hamlet he had left behind him.   (Ch. VIII)

Of course, all is not so restful as it at first appears, but for the moment, the contrast with the barrack life of a regiment of eighteenth-century Dragoons could not be more emphatic. Yet a latent violence is conveyed in the ambiguity of the architecture of the house, half castle, half peaceful country residence, where there is a place for decorative flourishes beside the musketry loopholes, battlements and bartizans in carefully tended grounds. The suspension of action is brought home in Scott's concluding sentence where he refers to the episode as 'a chapter of still life'.

The oscillation between peaceful and warlike appearances continues in the next chapter when Waverley opens a little oak door 'well clenched with nails' in the courtyard; 'it was only latched, notwithstanding its fortified appearance, and, when opened, admitted him into the garden, which presented a pleasant scene'. Waverley is still dreaming. He sees the place as an enchanted castle in Spenserian terms; the garden is 'not quite equal to the gardens of Alcina'; before they meet later in the novel he thinks of Fergus Mac-Ivor as 'a sort of Highland Jonathan Wild', and of Donald Bean Lean as 'a second Robin Hood, perhaps, or Adam o' Gordon'; when he first sees Bradwardine striding towards him he is reminded of the fairy-tale seven-league boots. At this stage of experience his mind, in spite of Dragoons, continues to observe obliquely whatever is before it through a literary veil. As he grows in stature, so the veil is removed and he begins to see clearly, face to face. Now he is moving into a new and dangerous period of isolation.

After Bradwardine's '*démêlé* with the law of high treason in 1715, he had lived in retirement' exercising 'a solitary and secluded authority', and his friendship towards Waverley is qualified with a hint of tolerant regret: ' "And so ye have mounted the cockade? Right, right; though I could have wished the colour different, and so I would ha' deemed might Sir Everard" ' (Ch. X). In the light of the whole novel we see Edward's sojourn with the Baron as a time of preparation. In their own relationship, as I have already suggested, widely opposed as they are in age, character, experience, allegiance and intellectual practice, they find common ground in history; even here, their approaches are different but they are mutually tolerable. As a solution to genuine opposition, however, it is not enough to share common ground, and Waverley very soon discovers that common ground held with anyone in discussion may well be reduced to the mortally negligible proportions of a no-man's-land in a world where decisions have to be taken and practically maintained. In the life he must lead once he leaves the shelter of Tully-Veolan, he will no longer be guided either by his turncoat father, or by his uncle whose Jacobitism 'had been gradually decaying' since 1715, or by the Baron, of whose youthful courage and conviction little more than elderly pedantry seem to remain at this stage, though he does serve later under Charles Edward. He will meet with his peers, alone, and be compelled to his own decisions in a continuing context of cultural estrangement.

At the end of his six weeks at Tully-Veolan, he is thrust into a landscape and a social context where for the first time he suffers a mental and moral, as well as a physical exposure to wholly unfamiliar forces. The Highland band of Donald Bean Lean raids Bradwardine's estate and carries off all his cattle. At once, Edward begins to discover new facets of his hosts. Rose, young as she is, has known violence from childhood.

For her, Tully-Veolan is not a refuge but an exposed place; it 'has never been a safe or quiet residence when we have been at feud with the Highlanders', she tells Waverley, and describes to him a raid she saw when she was ten, in which

Three of the Highlanders were killed, and they brought them in wrapped in their plaids, and laid them on the stone floor of the hall; and next morning, their wives and daughters came, clapping their hands and crying the coronach, and shrieking, and carried away the dead bodies, with the pipes playing before them. I could not sleep for six weeks without starting, and thinking I heard these terrible cries, and saw the bodies lying on the steps, all stiff and swathed up in their bloody tartans. (Ch. XV)

The reader, as well as Waverley, is suddenly introduced to one of the ancient functions of women in a relatively primitive society, though Rose has been aware of it all her life and would see it as her role now; that is, the duty after the fighting of identifying, removing and burying their dead husbands, sons and brothers. It is not exclusive to Highland communities; the Border Widow laments

I sew'd his sheet, making my mane;
I watched the corpse, myself alane;
I watched his body, night and day;
No living creature came that way.

I took his body on my back,
And whiles I gaed, and whiles I sat;
I digg'd his grave, and laid him in,
And happ'd him with the sod sae green,

and after the Battle of Otterburn

Then on the morne they mayde them beerys
    Of byrche and haysell graye;
Many a wydowe, wyth wepynge teyres,
    Ther makes they fette awaye.

It is a Scottish girl's inescapable involvement in the action and ritual of a savage and bitter world, yet Waverley sees it with surprise and pleasure as no more than an illustration of his earlier daydreams of scenes of ancient times: 'I am actually in the land of military and romantic adventures, and it only remains to be seen what will be my own share in them'. He does not have to wait long.

The Baron has been safe for some time from Highland depredations because he has been paying black mail, or protection money, to Fergus Mac-Ivor, in whose territory Donald and his caterans operate. 'The boldest of these robbers', Rose tells Waverley, 'will never steal a hoof from any one that pays black mail to Vich Ian Vohr', and she goes on to outline to him the elaborate system of hierarchical relationships existing in the Highlands between the clan chieftain and his followers and dependants; a gentle introduction, later continued by his Highland guide, for the young English soldier to the protocol, ritual, allegiance and danger of the life he is soon to enter.

The immediate consequences of Donald Bean Lean's raid is the arrival of an emissary, Evan Dhu Maccombich, from Fergus Mac-Ivor, to negotiate a settlement. This he does, but his presence serves the more important literary purpose of introducing new dress, new speech, new manners to Waverley, which excite his interest in Highland life. He

> started at the sight of what he had not yet happened to see, a mountaineer in his full national costume. The individual Gael was a stout, dark, young man, of low stature, the ample folds of whose plaid added to the appearance of strength which his person exhibited. The short kilt, or petticoat, showed his sinewy and clean-made limbs; the goatskin purse, flanked by the usual defences, a dirk and steel-wrought pistol, hung before him; his bonnet had a short feather, which indicated his claim to be treated as a Duinhé-wassel, or sort of gentleman; a broadsword dangled by his side, a target hung upon his shoulder, and a long Spanish fowling-piece occupied one of his hands. With the other hand he pulled off his bonnet, and the Baron, who well knew their customs, and the proper mode of addressing them, immediately said, with an air of dignity, but without rising, and much, as Edward thought, in the manner of a prince receiving an embassy, 'Welcome, Evan Dhu Maccombich; what news from Fergus Mac-Ivor Vich Ian Vohr?' (Ch. XVI)

In the end, a settlement is reached, and solemnized by the drinking of usquebaugh. One of its consequences is that Waverley makes a further tour, this time on foot into the mountains some fifteen miles distant with Evan Dhu as his guide and instructor in Highland manners. Here he meets two kinds of outlaw: Donald Bean Lean, the cateran, and then Fergus Mac-Ivor, known as Vich Ian Vohr (the son of John the Great), soldier, Jacobite, clan chief who, with his sister Flora, is to have such a profound effect on Edward's life.

Scott's description of Donald Bean Lean's Highland refuge, a cave by a mountain loch, is unashamedly picturesque, though characteristically founded on an anecdote involving Rob Roy that Scott had heard about

1792 'from the mouth of the venerable gentleman who was involved in it'. The small party, led by Evan Dhu, reaches the place by moonlight, and Scott offers us a set piece of romantic chiaroscuro, with flickering firelight, pine torches, plaided and armed Highlanders and the spoils of their raid.

> Four or five active arms lifted Waverley out of the boat, placed him on his feet, and almost carried him into the recesses of the cave. He made a few paces in darkness, guided in this manner; and advancing towards a hum of voices which seemed to sound from the centre of the rock, at an acute turn Donald Bean Lean and his whole establishment were before his eyes.
>   The interior of the cave, which here rose very high, was illuminated by torches made of pine-tree, which emitted a bright and bickering light, attended by a strong, though not unpleasant odour. Their light was assisted by the red glare of a large charcoal fire, round which were seated five or six armed Highlanders, while others were indistinctly seen couched on their plaids in the more remote recesses of the cavern. In one large aperture, which the robber facetiously called his *spence* (or pantry), there hung by the heels the carcasses of a sheep, or ewe, and two cows lately slaughtered.   (Ch. XVII)

Though Waverley's helplessness is symbolically emphasised in the opening lines of this passage, one has the sense here that the author is not yet thinking and feeling his theme, only assembling it from the materials at hand, a suspicion which is confirmed by his introduction of the gang leader:

> The principal inhabitant of this singular mansion, attended by Evan Dhu as master of the ceremonies, came forward to meet his guest, totally different in appearance and manner from what his imagination had anticipated. The profession which he followed— the wilderness in which he dwelt—the wild warrior forms that surrounded him, were all calculated to inspire terror. From such accompaniments. Waverley prepared himself to meet a stern, gigantic, ferocious figure, such as Salvator would have chosen to be the central object of a group of banditti.
>   (Ch. XVII)

Donald Bean Lean turns out to be a little man, absurdly dressed, so puncturing another of Edward's romantic balloons, though the incongruity of his appearance helps to reinforce Scott's consistent emphasis on the importance of the natural harmony achieved by the unselfconscious. On such an occasion, moreover, Waverley's uniform of the *sidier roy* or red soldier is hardly the most tasteful or tactful attire. The matter of dress grows gradually in importance, and in relation to Waverley's affairs soon assumes a symbolic value which persists to the end of the novel. The cateran, having seen some service in the French army, has put aside his Highland dress in favour of 'an old blue and red uniform, and a feathered hat', by which he hopes to impress Waverley. Scott's touch is uncertain here, however. The dress image neatly places Lean on a lower social and intellectual level than Mac-Ivor, who makes no such show, and one does not really need to be told that 'he had served in some inferior capacity' in the French army. Scott's condescension here is identified with that of his hero, unaware of the impropriety of his own dress; the observation is both undeserved and unkind, since Lean is profusely hospitable and courteously apologises for missing elements in the meal: 'Where there are no bushes there can be no nuts, and the way of those you live with is that you must follow.' Waverley learns the truth of his words before very long.

Edward passes only one night in the company of the robbers but during this brief stay we become sensible of his isolation, his new experience of exposure. Although he is not of a gregarious nature, he has never been wholly alone or unprotected until this moment, and his growing awareness of alienation is now intensified by his ignorance of the Gaelic tongue which all about him speak. Communication, which he has always been able to take for granted, now depends on other wills than his own and he can be instantly excluded from the assembled company by a sudden change of language.

He must also attempt to reconcile himself to the forces which have shaped the moral code of the caterans and that of Mac-Ivor, and in doing so he must examine more closely his own increasingly frequent equivocations. Evan Dhu, accompanying him on the way to Mac-Ivor's house of Glennaquoich, continues his instruction in Highland ways and indignantly refutes the suggestion made to him by Waverley that Donald Bean Lean is no more than a common thief:

'He that steals a cow from a poor widow, or a stirk from a cottar, is a thief; he that lifts a drove from a Sassenach laird, is a gentleman drover. And, besides, to take a tree from the forest, a salmon from the river, a deer from the hill, or a cow from a lowland strath, is what no Highlander need ever think shame upon.'

'But what can this end in, were he taken in such an appropriation?'

To be sure he would *die for the law*, as many a pretty man has done before him.'

'Die for the law!'

'Ay; that is, with the law, or by the law; be strapped up on the *kind* gallows of Crieff, where his father died, and his goodsire died, and where I hope he'll live to die himsell, if he's not shot, or slashed, in a creagh.' (Ch. XVIII)

Politically too, Edward learns that the first loyalty for a Highlander is to his chieftain. 'We are for his king', says Evan Dhu of Mac-Ivor, 'and care not much which o' them it is.'

Unlike Donald Bean Lean, Fergus Mac-Ivor is unpretentious both in dress and in *ménage*, unwilling to appear before his visitor with any show of ostentatious dignity, though his attitude arises from pride rather than from modesty. The friendship of the two men grows quickly, nurtured by mutual respect yet restrained by opposing loyalties. Hitherto, Edward has had no experience of true commitment; no close acquaintance with men and women whose lives are dominated by a total involvement in the manipulation of contemporary history. Mac-Ivor has been, up to a point, a loyal Hanoverian subject, exercising his own considerable power to bring the rule of law to the Highlands, but exercising it in such a way as to bring government suspicion upon himself and the eventual withholding of his commission. His deeper loyalty is with the exiled family of Stuart and his attempts to bring order to the Highlands have been dictated by the hope of raising a Highland army to support Charles Edward, not by any feeling for the value of Hanoverian rule. The Stuart cause has occupied him from infancy (and we remember that nothing has occupied Waverley for very long) and he and Edward eventually become close friends and political allies when the Englishman finds himself utterly alone, his father disgraced and dismissed, himself deprived of his commission and a wanted man. He joins the Jacobite cause. Unlike Fergus, however, he is a convert, not a born Jacobite, and his allegiance is temporary and uneasy; urged and restrained in turn by reason rather than by passion, a state of mind symbolised by his failure, or refusal, to adopt completely the Highland dress. When he takes part in a stag-hunt, he 'complied so far with the custom of the country as to adopt the trews (he could not be reconciled to the kilt), brogues, and bonnet, as the fittest dress for the exercise in which he was to be engaged, and which least exposed him to be stared at as a stranger when they should reach the place of rendezvous' (Ch. XXIV). Nevertheless the decision represents an evolutionary development even if he does for the time see it as no more than protective camouflage.

Fergus, however, like Redgauntlet in the later novel, remains irrationally loyal in his total devotion to the King across the water. In a finely conceived passage introducing Flora Mac-Ivor, Scott outlines the subtle internal balances of their commitment to the house of Stuart:

Early education had impressed upon her mind, as well as on that of the Chieftain, the most devoted attachment to the exiled family of Stuart. She believed it the duty of her brother, of his clan, of every man in Britain, at whatever personal hazard, to contribute to that restoration which the partizans of the Chevalier de St George had not ceased to hope for. For this she was prepared to do all, to suffer all, to sacrifice all. But her loyalty, as it exceeded her brother's in fanaticism, excelled it also in purity. Accustomed to petty intrigue, and necessarily involved in a thousand paltry and selfish discussions, ambitious also by nature, his political faith was tinctured at least, if not tainted, by the views of interest and advancement so easily combined with it; and at the moment he should unsheath his claymore, it might be difficult to say whether it would be most with the view of making James Stuart a king, or Fergus Mac-Ivor an earl. This, indeed, was a mixture of feeling which he did not avow even to himself, but it existed, nevertheless, in a powerful degree.

In Flora's bosom, on the contrary, the zeal of loyalty burned pure and unmixed with any selfish feeling.   (Ch. XXI)

Scott's hand, however, is inconsistent and a number of scenes in which she appears as a stereotyped romantic heroine, speaking an absurd language of high culture ('A truce, dear Fergus! spare us those most tedious and insipid persons of all Arcadia. Do not, for Heaven's sake, bring down Coridon and Lindor upon us') detract from his initial conception of her as the dedicated and ruthless rebel, even accepting that she, like so many of her class, has had a courtly education in France. Flora's commitment is gallows high, though it brings her in the end only the quietude of a Benedictine convent. Until late in the novel, neither her brother nor Waverley fully recognises or believes the strength of this political passion, in spite of her early and firm rejection of Edward's proposal of marriage. 'From infancy till this day', she tells him, 'I have had but one wish—the restoration of my royal benefactors to their rightful throne. It is impossible to express to you the devotion of my feelings to this single subject; and I will frankly confess, that it has so occupied my mind as to exclude every thought respecting what is called my own settlement in life' (Ch. XXVII).

For some time after this rejection, Edward endures other forms of isolation and exposure as a suspected traitor to King George, a series of experiences which stretch both his mind and his loyalties to the point at which, rescued from the English law by a Scots outlaw he at length finds himself again in the company of Vich Ian Vohr, but this time in the presence of Prince Charles Edward at the Palace of Holyrood: a Prince euphoric after his victorious march from Moidart. Now, 'rejected, slandered, and threatened upon the one side, he was irresistibly attracted to the cause which the prejudices of education, and the political principles of his family, had already recommended as the most just . . . and Waverley, kneeling to Charles Edward, devoted his heart and sword to the vindication of his rights' (Ch. XL). He now follows his Prince loyally through the battle of Prestonpans and south as far as Derby, outwardly signifying his complete change of heart by wearing the full battle tartan of Vich Ian Vohr. He is now, as Fergus says, 'a complete son of Ivor'. By this time, too, 'he equalled the Highlander in the endurance of fatigue, and was become somewhat acquainted with their language' (Ch. LVII). Such an assumption of protective colouring gives an economical indication of how far, both physically and philosophically, he has been absorbed into his environment. A logical progression; a phase completed.

From the time of the stag-hunt (Ch. XXIV) and Waverley's abduction, landscapes are for the most part conventionally presented, either to locate an incident or to romanticise a prospect; action and reflection are suspended while, with the hero, we look at the view.

After the retreat from Derby, other factors come into play. Fergus, in the first place, loses heart entirely, not, as might be supposed, from the weariness of defeat—the hopelessness of his cause has never disturbed him—but from the certainty of superstition. He has seen the Bodach Glas, the Grey Spectre and believes his death is now certain. We remember his respect for the spells uttered over Waverley's stag-hunting injuries:

> Edward observed, with some surprise, that even Fergus, notwithstanding his knowledge and education, seemed to fall in with the superstitious ideas of his countrymen, either because he deemed it impolitic to affect scepticism on a matter of general belief, or more probably because, like most men who do not think deeply or accurately on such subjects, he had in his mind a reserve of superstition which balanced the freedom of his expressions and practice upon other occasions.
>
> (Ch. XXIV)

In extremity, the great Highland chief, Vich Ian Vohr, cosmopolitan by birth and education, polished in manner and skilled in the ways of the world, returns to the fears and the faith of his forebears; nature, not improbably, overrides nurture. He is captured at the last Jacobite battle in England, at Clifton Moor near Penrith, and later philosophically suffers a traitor's end in Carlisle. Here, too, ends Edward Waverley's military career. 'The plumed troops and the big war', he confesses later, echoing Othello, 'used to enchant me in poetry; but the night marches, vigils, couches under the wintry sky, and such accompaniments of the glorious trade, are not at all to my taste in practice' (Ch. LXII).

Can the author rescue his hero from what looks like moral dereliction on both sides of the border? Not, it appears, without a sentimental compromise which conceals an unexpected irony. Edward marries Rose Bradwardine and they live happily on the Bradwardine estate, restored to its former splendour after the rebellion by the generosity of Colonel Talbot, whose life Edward had saved at Prestonpans, and to whose intercession with the King he owes his own pardon. The clue to the compromise, however, is the one addition to Tully-Veolan Talbot has made, 'a large and spirited painting, representing Fergus Mac-Ivor and Waverley in their Highland dress, the scene a wild, rocky and mountainous pass, down which the clan were descending in the background'. Nothing could be more revealing of Scott's dilemma, from which he extricates himself but lamely. Fergus, the mountains, the clan, the Highland dress, are all of a piece; they represent one allegiance, for which Fergus and his men died, and for which his sister renounced the world. Waverley here is merely a curious English tourist, wearing fancy dress, who for all his adventures loses nothing.

Almost the last words of the novel are uttered by the Baron Bradwardine; he proposes a cup of gratitude to Colonel Talbot and 'the Prosperity of the united Houses of Waverley-Honour and Bradwardine'. The union is an obvious reference to the Act of 1707 but the price, in moral terms, is not shown.

CHAPTER IV

Guy Mannering (1815)

'I want to shake myself free of Waverley, and accordingly have made a considerable exertion to finish an odd little tale . . . It is a tale of private life, and only varied by the perilous exploits of smugglers and excise-men . . .', Scott wrote to his friend John Morritt in January, 1815.[1] He had just completed *Lord of the Isles*, and a few weeks later, on 24 February, *Guy Mannering* was published, 'the work of six weeks at a Christmas'.[2]

The remark to Morritt isolates an essential characteristic of Scott's second novel which not only distinguishes it from *Waverley*, but signposts a new direction for his fiction. Though most of the action takes place towards the end of the American War of Independence, nothing in this novel relates to the broad movement of history; it is no tale of armies, battles, thrones and powers; its major actors are not princes, potentates or generals, but gipsies, farmers, lawyers, smugglers, and the epigoni of Scottish nobility, who play out their violent and intriguing roles along the northern shores of the Solway Firth, in Dumfriesshire and Galloway, and in the western Borders where Scott moves easily and familiarly. He was to use the region again and even more vitally in *Redgauntlet*, almost a decade later. A consequence of this contraction of view is that one can see the almost organic gestation of the novel from Scott's own youthful excursions and from the anecdotes of folk life he was so fond of collecting.

As a boy, he heard the tale of the astrologer from John MacKinlay, an old Highland servant of his father's; this was brought to his mind again in 1814, when he became acquainted with Joseph Train, Supervisor of Excise at Newton-Stewart and a collector of local anecdote and historical material. Train provided him with stories of the Galloway gipsies and a 'local story of an astrologer who, calling at a farm-house at the moment when the good-wife was in travail, had, it was said, predicted the future fortune of the child, almost in the words placed in the mouth of John MacKinlay, in the Introduction to *Guy Mannering*'.[3] After Scott's death, Train discovered *The Durham Garland*, a ballad recording the same incident, but with much more detail;[4] it is thin brose as a ballad, of

F

indifferent broadsheet quality, but it does introduce into MacKinlay's version the theme of lost identity, the suspicion of the hero's villainy, and the eventual marriage of the hero with the astrologer's daughter. Lockhart presumes that Scott must have read this Durham broadsheet in boyhood and failed to mention it in his Introduction of 1829 simply because of the haste with which those Introductions were compiled.

Other major elements in *Guy Mannering* are drawn directly from Scott's own experience as a traveller in the Borders, or from his work and reading as an Edinburgh advocate.[5] Such sources, however, provide structures only and the heart of *Guy Mannering* does not beat in its structure but in its feeling for locality. The pulse is felt at two kinds of pressure point: the evocation, in terms of landscape and people, of the region in which the plot evolves, and the rich dialogue of those people as distinct from the pallid and formal exchanges of the gentry. Scott draws here on his own knowledge of the Borders and its folk.

In 1797 he spent some time in Cumberland, exploring a wide region, including the Roman Wall, and staying for a time in what was then the spa town of Gilsland, absorbing impressions which later enriched *St Ronan's Well*, and provided ideas for *The Bridal of Triermain*. The region gave him the original of Mump's Ha', and more tales, including 'Fighting Charlie of Liddesdale' which provided some colour for his development of Dandie Dinmont.

His own Border locality gave him Meg Merrilies, one of the most vital figures in the novel; she exists as a brilliant character in her own right but also, and, equally important, as part of a gipsy community whose role in the Border society of the day Scott represents here with some elaboration. He had known the race from childhood, both in the stories of his Sandyknowe days, from the mouth of his grandfather, as well as from the constant presence of gipsies in the Borders, where they had first appeared in the sixteenth century. Their headquarters were at Kirk Yetholm, just on the Scottish side of the border between Northumberland and Roxburgh. 'My memory', he writes in his Introduction, 'is haunted by a solemn remembrance of a woman of more than female height, dressed in a long red cloak, who commenced acquaintance by giving me an apple.' This woman he believes to have been Madge Gordon, grand-daughter of Jean Gordon, queen of the gipsies, from whom Meg is drawn. Jean, a Jacobite supporter, made her allegiance too obvious in Carlisle after the 1745 rising, and was ducked to death in the River Eden by a local mob, crying as often as she could get her head above water, 'Chairlie yet! Chairlie yet!' until the end. It is a sickening story which Scott must have had in mind when he came to write of Madge

Wildfire and her mother in the same city, in *The Heart of Midlothian* three years later.

Scott had maturer dealings with gipsies too, both as sheriff and as the owner of Abbotsford, about whose grounds they moved unmolested, though Scott's man Tom Purdie (himself a former poacher whom Scott had taken into his service) found them less tolerable. 'If folk but kenned them as I ken them', he said, 'there would be less trock wi' sic a crew.'[6] In his later years, ill and anxious, Scott made a journey to Edinburgh, stopping at an inn on the way and recording in his journal, 'Ah! good Mrs Wilson, you know not you are like to lose an old customer', to which Lockhart adds the note: 'Mrs Wilson, landlady of the inn at Fushie, one stage from Edinburgh,—an old dame of some humour, with whom Sir Walter always had a friendly colloquy in passing. I believe the charm was that she had passed her childhood among the gipsies of the Border.'[7] The narrative that Scott generated from such material is soon traced.

As a young tourist, just down from Oxford, Guy Mannering, benighted in Dumfriesshire, is given hospitality by Godfrey Bertram, Laird of Ellangowan, on the eve of the birth of his first child, Harry. Mannering indulges his hobby and half-jokingly casts the horoscope of the child, but he is alarmed at what he sees and asks the parents not to look at the prediction he has written down until the boy's fifth birthday. When that day comes, Harry is abducted by smugglers, taken to Holland, and is henceforth known as Vanbeest Brown. Later, he is sent to India as an agent for a Dutch firm and when it collapses he joins the army. There he rises to the rank of captain in Colonel Mannering's regiment. The Colonel suspects Brown of having an affair with his wife and eventually challenges him to a duel (ostensibly over a game of cards). Brown is left for dead, but is alive; he is captured by Indians, escapes, and finally follows Mannering to Scotland where, following the death of his wife and the illness of his daughter he has taken up residence near Ellangowan. It is, of course, the daughter, Julia Mannering, with whom Brown has been in love all along. He goes through many trials before he can be accepted by her, discovering on the way that he is not Vanbeest Brown, but Harry Bertram, heir to Ellangowan which has, for seventeen years, been in the hands of the sly lawyer, Gilbert Glossin. In the end, through the agency of Meg Merrilies, who was also present with predictions at his birth, he is recognised, rescued from false imprisonment and restored to his property. Mannering is reconciled to him and he marries Julia. His original kidnappers make another attempt to remove him, but lose their own lives. Meg is destroyed in the final affray.

The seriousness of the novel lies elsewhere than in its melodramatic plot: in the gipsy settlement at Derncleugh, in Dandie Dinmont's Liddesdale farm, in Bewcastle Waste, in Edinburgh's Old Town, and in the kitchen of the Gordon Arms at Kippletringan. In these places Scott shows us, as if he were demonstrating the anatomy of a living organism, how a community lives, and how all the cells in that community must function in moral as well as material concord if it is to survive.

Derncleugh (the name is intended to evoke the picture of an obscure and gloomy wooded glen) is a lonely defile where a gipsy colony has settled and erected a few huts which they called their 'city of refuge'. Here, on the estate of Ellangowan,

> they had been such long occupants, that they were considered in some degree as proprietors of the wretched shealings which they inhabited. This protection they were said anciently to have repaid, by service to the laird in war, or, more frequently, by infesting and plundering the lands of those neighbouring barons with whom he chanced to be at feud. Latterly their services were of a more pacific nature. The women spun mittens for the lady, and knitted boot-hose for the laird, which were annually presented at Christmas with great form. The aged sybils blessed the bridal bed of the laird when he married, and the cradle of the heir when born. The men repaired her ladyship's cracked china, and assisted the laird in his sporting parties, wormed his dogs, and cut the ears of his terrier puppies. The children gathered nuts in the woods, and cranberries in the moss, and mushrooms on the pastures for tribute to the Place. These acts of voluntary service and acknow- ledgements of dependence, were rewarded by protection on some occa- sions, connivance on others, and broken victuals, ale and brandy, when circumstances called for a display of generosity; and this mutual inter- course of good offices, which had been carried on for at least two centuries, rendered the inhabitants of Derncleugh a kind of privileged retainers upon the estate of Ellangowan.   (Ch. VII)

This symbiotic relationship is brought to an end early in the novel by the Laird, the inane Godfrey Bertram, by an act that proves mortal to both parties. The gipsies become an embarrassment to Bertram when he is elevated to the Bench and feels he must sacrifice his indolent indiffer- ence to the life of his estate in order to preserve his dignity. Their depredations confront him with an unwelcome moral problem which he attempts to solve first by harassing and eventually by evicting them. The curious bond, of affection and distrust, which is seen throughout history to bind in its reciprocal coils so many people and institutions, is thus hastily and clumsily severed. Bertram, acting strictly in accordance with the law, perpetrates an injustice, and the consequences of such an abrupt disturbance of the delicate ecological balance of Ellangowan's inhabitants are extensive and entirely detrimental. Scott's own solution to Bertram's difficulty is never in doubt; it is at the same time an interesting revelation of the author's attitude to a certain kind of organic community, and of his view of the proper relationship that should exist between laird and dependents.

> Ought the mere circumstances of Bertram's becoming a magistrate to have made at once such a change in his conduct towards them? Some means of reformation ought at least to have been tried, before sending seven families at once upon the wide world, and depriving them of a degree of countenance which withheld them at least from atrocious guilt.   (Ch. VIII)

The hint here is vital to an understanding both of the nature of the relationship and of the sensitive social balance that sustains it. The Laird's tolerance of the gipsies may in one view be seen as a condonement of vice; in Scott's view it is an agency of moral restraint on a people whose crimes are not always petty. The sympathy we may feel for the evicted gipsies, whose punishment seems excessive, Scott carefully balances by throwing into the scale other members of the tribe whose lives as smugglers or footpads are shot through with treachery, dishonesty, violence and cruelty. When Mannering, on first seeing Meg Merrilies, asks who she is, Dominie Sampson replies succinctly, 'Harlot, thief, witch, and gipsy' (Ch. III). Bertram may misjudge his problem and exercise his powers clumsily; but his problem is a real one, and he is not dealing with a tame tribe. The eviction is carried out with the customary heartlessness of such ceremonies, on Martinmas Day, after the gipsies of Derncleugh have refused all orders to move,

> A strong posse of peace-officers, sufficient to render all resistance vain, charged the inhabitants to depart by noon; and, as they did not obey, the officers, in terms of their warrant, proceeded to unroof the cottages, and pull down the wretched doors and windows,—a summary and effectual mode of ejection, still practised in some parts of Scotland, when a tenant proves refractory.   (Ch. VIII)

The gipsies leave, meeting the Laird with sullen contempt, and here, for a moment, Scott's realism slips to one side. 'The group would have made an excellent subject for the pencil of Calotte',[8] he comments, and at once the banished families (having already, in addition, suffered the attentions of the press-gang) become objects not of sympathy but of tourist curiosity. Familiar though he was with their kind in real life, this group does not inhabit the literary part of his mind. A year later, with the Mucklebackits in his next novel, The Antiquary, Scott was to approach much nearer the truth of fiction. One finds the same uncertainty of touch in his presentation of Meg Merrilies, the same havering between a picturesque theatricality and a genuinely dramatic realism. When the gipsies leave, she stands on a bank above Bertram as he goes his way and her folk theirs. 'Her attitude was that of a sybil in a frenzy', but the rhetoric of her malediction is dignified, powerful and effective:

> 'Ride your ways', said the gipsy, 'ride your ways, Laird of Ellangowan—ride your ways, Godfrey Bertram!—this day have ye quenched seven smoking hearths—see if the fire in your ain parlour burn the blither for that. Ye have riven the thack off seven cottar houses—look if your ain roof-tree stand the faster.—Ye may stable your stirks in the shealings at Derncleugh—see that the hare does not couch on the hearthstane at Ellangowan.—Ride your ways, Godfrey Bertram— what do ye glower after our folk for?—There's thirty hearts there, that wad hae wanted bread ere ye had wanted sunkets, and spent their life-blood ere ye had scratched your finger. Yes—there's thirty yonder, from the auld wife of an hundred to the babe that was born last week, that ye have turned out o' their bits o' bields, to sleep with the tod and the blackcock in the muirs!—Ride your ways, Ellangowan . . .'
>
> (Ch. VIII)

Here, however, the gipsy community disappears from the novel, leaving only Meg and Tod Gabbie to play their individual parts.

But Meg's words are not mere rhetoric. Throughout the novel, the dialogue of country folk and gipsies, in particular the speech of Meg, Dandie Dinmont, Mrs MacCandlish and Jock Jabos reveal a linguistic virility totally absent from the genteel interchanges of their superiors, and sometimes from Scott's own narrative. When the gipsies gather at Derncleugh, which they continue to use as a secret rendezvous, they speak a mixture of Border dialect and thieves' cant:

> 'Why', replied Jack, 'the people got rusty about it, and would not deal and they had bought so many brooms that—'
> 'Well, for all that', said the other, 'I think we should be down upon the fellow one of these darkmans, and let him get it well.'
> 'But old Meg's asleep now', said another; 'she grows a driveller and is afraid of her shadow. She'll sing out some of these odd-come-shortlies, if you don't look sharp.'
> 'Never fear', said the old gipsy man; 'Meg's true-bred; she's the last

in the gang that will start—but she has some queer ways, and often cuts queer words.'

With more of this gibberish, they continued the conversation, rendering it thus, even to each other, a dark obscure dialect, eked out by significant nods and signs, but never expressing distinctly or in plain language the subject on which it turned. (Ch. XXVIII)

Though Scott here does make concessions to gentility, it is clear both from the language of the passage as a whole, and from his concluding gloss that he is conscious of the problem of rendering the occasion in speech and is attempting to resolve it. An even more telling instance of this distinction of styles occurs later in a dialogue between Meg and young Hazlewood before the Portanferry rescue.

'Good God! what do you mean?' said young Hazlewood; 'your words and manner would persuade me you are mad, and yet there is a strange combination in what you say.'

'I am not mad!' exclaimed the gipsy; 'I have been imprisoned for mad—scourged for mad—banished for mad—but mad I am not. Hear ye, Charles Hazlewood of Hazlewood: d'ye bear malice against him that wounded you?'

'No, dame, God forbid! My arm is quite well, and I have always said the shot was discharged by accident. I should be glad to tell the young man so himself.'

'Then do what I bid ye', answered Meg Merrilies, 'and ye'll do him mair gude than ever he did you ill; for if he was left to his ill-wishers he would be a bloody corpse ere morn, or a banished man—But there's ane abune a'.—Do as I bid you; send back the soldiers to Portanferry. There's nae mair fear o' Hazlewood House than there's o' Cruffelfell.'

And she vanished with her usual celerity of pace. (Ch. XLVII)

Here, without heavily loading Meg's speech with dialect terms, or introducing typographical devices to point the expression, Scott effectively differentiates, largely through rhythm and pace, the energy of the gipsy and the effeteness of the young gentleman. The distinction is made even more clear by the language of the next paragraph:

It would seem that the appearance of this female, and the mixture of frenzy and enthusiasm in her manner, seldom failed to produce the strongest impression upon those whom she addressed. Her words, though wild, were too plain and intelligible for actual madness, and yet too vehement and extravagant for sober-minded communication. She seemed acting under the influence of an imagination rather strongly excited than deranged; and it is wonderful how palpably the difference, in such cases, is impressed upon the mind of the auditor.

The ponderous and verbose condescension of the passage adds nothing at all to what has gone before, though its absurdity accidentally intensifies the realism of Meg's words. These again recall us to the fact that after the murder of Kennedy and Harry's abduction she was, though innocent,

> long confined in jail under the hope that something might yet be discovered to throw light upon this dark and bloody transaction. Nothing, however, occurred; and Meg was at length liberated, but under sentence of banishment from the county as a vagrant, common thief, and disorderly person.   (Ch. X)

Cruelty and ignorance, Scott suggests here, and indeed throughout, are not the prerogative of nomads and smugglers, and we become increasingly aware, through the very consistency of Meg's language, that he has here characterised one who has 'the savage virtue of fidelity in the same per-fection' as Jean Gordon of Yetholm.[9]

The Derncleugh material is rich, especially in Scott's apprehension of it as a working, organic landscape, a kind of Debatable Land on the Ellangowan estate. He communicates with wit and sympathy the func-tional balance between the gipsies and the other groups in this small society. Derncleugh itself features only occasionally, though in the end, Meg, shot by the smuggler Dirk Hatteraick, asks to be taken to the Kaim of Derncleugh, a ruined tower on the edge of the glen, to die. This too is where Hatteraick's lieutenant, Brown (Harry's namesake), shot in the raid on Woodbourne, ends his life in Meg's care. In death, Derncleugh is still a place of belonging but the old relationship with the big house is never re-established.

When Meg leads Harry and Dinmont to capture Hatteraick, they pass the ruined settlement on the way to the Kaim of Derncleugh, and there,

> pausing with a look of peculiar and softened interest before one of the gables which was still standing, she said, in a tone less abrupt, though as solemn as before, 'Do you see that blackit and broken end of a sheeling?—There my kettle boiled for forty years—there I bore twelve buirdly sons and daughters—Where are they now?—Where are the leaves that were on that auld ash-tree at Martinmas?—the west wind has made it bare—and I'm stripped too.—Do you see that saugh-tree? —it's but a blackened rotten stump now—I've sat under it mony a bonnie summer afternoon, when it hung its gay garlands ower the poppling water—I've sat there, and' (elevating her voice) 'I've held you on my knee, Henry Bertram, and sung ye sangs of the auld barons

and their bloody wars—It will ne'er be green again, and Meg Merrilies
will never sing sangs mair, be they blithe or sad. But ye'll no forget
her?—and ye'll gar big up the auld wa's for her sake?—   (Ch. LIII)

This is not a romantic, nostalgic recollection, a piece of melancholy self-
indulgence; it is a lament, profoundly felt, for a way of life that has been
irrecoverably damaged by selfishness, ignorance and vanity; a lament
Scott was to echo four years later in the words of Old Alice, victim of a
similar insensitiveness, in The Bride of Lammermoor.

Later, after Meg's death, Dinmont recalls her words as he and Bertram
ride past the ruins of the old settlement. ' "I'm sure when ye come into
your ain again, Captain," ' says the farmer, ' "ye'll no forget to big a bit
cot-house there?" ' (Ch. LV). And in the last chapter we find that
Bertram is indeed planning such a cottage, but it is unlikely ever to be a
gipsy refuge; those families and all they represented on the estate of
Ellangowan are irretrievably dispersed, and they have no place in the
heart of the young heir.

The nomadic tendencies of the gipsies, notwithstanding their occupation of Derncleugh, appears in strong contrast to the settled and ancient
tenure of the Bertrams of Ellangowan. Like old Ravenswood in The Bride
of Lammermoor, Godfrey Bertram 'succeeded to a long pedigree and a
short rent-roll'. In his second chapter, Scott introduces the Laird by way
of a lengthy genealogical history of the castle and its family, punctuated
by references to significant dates in Scottish history and events in which
the family had taken part, having 'made war, raised rebellions, been
defeated, beheaded, and hanged, as became a family of importance, for
many centuries'. The mild rhetoric of the passage ironically links them
with the smugglers whom their captain, Hatteraick, describes as 'all dead,
shot, hanged, drowned, and damned' (Ch. XXXIV). The sequel dis-
appoints, however. Scott establishes the degeneracy of the present owner
by this means, but for the remainder of the novel the past plays no part
in giving the action a living context. Similar historical circumstances
obtain in the case of the family of Ravenswood, but Scott weaves them
into the fabric of the later novel in a very different way.

The immediate source for Ellangowan Castle, Scott explains in a note,
is Caerlaverock Castle, still a splendid ruin on the Solway coast a few
miles south of Dumfries, though he places it on a coastline more like the
rugged cliffs of Galloway further to the west. His description of the front
of the castle corresponds closely with the appearance of Caerlaverock
from the north:

It consisted of two massive round towers, projecting deeply and darkly,
   at the extreme angles of a curtain, or flat wall, which united them,

and thus protecting the main entrance, that opened through a lofty arch in the centre of the curtain into the inner court of the castle. The arms of the family, carved in freestone, frowned over the gateway, and the portal showed the spaces arranged by the architect for lowering the portcullis and raising the drawbridge.   (Ch. IV)

The language of this is concise and accurate, a workmanlike description, without excess or extravagance, simply of what is there. And what is there, however ruinous, represents place and history in the family of Ellangowan, the crumbling but dignified record of an epoch, a phase in the continuity of the community. Near it is the New Place, 'an awkward mansion, indeed, in point of architecture', but a suitable emblem of its most recent tenants. At the close of the novel, however, Scott offers us an equivocal and possibly bizarre building to be the dwelling of the new Laird; in Chapter LVIII we discover Mannering studying plans 'relating to a large and splendid house, which was to be built on the site of the New Place of Ellangowan, in a style corresponding to the magnificence of the ruins in its vicinity'. So far, the reader might reasonably expect Harry Bertram's return to reunite and revitalise the community, but Scott's concluding concern with such matters is quite perfunctory, having been wholly subdued by the romances of the Bertrams, Mannerings and Hazlewoods. The plans (which do not escape Pleydell's irony) have been made by Mannering, and they represent an abrupt, backward-looking change, not an evolutionary process in which provision may be made for the estate dependents as well as respect for the family. Harry Bertram might conceivably have given the place new dignity; all Mannering can do is imitate old pride. It is a piece of hurried writing in which Scott once again misses an opportunity of bringing together in consistent and realistic harmony the three main groups in the novel: Laird, villagers, and the younger generation of the large houses.

Even the degeneracy of the old Laird is reflected not in the ruin of the old castle, or in the tawdriness of the New Place, to any significant degree; it lies in his alienating his humble neighbours as soon as he achieves his long-cherished ambition and becomes a justice of the peace. With a sweep of his new broom he rids the locality of petty law-breakers whose depredations, though real enough, were relatively harmless, hallowed by time and the indolence of Ellangowan. Godfrey Bertram, J.P., 'ruthlessly commenced his magisterial reform, at the expense of various established and superannuated pickers and stealers, who had been his neighbours for half a century' (Ch. VI). By this means he wins the applause of the Bench, and the contempt of the community; 'even the admitted nuisance', Scott comments with characteristic humanity, 'of ancient standing, should not be abated without some caution'. Bertram's zeal in carrying out his new duties shows an insensitivity to local relationships which soon disrupts irremediably the long-standing pattern of life there.

> We are not made of wood or stone, and the things which connect themselves with our hearts and habits cannot, like bark or lichen, be rent away without our missing them. The farmer's dame lacked her usual share of intelligence,—perhaps also the self-applause which she had felt while distributing the *awmous* (alms) in shape of a *gowpen* (handful) of oatmeal, to the mendicant who brought the news. The cottage felt inconvenience from interruption of the petty trade carried on by the itinerant dealers. The children lacked their supply of sugar-plums and toys; the young women wanted pins, ribbons, combs and ballads; and the old could no longer barter their eggs for salt, snuff and tobacco.   (Ch. VI)

In its separate details, this complex network may seem trivial; in fact, the smooth operation of unwritten rules, the well founded expectation of the way certain members of the community pursue their peripatetic lives, the necessity of personal communication and the barter of goods is the very life of a sparse and dispersed society, unobtrusively monitored and adjusted by the Laird. 'The relationship of master and tenant, like prince and people, implies a reciprocal duty and mutual affection; beneficence to tenants is the best privilege of landed property.'[10] It was a theme Scott took seriously in his own practice as a laird. In 1818 he had the idea, which seems to have come to nothing, of establishing a small hamlet of workpeople on the Abbotsford estate, to be called Abbotstown.

> I would [he wrote to William Laidlaw] give them some advantages sufficient to balance the following conditions, which, after all, are conditions in my favour:—1st, That they shall keep their cottages and little gardens, and doors, tolerably neat; and 2nd, That the men shall on no account shoot, or the boys break timber or take birds' nests, or go among the planting. I do not know any other restrictions, and these are easy. I should think we might settle a few families very happily there, which is an object I have much at heart, for I have no notion of the proprietor who is only ambitious to be lord of 'the beast and the brute', and chases the human face from his vicinity.[11]

During the life of the former Laird of Ellangowan,

> 'the muckle chumlay in the Auld Place reeked like a killogie in his time, and there were as mony puir folk riving at the banes in the

court, and about the door, as there were gentles in the ha'. And the leddy, on ilka Christmas night as it came round, gae twelve siller pennies to ilka puir body about, in honour of the twelve apostles like. They were fond to ca' it papistrie; but I think our great folk might take a lesson frae the papists whiles. They gie another sort o' help to puir folk than just dinging down a saxpence in the brod on the Sabbath, and kilting, and scourging, and drumming them a' the sax days o' the week besides.'   (Ch. VI)

But Bertram senior is deaf to such gossip over the twopenny ale in the Gordon Arms (and there is very little reason to believe that young Harry will be any more willing an auditor) and he drives forward until his activities culminate in the expulsion of Meg Merrilies and her people. One looks, at the end of the novel, for some rehabilitation, some re-integration of total, homogeneous, communal life, but apart from a few glimpses into the kitchen of the Gordon Arms at Kippletringan, and the conversation of Mrs MacCandlish and her customers, we learn little more of the community. It fades out, only to be dragged clumsily on stage again in Chapter LV, like the rustic chorus of an operetta, to cheer the young heir in the recognition scene in an utterly unconvincing rally.

Derncleugh and Ellangowan polarise the community life represented in *Guy Mannering*; between them lie the smuggling fraternity, a lawyer's Edinburgh and, most explicit and convincing of all, the domestic manners of Dandie Dinmont, Liddesdale farmer, at Charlies-hope.

Smugglers are not unfamiliar in Scott's novels; particularly interesting examples are Robertson and Wilson in the *Heart of Midlothian*, and Nanty Ewart in *Redgauntlet*. Their activities, especially in the eighteenth century, have formed the basis of much romantic and children's fiction, and it is interesting to see Scott working out a role for them which, though often stagey, is neither romanticised beyond recognition nor insufferably moralised. Dirk Hatteraick, for example, and his jailer MacGuffog are good examples of a completely amoral and brutalised mentality, interestingly set over against the smooth cunning of Glossin and the more complex mixture of harshness and compassion we find in Meg. Scott was in his own life and conduct a man of profound moral awareness, though apart from the triumph of *The Heart of Midlothian* he never really successfully embodied his views in the subtleties of fiction. In assessing his scenes and characters, however, we do well to remember two of his precepts. The first he notes at the end of the first chapter of *Waverley*, where he writes: 'Some favourable opportunities of contrast have been afforded me, by the state of society in the northern part of the island at the period of my history, and may serve at once to vary and to illustrate the moral lessons, which I would willingly consider as the most important of my plan.' This must have been written, at the latest, in 1814, but is more likely to have been set down as early as 1805 when the work was begun and put aside. The second appears twenty years later, in a letter to his son-in-law: 'We shall never learn to feel and respect our real calling and destiny, unless we have taught ourselves to consider everything as moonshine, compared with the education of the heart.'[12] Victorian readers and educators trivialised Scott's moral lessons and their insistence that Scott was good for children is a syndrome from which we have not fully recovered. Harriet Martineau went so far as to claim reverently that Scott had done more for our society than all the divines and moral teachers of the century past, and that his influence was just beginning its course of a thousand years.[13]

The smugglers, consequently, play a brutal, not a romantic role in the novel and in this sense Scott anticipates Dickens's view in *Oliver Twist*, where he seeks to deprive the squalid metropolitan underworld of Fagin and Bill Sikes of any comforting romantic glossiness; Hatteraick, MacGuffog and Glossin are not Beggar's Opera villains, and though Scott may cast a humorous and condoning eye on the act of smuggling as a time-honoured method of evading oppressive taxes, it is a view he expresses mainly through the naïve receivers of the contraband goods; the smugglers themselves he sees with a kind of ethical squint, which enables him to dissociate the morality of their activities from that of their bucolic consumers. Their ends come by violence, out of despair; Hatteraick, having murdered Glossin, hangs himself.

This is one small ripple of the moral undercurrent which seems at first barely to disturb the romantic surface of the novel; but the materials of a serious moral fable are perhaps more compellingly present in *Guy Mannering* than in *Waverley* where, as I have suggested, Edward's waverings are easily shrugged off in a fairytale happy ending for the hero and a barbed compromise on the part of the author. In *Guy Mannering*, however, we can see Glossin's conscience at work over his own turpitude; as one critic has pointed out, Scott bestows almost as much psychological description on Glossin as he gave to Edward Waverley[14] and it is doubtful whether we are invited wholeheartedly to support Kennedy, the murdered exciseman. Scott's concern, in fact, is not at all with the law and the breaking of the law but entirely with the way in which people behave towards each other. Consequently, those who are motivated by selfishness, greed, cruelty or malice, knowingly and intelligently so, like Glossin and Hatteraick, are in the end made victims of their own destructive philosophies; MacGuffog, brutal and brainless, without the intellect necessary for malice, is merely dismissed. Hatteraick is placed, too, by his environment, which in terms of the novel is not the sea, as we might expect, but stone: the chill vault of the ruins of Ellangowan, a bleak and isolated cave among the wintry cliffs of Galloway, the prison at Portanferry. His morality, if he can be said to have one, echoes this cold, pitiless exposure, and, just before the fight in the cave, and Hatteraick's capture, Scott makes the association explicit: 'Hatteraick's savage and rugged cast of features, now rendered more ferocious by the circumstances of his situation, and the deep gloom of his mind, assorted well with the rugged and broken vault which rose in a rude arch over and around him' (Ch. LIV).

Glossin is simply a misfit, in a sense a man without environment; the villagers distrust him, the gentry despise him, and he lives as a usurper in the house of Ellangowan, a laird without an identity, since no-one gives him the territorial name 'Ellangowan' that he longs for, but all persist in calling him plain Glossin; indeed, he 'was known to give half-a-crown to a beggar because he had thrice called him Ellangowan, in beseeching him for a penny' (Ch. XXXII). A similar social contempt is exercised by the community in *The Bride of Lammermoor*, in that Sir William Ashton. who like Glossin with Ellangowan, has acquired the Ravenswood estates by devious means, is never addressed as Ravenswood, the title being reserved entirely for the hereditary family.

Like Hatteraick, Meg Merrilies is another wanderer, in a different element, though, unlike the smuggler, her vagrancy has social overtones which beget compassion rather than condemnation. She is 'the mad randy gipsy, that had been scourged and banished, and branded—that had begged from door to door, and been hounded like a stray tike from parish to parish' (Ch. LV). This is a much more convincing and moving context than the melodramatic limbo in which we sometimes discover her as 'the Sybil', and where 'the attitudes into which she naturally threw herself were free, unconstrained, and picturesque' (Ch. XXIII).

In their different ways, both Hatteraick and Glossin are rootless; morally, historically and environmentally unplaced; beyond their self-interest they remain wholly unattached. Meg has a tribal history which locates her in time and in spite of the nomadic habits of her people we find in her a strange yearning link with Derncleugh; in this, she provides yet another example of a typical Scott character who must live in two worlds, owe two allegiances, submit to twin, equivocal moralities, and never wholly belong in or to either. Happiness in Scott's fiction, if it exists at all aside from conventional conclusions, is not a simple state; it is barely attainable, always shadowed.

The characters who live closest to this condition, however, are undoubtedly Dandie Dinmont and Paulus Pleydell. Of all the figures in the novel, these two especially come to life, each in his way moulded by tradition, history and place, clinging in the work and conversation of daily life to beliefs and customs long established, having their foundations in the neighbourly morality of convivial warmth and personal integrity.

Pleydell, as county sheriff at the time when Kennedy was murdered and Harry taken, had been involved in the investigations, and hence is linked by time as well as friendship with the fortunes of Ellangowan. Mannering, accompanied by Dominie Sampson, visits him at his home in Edinburgh, to enlist his help in the interest of Lucy Bertram, on the death of a relative from whom she may inherit. The journey to Edinburgh (during which Sampson is allowed a visit to Rullion Green in the Pentland Hills, where a Presbyterian army was defeated by Royalist troops in 1666) is hardly necessary to the prosecution of the plot, but one cannot wish it otherwise, so rich is Scott's evocation of the world of an eighteenth-century lawyer. This was the Edinburgh of Scott's childhood, a city gradually being transformed from one of the most notorious of slums to one of the most elegant cities in Europe. The New Town, north of what is now Princes Street, was begun in 1767, and joined to the warren-like Old Town by the North Bridge in 1772. Migration to the New Town by the more prosperous was slow and Pleydell characteristically lives in the Old, in one of its misleadingly squalid, exceptionally tall and crowded tenement buildings. (Even as early as 1700, some of these dwellings, built on steep slopes, reached fourteen storeys.) To Mannering, the High Street was

a spectacle which, though composed of the most vulgar materials when they are separately considered, has, when they are combined, a striking and powerful effect on the imagination. The extraordinary height of the houses was marked by lights, which, glimmering irregularly along their front, ascended so high among the attics that they seemed at length to twinkle in the middle sky. This *coup d'oeil*, which still subsists in a certain degree, was then more imposing, owing to the uninterrupted range of buildings on each side, which, broken only at the space where the North Bridge joins the main street, formed a superb and uniform Place, extending from the front of the Luckenbooths to the head of the Canongate, and corresponding in breadth and length to the uncommon height of the buildings on either side.   (Ch. XXXVI)

Mannering is led to a shabby tavern where he can find Pleydell by a 'cadie' a member of that 'brotherhood of unofficial guides who carried messages and letters, who helped strangers find their way or find suitable lodgings, and who knew every address in town: "wretches that in rags lie upon the stairs and in the streets at night, yet they are often considerably trusted" '.[15]

On reaching the inn, Mannering is understandably discomposed at first when he finds Pleydell engaged in the game of High Jinks but, to his credit, he does his best to enter into the spirit of the occasion.

The advocate embodies all those qualities which Scott admired in the intellects of his own profession: eloquence, knowledge, especially of history and letters, humour, and a compassionate understanding of human weakness (all noticeably absent in Glossin and Hatteraick). That the scene is wholly in keeping with the manners of the period is evident from several sources, and in particular from Lord Cockburn's account of High Jinks at the Middleton Inn, in the late eighteenth century:

> People sometimes say that there is no probability in Scott's making the party in *Waverley* retire from the Castle to the Howf; but these people were not with me at the inn at Middleton, about forty years ago [i.e. about 1780]. The Duke of Buccleuch was living at Dalkeith; Henry Dundas at Melville; Robert Dundas, the Lord Advocate, at Arniston; Hepburn of Clerkington at Middleton; and several of the rest of the aristocracy of Midlothian within a few miles; all with their families, and luxurious houses; yet they, to the number of twelve or sixteen, congregated in this wretched ale-house for a day of freedom and jollity. We found them roaring and singing, and laughing, in a low-roofed room scarcely large enough to hold them, with wooden chairs and sanded floor. When their own lacqueys, who were carrying on high life in the kitchen, did not choose to attend, the masters were served by two women. There was plenty of wine, particularly claret, in rapid circulation on the table; but my eye was attracted by a huge bowl of hot whisky punch, the steam of which was almost dropping from the roof, while the odour was enough to perfume the whole parish. We were called in and made to partake, and were very kindly used, particularly by my uncle Harry Dundas. How they did joke and laugh! with songs and toasts, and disputation, and no want of practical fun . . .[16]

It is this atmosphere that Scott evokes in his Pleydell scenes, this Edinburgh of convivial mirth, stinking squalor, and energetic intellectualism.

On the whole, however, the Edinburgh scenes in *Guy Mannering* remain scenes; at best, passages of irresistible descriptive prose, but self-contained in their elegantly informative place. In his creation of Dandie Dinmont, Scott finely transcends this.

'He is kin', John Buchan wrote admiringly of this character, 'both to poetry and reality', and there can be no doubt that in this novel Scott is most at home with Dinmont. Chapters XXII–XXIV where he is introduced place him precisely as no one else in the novel is placed, as a Borderer, and though Brown's stay at Charlie's-hope has all the elements of a pastoral idyll, the shadows of violence and brutality, as in Edward Waverley's experience of Tully-Veolan, are close both in Dinmont's life and in the turbulent history of the region. Scott's development of the whole Dinmont episode is underpinned by references to the history, manners and balladry of the wasteland lying between Mump's Ha', near Gilsland, where Brown meets him on his return from Stagshawbank Fair in Northumberland, and his farm in upper Liddesdale. They are beset by 'landloupers' in Bewcastle Waste, on their northward journey through Conscouthart Moss where Hobbie Noble in the ballad fights a losing battle with the land-sergeant and his men, but breaks his sword over Jersawhigham's head. Even today, the area is devoid of roads. Brown and Dinmont have some difficulty in navigating it until they strike the old Roman road, the Maiden Way, used for centuries as a drove road from Scotland, though no trace of it now remains north of Bewcastle. The route is presumably the one through 'the Waste' and past Christenbury Crag which Harry Wakefield and Robin Oig follow in Scott's magnificent late story, The Two Drovers (1827). Dandie's house, too, stands in clear contrast to the dilapidation of Ellangowan, as well as to the gentry homes of Hazlewood and Woodbourne; it is a live environment, a working farm, not a picturesque item in the landscape:

All was rough and neglected in the neighbourhood of the house;—a paltry garden, no pains taken to make the vicinity dry or comfortable, and a total absence of all those little neatnesses which give the eye so much pleasure in looking at an English farmhouse.

One remembers Edward Waverley's similar reaction on first seeing the village of Tully-Veolan. Charlies-hope, however, is well stocked, and bears all the signs of profitable activity; 'in a word, an air of liberal though sluttish plenty indicated the wealthy farmer' (Ch. XXV).

The immediate environment of the farm has all the evocative Border traces of other days, most of which still exist: ruined pele towers and place names which commemorate local history and personalities, as that where the children play, building houses of peats 'around a huge doddered oak-tree, which was called Charlie's-Bush, from some tradition respecting an old freebooter who had once inhabited the spot' (Ch. XXV). Such place names abound in the area: Dand's Pike, Elliot's Pike, Davy's Round, Hobb's Flow, Robbie's Rigg; perhaps Scott even took Dandie's surname from Dinmontlair Knowe, to the east of Newcastleton

G

in Liddesdale, though the name also signifies a sheep. The farmer's first name, incidentally, is a local affectionate form of Andrew (as in Dand's Pike), and has nothing to do with sartorial extravagance.

During his stay, Brown is introduced to Border customs and sports, and the leisure activities of a scattered but homogeneous community; he hunts a fox, shoots, engages in coursing and salmon-spearing, and has the ancient Border system of to-names explained to him:

> 'Ye see, sir', said an old shepherd rising and speaking very slow, 'the folks hereabout are a' Armstrongs and Elliots, and sic like—twa or three given names—and so, for distinction's sake, the lairds and farmers have the names of their places that they live at—as for example, Tam o' Todshaw, Will o' the Flat, Hobbie o' Sorbietrees, and our good master o' the Charlies-hope.—Aweel, sir, and then the inferior sort o' people, ye'll observe, are kend by sorts o' by-names some o' them, as Glaiket Christie, and the Deuke's Davie, or maybe, like this lad Gabriel, by his employment; as for example, Tod Gabbie, or Hunter Gabbie.' (Ch. XXVI)

And by this means, Scott quietly reintroduces the gipsy Gabriel whose information to Dinmont is to play an important part in the rescue of Brown from the jail at Portanferry. Dinmont, in fact, is contained firmly in his country and his time, like the vision in a sculptor's block; as if Scott has sliced through the stone to let us see both the finished work and the inside of the block from which it is hewn and which, from the beginning dictates the essential outlines of its form.

Brown reaches Charlies-hope at a crucial stage in his metamorphosis from the virtually nomadic, kinless, Captain Vanbeest Brown to the native Harry Bertram, heir to an ancient Scottish line, securely placed in the land among the people from whom he has sprung. When he arrives in England, even the vague knowledge that he is of Scots birth is no consolation to him, as he writes from Westmoreland to a Swiss regimental colleague: 'You and I Delaserre, foreigners both—for what am I the better that I was originally a Scotchman, since, could I prove my descent, the English would hardly acknowledge me a countryman?' (Ch. XXI). Yet we see that though he is unaware of his true identity, the growth of self-knowledge, which will lead him to that identity and at the same time test his fitness to bear it, is clearly associated with his sense of place: 'Despite my Dutch education, a blue hill to me is a friend, and a roaring torrent like the sound of a domestic song that hath soothed my infancy' (Ch. XXI). (We remember that it is the wild Meg who has sung him the old songs.) And Scott implies that it is this affinity which opens to him the doors of Charlies-hope and the friendship of Dinmont, not simply the event of his having helped the farmer when he was attacked on the Waste. Brown is not simply entertained as a guest at the Liddesdale farm, he is accepted as a friend and, by the time he leaves, the first signs of his metamorphosis become visible when he asks if Dinmont's wife ' "would have the kindness to weave me, or work me, just such a grey plaid as the goodman wears?" He had learnt the language and feelings of the country even during the short time of his residence, and was aware of the pleasure the request would confer' (Ch. XXI). The point is acutely made, in that the plaid or *maud* is what Dinmont wears when he is out of doors on the farm, as distinct from the jockey-coat used when he travels away.

As he moves into Scotland, Brown's feeling of nonentity is increased by his becoming lost and by the theft of his papers, though still, and for some time to come, he is consciously concerned to establish only his rank and character; the deeper feeling comes to the surface later. At the time of his inauspicious arrival, Meg Merrilies shelters him, recognises him as belonging, and in a strange fashion her transfer to him of the purse containing, as well as cosmopolitan currency, rings and jewellery of his own family, takes upon itself the nature of a ritual of adoption, a kind of redemption. The incident ends on a further symbolic note as Brown, 'placing the purse of the gipsy in a private pocket . . . strode gallantly on through the wood in search of the promised highroad' (Ch. XXVIII).

But he does not get out of the wood easily. After being taken for a vagrant and accidentally shooting Charles Hazlewood, though Julia Mannering recognises in him the man she has known as Captain Brown, he retreats into West Cumberland, returns to Scotland by sea from Allonby, and is put ashore not far from the place where he had been kidnapped some seventeen years before. Now, having proved his quality at Charlies-hope, having been symbolically reinstated by Meg at Derncleugh, he is ready to experience the third stage of his process of change. He finds himself before the ruins of the Old Place of Ellangowan, the castle of his ancestors, and reflects on the feeling that he has some early recollection of them. It is a magnificent opportunity, but Scott misses it; the language of Bertram's response is little better than conventional tourist platitude: ' "Nor can I divest myself of the idea, that these massive towers, and that dark gateway, retiring through its deep-vaulted and ribbed arches, and dimly lighted by the courtyard beyond, are not entirely strange to me" ' (Ch. XLI). Unsuccessful though the episode may be, the interest remains that Scott is attempting to secure identity for Bertram in terms of place and intensity of response; papers and documents are not enough, and in any case those that Bertram possesses only tell him that he is someone else.

Just before the final recognition, when Bertram is for the first time in the company of Colonel and Julia Mannering, Lucy Bertram (his sister, born on the day of his abduction), and Pleydell, Scott intensifies the confusion of identity by presenting a brief episode in what we should now regard as cinematic terms: 'Mannering saw before him the man whom he supposed he had killed in India; Julia beheld her lover in a most peculiar and hazardous situation; and Lucy Bertram at once knew the person who had fired upon young Hazlewood' (Ch. L). Then with Pleydell's question, 'my dear boy, do you know who or what you are?' the dénouement begins.

For Guy Mannering, by this time we begin to see a slight modification of his prejudice and imperiousness, an increased tolerance, a more pronounced good humour. Perhaps he has begun to respond to the mild, persistent, ancient pressures of a folk community; no small development if James Hogg was right. 'Colonel Mannering', he said on first reading the novel, 'is just Scott painted by himself.'[17]

CHAPTER V
The Antiquary (1816)

In his 1829 Advertisement to this novel. Scott described it as completing 'a series of fictitious narratives, intended to illustrate the manners of Scotland at three different periods. *Waverley* embraced the age of our fathers, *Guy Mannering* that of our own youth, and *The Antiquary*, refers to the last ten years of the eighteenth century'. Each of the three, moreover, embodies an aspect of the author's own personality. In the character of Edward Waverley, Scott revealed something of himself as a youth; in that of Mannering, he revealed, in John Buchan's words, 'the imperious element . . . which underlay his habitual good nature';[1] while in *The Antiquary* he redressed the balance by offering, in the central character, Jonathan Oldbuck, a whimsical, affectionately mocking portrait of himself as antiquary, the compiler of *Reliquiae Trottcosianae—or the Gabions of the late Jonathan Oldbuck, Esq.*,[2] though commentators, including Scott himself, have brought forward a variety of originals. Consequently, this novel is in many ways a self-indulgence; a *jeu d'esprit* in which the author rides his hobby-horse with a light satirical rein in all directions. He allows Oldbuck to ramble interminably, he laughs at spurious antiquarianism (pointing the finger at himself as well as at others), almost wholly disregarding matters of structure and plot. Yet, amid all this, he creates a bitterly realistic picture of poverty among the fisher folk of the east coast, and the skilful actuality he brings to his narrative of the Mucklebackit family stands out the more movingly against the conventional vacuities of the romantic episodes and the black gothic gloom of the perversely penitential Glenallan.

Lockhart recalls that this became Scott's favourite novel, but the author's own comments, couched in terms of guarded uncertainty, convey some dissatisfaction with it. He wrote to John Morritt in December 1815, that the three-week recess of the courts would allow him time to make a serious start on *The Antiquary*. 'When once I get my pen to paper it will walk fast enough. I am sometimes tempted to leave it alone, and try whether it will not write as well without the assistance of my head as with it.'[3] Perhaps this is what happened, in fact, and though it sold 6000 copies within a week of publication in May 1816, Scott wrote shortly afterwards to Morritt: 'It is not so interesting as its predecessors —the period did not admit of so much romantic situation.'[4] The remark is enigmatic, and reads more like an embarrassed excuse than an explanation. His somewhat casual approach (he never revised his prose) is further suggested by his attitude to epigraphs, which must have lured many a reader into vain searches. It was in correcting the proof-sheets of *The Antiquary*, Lockhart observes, that 'Scott first took to equipping his chapters with mottoes of his own fabrication'.[5]

The threads of the tale are tangled. Oldbuck is accompanied on his journey home from Edinburgh to Monkbarns by young William Lovel, who is bound for the nearby fishing town of Fairport. Lovel has come to seek the hand of Isabella Wardour, whom he has met in Yorkshire but who has been forbidden his advances because her father believes him to be of low birth. In the end, he turns out to be not only the gallant Major Neville but also Lord Geraldin Glenallan, and he marries Isabella. Once more, though the consequences are not so finely wrought in terms of individual psychology, we have not only the lost heir, but the hero of Scottish descent who is brought up in England; Scott was to treat the theme again, more profoundly, when he came to write of Darsie Latimer in *Redgauntlet*.

Isabella's father, Sir Arthur Wardour, is, like Ellangowan, a man of ancient descent, honourable family and embarrassed fortune. He is, too, a foolish antiquarian, deceived by the German Dousterswivel and by his own greed into parting with his money and that of his friends to find treasure by necromantic means. Just as Oldbuck is a mocking portrait of Scott the antiquary, so is Wardour of Scott the upholder of the absolute value of hereditary rank and status.

The third family of rank is that of the Earl of Glenallan. He is the son of the Countess Joscelin, a devout Roman Catholic and father of Lovel. Glenallan loved and secretly married Eveline Neville. His mother, knowing of the attachment but not of the marriage discouraged it viciously, finally hinting that the relationship was incestuous.[6] But Eveline is already with child. She tries to drown herself, and before she dies the child, Lovel, is born. Glenallan then retreats into a penitential asceticism which is not to be broken until the truth is out, more than twenty years later.

The agent of this revelation is old Elspeth Mucklebackit, formerly servant to the Countess Joscelin and a party to the deception. She too has nursed her guilt and confesses to Glenallan just before she dies. For the rest, in a novel rich in minor figures, one major character remains: the bedesman, Edie Ochiltree. As a wanderer he serves to link the fortunes and events of the novel's various locations, moving between Fairport,

Monkbarns, Knockwinnock House, the home of the Wardours, and Glenallan House.

In terms of environment, two aspects of the novel stand out; the first is Scott's satire on antiquarian obsession, and the second, the brilliant recreation of the life and locality of the Mucklebackit family.

Oldbuck is a maverick antiquarian, an indiscriminate collector of old objects with which he clutters his old house. He is one of the tribe of which Dr Johnson was perhaps thinking when he wrote to Boswell: 'A mere antiquarian is a rugged being.'[7] He is the focus of a series of lessons by Scott on how *not* to look at a landscape. The first instance of this occurs in Chapter IV when the Antiquary conducts his guest, the colourless Lovel, round his estate.

He led the way briskly through one or two rich pasture meadows, to an open heath or common, and so to the top of a gentle eminence. 'Here', he said, 'Mr Lovel, is a truly remarkable spot.'

'It commands a fine view', said his companion, looking around him.

'True: but it is not for the prospect I brought you hither: do you see nothing else remarkable?—nothing on the surface of the ground?'

'Why, yes; I do see something like a ditch, indistinctly marked.'

'Indistinctly!—pardon me, sir, but the indistinctness must be in your powers of vision. Nothing can be more plainly traced—a proper *agger* or *vallum*, with its corresponding ditch or *fossa*.'

And the Laird launches into a thousand word discourse on the conjectured history of the site, and his favourite theme of castrametation.

'Yes, my dear friend, from this stance it is probable—nay, it is nearly certain, that Julius Agricola beheld what our Beaumont has so admirably described!—From this very Praetorium'—

A voice from behind interrupted his ecstatic description—

'Praetorian here, Praetorian there, I mind the biggin o't.'

And the cold voice of reason, proceeding from Edie Ochiltree the Bedesman whom we meet here for the first time, explains how he and a few friends built it twenty years before 'just for a bield at auld Aiken Drum's bridal' (Ch. IV).

According to Lockhart, the incident is founded on an actual occurrence in which some English visitors were being shown a supposed Roman camp in Dumfriesshire. 'This', said their guide when they reached a certain spot, 'I take to have been the Praetorium', when a herdsman nearby called, 'Praetorium here, Praetorium there, I made it wi' a flaughter spade.'[8]

It is possible, however, that Scott took a hint for the episode from Robert Bage's novel, *Hermsprong* (1796), in which Dr Blick shows the hero, Hermsprong, the locality in circumstances very like those in *The Antiquary*.

'This place, sir', says Blick, 'seems to take your attention, and is indeed worthy of it. I presume you know this was once a Roman camp?'

'No, sir', the stranger replied, 'I do not know it.'

'Nothing can be plainer, sir. You see it was a square. Here must have stood the praetorium, here the augurale; that, sir, must have been the decuman gate.'

'I see, indeed, ground on which these things might have been,— nothing to indicate with certainty that they were.'

'I have studied the place so long, sir, and with so much attention, that I can demonstrate it. I can tell you exactly where were the stations of the *volites*, the *hastati*, the *triarii*; their centurions and tribunes.'

'They cannot arise to contradict you, sir; nor shall I.'

'I wish to convince you.'

'Do not take the trouble, sir. I have seen many places of encampment like this; some where Romans never were. But they shall be all Roman, to oblige you.'[9]

Bage died in 1801, and Scott wrote a piece on him for the proposed *Ballantyne's Novelists' Library* in 1824. It seems likely that he was acquainted with this work before 1816, the year of *The Antiquary*. Though Scott found Bage's view of men and manners decidedly uncomfortable in its radicalism, he nevertheless thought highly of him as a writer.

The prospect of ruins in a landscape, the observation and handling of the relics of old wars, old occupations, old beliefs, naturally inspires reflections on time, mutability, mortality. It seems odd, therefore, that Oldbuck is moved to such moods not directly by the influence of the ancient objects with which he has surrounded himself but indirectly and personally. He shows Lovel into the Green Room at Monkbarns where he is to spend the night. It contains a sixteenth-century Arras tapestry of a hunting scene. Later, we discover that certain lines from Chaucer which have been added were supplied by Eveline Neville with whom Oldbuck had been in love as a young man, a rival to Glenallan. As a rule, Oldbuck's response to the past is argumentative rather than reflective; in the Green Room, however, consciousness of time first as a disappointed lover leads him to reflect on a vanished childhood.

'I am seldom in this apartment', he said, 'and never without yielding to a melancholy feeling . . . owing to circumstances of an early and unhappy attachment. It is at such moments as these, Mr Lovel, that we feel the changes of time. The same objects are before us—those inanimate things which we have gazed on in wayward infancy and impetuous youth, in anxious and scheming manhood—they are permanent and the same; but when we look upon them in cold and unfeeling old age, can we, changed in our temper, our pursuits, our feelings—changed in our form, our limbs, and our strength,—can we be ourselves called the same? or do we not rather look back with a sort of wonder upon our former selves, as being separate and distinct from what we now are?' (Ch. X)

It is difficult not to associate such a passage with Scott's own unfortunate love for Williamina Belsches, a young greenmantled lady whom he once hoped to marry. She reappears in *Redgauntlet*. He was desolated when she married another in 1796, though she in no way deceived him. He never forgot this love. Unlike Oldbuck, Scott married a year afterwards, with more haste than passion; it was a union, he wrote to Lady Abercorn twelve years later, 'something short of love in all its fervour which I suspect people only feel *once* in their lives. Folks who have been nearly drowned in bathing rarely venturing a second time out of their depth';[10] and in his last years, he wrote in his *Journal*: 'Broken-hearted for two years, my heart handsomely pieced again, but the crack will remain to my dying day.'[11]

Oldbuck, however, is not enriched by his creator's experience here; Scott's horizons seem always too close for extensive contemplation. From the very beginning, though one senses at times the possibility of a longer view, only another limiting skyline appears. One has this feeling again, for example, in Chapter XVII, when a party including Oldbuck, the Wardours and Lovel visit the ruins of St Ruth's priory.

The approach to the abbey is described in some detail, and Scott presents with both accuracy and insight the topographical, architectural and historic features of the place, moving easily from one to the other and introducing without undue labour or emphasis, asides like: 'The side of these buildings which overhung the brook, was partly founded on a steep and precipitous rock; for the place had been occasionally turned to military purposes, and had been taken with great slaughter during Montrose's wars.' The reference is not directly historic, though Montrose did campaign in the Arbroath area in 1645; it is, however, an example of Scott's technique of making probable history sustain the framework of his fiction.

Naturally, the ruins provoke discussion and speculation among the visitors and at one point Isabella Wardour asks why tradition has been so little influenced by the great and good men who lived here in the past, and yet preserves in some detail the exploits of freebooters of the meanest kind. Only Lovel has an answer (another instance of Oldbuck's un-reliability as an antiquarian theorist) and it is in the voice of Scott:

> 'The eras by which the vulgar compute time, have always reference to some period of fear and tribulation, and they date by a tempest, an earthquake, or burst of civil commotion. When such are the facts most alive in the memory of the common people, we cannot wonder,' he concluded, 'that the ferocious warrior is remembered, and the peaceful abbots are abandoned to forgetfulness and oblivion.'

Though in no way as successful, or as consistent, as in other Waverley novels, the presentation in *The Antiquary* of the vital interrelationship of time and landscape should be noticed. When the two become separated, Scott sinks to the sluggishly conventional, as for example when the Wardours are cut off by the tide, 'longing doubtless to exchange the easy curving line, which the sinuosities of the bay compelled them to adopt, for a straighter and more expeditious path, though less conformable to the line of beauty' (Ch. VII).

Time and place are fairly joined in the person of Edie Ochiltree. Like Meg Merrilies, he has the twofold function of helping on the plot by his convenient peregrinations and of representing the people, indigenous in their speech, customs and beliefs. 'I gang about a' gates', he says, 'like the troubled spirit.' Both of these roles make him the indispensable bearer of news and gossip in a dispersed community. The Praetorium incident is not an isolated and idle gibe at pretentious antiquarianism; even Oldbuck, in a cooler moment, respects Edie's calling, recognising that he is

> 'One of the last specimens of the old fashioned Scottish mendicant, who kept his rounds within a particular space, and was the news-carrier, the minstrel, and sometimes the historian of the district. That rascal, now, knows more old ballads and traditions than any other man in this and the four next parishes'.   (Ch. IV)

It is integral to the novel that Ochiltree's knowledge and interpretation of the landscape should represent the man who belongs, Oldbuck's that of the spiritual outsider; however much time may have familiarised him with his homeland, in spite of Scott's assertion that 'his countenance was of the true Scottish cast', there remains something in him of the foreigner; his German Protestant ancestors had settled in Scotland shortly after the Reformation and though his family 'had been established for several generations, as landowners in the county, and in most shires of England would have been accounted a family of some standing . . . the shire of —— was filled with gentlemen of more ancient descent and larger fortune'. In tradition, if not in wealth, Ochiltree occupies a corner here. His origins, like those of Meg Merrilies, are tribal rather than aristocratic, but in his own kind his descent is long, probably bardic, and he is proud of his calling. His part in the plot is substantial, even leaving aside the trivial treasure-hunting episodes, and it is clear from the extensive discussion of him and his kind in the Introduction that Scott thought him a figure of some importance in the history and life of an eighteenth-century rural community.

In Chapter IX, for example, it is the local knowledge of Edie and the Mucklebackits that saves the lives of Isabella Wardour and her father, cut off by the tide, when the conventional heroics of Lovel, though helpful, are of limited scope, and Oldbuck merely gets in the way: 'I'se warrant we'll sune heave them on board, Monkbarns, wad ye but stand out o' the gate', says the fisherman (Ch. VIII). Indeed, throughout the novel, the lords, lairds and their like seem incapable of moving out of their own light or looking anywhere but into the past: Oldbuck sees the antiquity that he wants to see; Wardour's impoverished head is turned permanently to a departed family glory, and Glenallan lives and dies to expiate a sin long past which, it turns out, he never committed. The common people see more clearly and live, like the inhabitants of Wolf's-hope in *The Bride of Lammermoor*, in a present of their own making, because their past is indistinguishable from it in terms of their occupations of mendicant and fisherman. (Mucklebackit, it is worth observing in passing, is a smuggler too.) Ochiltree now and again glances back to his soldiering days but he does so with no sense of departed glory: his business is with the present, and he does not repine.

He is conscious too, of his service to the community. When the Wardours offer him, as a reward for his rescuing them, 'a neat cottage and a garden, and a daily dole, and nothing to do but dig a little in your garden when you pleased yourself', he refuses with a dignified consciousness of his function:

'But I am no that sair failed yet', replied the mendicant. 'Od, ance I gat a wee soupled yestreen, I was as yauld as an eel. And then what wad a' the country about do for want o' auld Edie Ochiltree, that brings news and country cracks frae ae farm-steading to anither, and gingerbread to the lasses, and helps the lads to mend their fiddles, and the gudewives to clout their pans, and plaits rush-swords and grenadier caps for the weans, and busks the laird's flees, and has skill o' cow-ills

and horse-ills, and kens mair auld sangs and tales than a' the barony
besides, and gars ilka body laugh wherever he comes? Troth, my leddy,
I canna lay down my vocation; it would be a public loss.' (Ch. XII)

The wily old bedesman does, however, have his eye on an old cottage
where he may rest when his joints grow too stiff for his calling. 'This is
a gay bein place, and its a comfort to hae sic a corner to sit in in a bad
day.' It belongs to Caxon the wig-maker who provides in Edie's case the
ease after toil that the Lady bestows on the Last Minstrel, and young
Redgauntlet on Wandering Willie, so that he may end his days 'unco
beinly in the ha' neuk'.

The opposition of past and present is brought out most strongly and
most seriously in the various interchanges that take place between
Oldbuck and the Mucklebackits. The Antiquary looks at people much as
he looks at landscape, with an irrelevant eye, and Scott deliberately
opposes the two households to reinforce what he has to say about time,
the land, men and manners, illusion and reality. Oldbuck, Wardour and
Glenallan inhabit a world of make-believe, though each sees different
things in it; as a result, communication between them is trivial, or fails.
The Mucklebackits act and suffer in a world where pain is unbuffered and
death a family disaster, not a romantic achievement.

I have suggested how the two are opposed when we first meet them
together at the rescue of the Wardours, where the practical good sense,
local knowledge and modest courage are most apparent in those who
daily have to compete with nature for their survival. On another level,
humorously treated yet fundamentally telling, is the distinction between
the misogyny of the Monkbarns ménage, which runs like a ground bass
through the tale, and the regiment of women in the fisher families, on
which Scott is careful to provide a documentary footnote of some length
to establish that 'in the fishing villages in the Friths of Forth and Tay,
as well as elsewhere in Scotland, the government is gynecocracy, as
described in the text' (Ch. XXVI). The difference becomes more voci-
ferously apparent when Monkbarns bargains ineffectually with Maggie
Mucklebackit for fish:

'How much for the bannock-fluke and cock-padle?' demanded the
Antiquary.
'Four white shillings and saxpence', answered the Naiad.
'Four devils and six of their imps', retorted the Antiquary, 'do ye
think I am mad, Maggie?'
'And div ye think', rejoined the virago, setting her arms akimbo,
'that my man and my sons are to gae to the sea in weather like
yestreen and the day—sic a sea as it's yet outby—and get naething for

their fish, and be misca'd into the bargain, Monkbarns? It's no fish ye're buying—it's men's lives.' (Ch. XI)

The passage in its entirety is humorously and lightly conducted and the bargain is eventually struck for 'half-a-crown and a dram', but it looks forward to one of the most realistic, most dramatic events in the whole of Scott's fiction: the death and funeral of Steenie Mucklebackit, and the reaction of his father.

There are two storms in *The Antiquary*. The first, in which the tide-trapped Wardours and Ochiltree are rescued, allows, with a dressing of picturesque description, a romantic episode whose safe and happy outcome is never seriously in doubt. During this episode Lovel is repeatedly referred to as 'the adventurer', and Scott takes prolix pains to force the stress:

> ... they paused upon the highest ledge of rock to which they could attain; for it seemed that any attempt to move forward could only serve to anticipate their fate. Here, then, they were to await the sure though slow progress of the raging element, something in the situation of the martyrs of the early church, who, exposed by heathen tyrants to be slain by wild beasts, were compelled for a time to witness the impatience and rage by which the animals were agitated, while awaiting the signal for undoing their gates, and letting them loose upon the victims. (Ch. VII)

A second storm capsizes the Mucklebackit boat and drowns Steenie. This disaster, like the climax of a Greek tragedy, occurs off-stage, and we learn of it, with Ochiltree, when the news interrupts a village game of bowls. In this instance, Scott stresses not the event but the effect; and the effect is one not simply of grief, but of ceremony; this is what, to the poor, makes the bereavement tolerable, this process of blending inconsolable grief with the commonplaces of everyday life.

Monkbarns follows tradition in attending, as Laird, the funeral of one who has lived on his lands. (The occasion is facetiously teased out when his military nephew, Hector McIntyre who accompanies him, gets involved in a fight with a seal, and loses.) After the burial, during which the parents remain in their cottage, he returns to the beach and finds the father repairing his boat.

> 'I am glad', he said, in a tone of sympathy—'I am glad, Saunders, that you feel yourself able to make this exertion.'
> 'And what would ye have me to do', answered the fisher gruffly, 'unless I wanted to see four children starve, because ane is drowned? It's weel wi' you gentles, that can sit in the house wi' handkerchers

at your een when ye lose a friend; but the like o' us maun to our wark
again, if our hearts were beating as hard as my hammer.'

(Ch. XXXIV)

In the distraction of his grief, the man works clumsily and eventually,
throwing down a piece of wood which he cannot shape,

> After wiping his dim eye with his quivering hand, he exclaimed,
> 'There is a curse either on me or on this auld black bitch of a boat,
> that I have hauled up high and dry, and patched and clouted sae mony
> years, that she might drown my poor Steenie at the of them, an'
> be d——d to her!' and he flung his hammer against the boat, as if she
> had been the intentional cause of his misfortune. Then recollecting
> himself, he added, 'Yet what needs ane be angry at her, that has
> neither soul nor sense?—though I am no that muckle better mysell.
> She's but a rickle o' auld rotten deals nailed thegither, and warped wi'
> the wind and the sea—and I am a dour carle, battered by foul weather
> at sea and land till I am maist as senseless as hersell. She maun be
> mended though again' the morning tide—that's a thing o' necessity.'
>
> (Ch. XXXIV)

The modulation of rhetoric and realism is masterly.

Monkbarns, of course, is kindly and sympathetic but the urgent point
of the passage, and the one of literary interest, is Scott's articulate awareness of the plight of the working family whose lives, moulded by the
harsh palm of necessity, can ill accommodate the outward shows of pro-
longed grief such as Glenallan indulges. It is a new turn in fiction, a
representation of common people not to be matched, much less developed,
for a generation. The Mucklebackits are part of their environment, living
by and on the sea; their home is one of

> four or five huts inhabited by fishers, whose boats, drawn high upon
> the beach, lent the odoriferous vapours of pitch melting under a
> burning sun, to contend with those of the offals of fish and other
> nuisances usually collected round Scottish cottages. Undisturbed by
> these complicated steams of abomination, a middle-aged woman, with
> a face which had defied a thousand storms, sat mending a net at the
> door of one of the cottages.   (Ch. XI)

> inside, there was confusion,—there was dilapidation—there was dirt
> good store. Yet, with all this, there was about the inmates, Luckie
> Mucklebackit and her family, an appearance of ease, plenty, and
> comfort, that seemed to warrant their old sluttish proverb, 'The
> clartier the cosier.'   (Ch. XXVI)

In some respects this is a Dinmont world by the sea, but it is a poor one and Scott resolutely avoids the idyllic.

Of course, one cannot help thinking of the other celebrated fictional fisher family, the Peggotys in *David Copperfield*. The later work is incomparably greater in almost every way, yet one has no real apprehension in it of the father and son as fishermen. Dickens tells us, and tells us amusingly, about their lives but he does not make us feel the poverty of a family that has to live on the beach in an upturned boat. Nor are we made particularly conscious of the occupation of the men in terms of income, hardship, expertise and danger. All of these, Scott indicates with unobtrusive emphasis; in Luckie Mucklebackit's bargaining, in the condition of their dwelling, in the everyday dialogue of the family, and ultimately in Steenie's drowning when the boat capsizes. His is a working death and we have seen how his father responds; Ham Peggoty, on the other hand, drowns heroically in attempting to save the life of the cad, Steerforth, who has seduced and abandoned Emily, whom Ham was to have married. Ham remains in David's memory not as a drowned fisherman but as a mere abstraction, a 'broken heart that had found rest in the stormy sea' (Ch. LVIII), and in his father's, a tuft of grass from the grave, and a little earth 'for Em'ly'.

In *The Antiquary*, Scott's understanding of the common people achieves triumphant expression through his recognition that 'the antique force and simplicity of their language, often tinctured with the Oriental eloquence of Scripture, in the mouths of those of an elevated understanding, give pathos to their grief, and dignity to their resentment'.[12] Nevertheless, along with this distinction in his third novel, Scott appears to have acquired Mrs Podsnap's art of prancing in a stately manner without ever getting on. It is a perilous condition for a novelist to be in, especially when he has earned vast popular acclaim. But the work was not without its adverse critics and over the next two years Scott moved out of danger, first with the brilliant *Old Mortality* (published with *The Black Dwarf* as the first series of *Tales of my Landlord*), followed by *Rob Roy* and *The Heart of Midlothian*.

CHAPTER VI
The Heart of Midlothian (1818)

With *The Black Dwarf*, Scott took up once again a Border theme. Apart from the Dandie Dinmont chapters in *Guy Mannering*, he had not used such material since 1805 when he wrote *The Lay of the Last Minstrel*, and this was close under the influence of all the work he had done three years earlier to collect, edit, introduce and publish his pioneering, if eclectic, *Minstrelsy of the Scottish Border*. In this novel, though he is dealing with a land, a people and a history with all of which he was intimately acquainted, and though he bases his central character on personal observation of a certain David Ritchie who lived by the Manor Water in Peeblesshire, he fails to create from them a coherent work. Locality, history, topography appear in *The Black Dwarf* as no more than disparately informative insertions in an improbable and ill-considered romance. This is not to say that the elements themselves are negligible. In his conception of the character of the Black Dwarf, for example, one may see a lame Scott exploring the Byronic psychology of an intelligent, energetic but misshapen man, 'residing in solitude, and haunted by the consciousness of his own deformity, and a suspicion of his being generally subjected to the scorn of his fellow-men' (Introduction). The promise of an understanding glimpse inside the mind of such a person is, however, never fulfilled, being dissipated in skilfully contrived misanthropic rant.

In various ways, a number of other characters in the Waverley Novels exist outside the norms of their community: Dominie Sampson in *Guy Mannering*, Davie Gellatley in *Waverley*, Rashleigh Osbaldistone in *Rob Roy*; perhaps the most moving, and certainly the most personal to Scott[1] is Conachar, the constitutionally timid clan chief in *The Fair Maid of Perth*. His interest in the mind of the Dwarf, however, is not sustained.

The events take place in 1708, at the time of the attempted Jacobite landing from France, a background prospect which animates but does not vitalise a number of characters. The main plot centres on Elshie, the Black Dwarf of Mucklestane Moor, really the wealthy Sir Edward Mauley. His Timon-like misanthropy lies at the weak heart of a tale of

Border reiving, family feud and superstition, involving the adventures of the Laird of Ellieslaw, Hobbie Elliot of the Heugh-foot and Willie Graeme of Westburnflat, indigenous Border families nursing long grievances. These are Ballad themes but Scott clearly felt he had drawn that well dry long ago. 'I began a border tale well', he wrote to Lady Louisa Stuart, 'but tired of the ground I had trode so often ... So I quarrelled with my story and bungled up a conclusion, as a boarding school Miss finishes a task which she had commenced with great glee and accuracy.'[2] He never again drew from this source, though it is never very far away. The tale was published together with *Old Mortality* in November 1816.

This second work pleased Scott much more. 'I am complete master of the whole history of these strange times both of persecutors and persecuted', he wrote confidently to Lady Louisa Stuart, 'so I hope I have come decently off.'[3]

It would be otiose to examine in detail the local and environmental features of these two novels; they have their place, but Scott is not here engaged in any new exploration of their possibilities in fiction. In *Old Mortality*, landscape remains largely a matter of description, 'done in smooth washes of sepia and burnt sienna';[4] beyond this it is simply functional, seen with the soldier's, rather than the novelist's eye.

The events take place in 1769 and record the Covenanting struggles of that rhetorical and bloody time. Scott triumphs once again, both in his use of dialect and in his resounding reconstruction of the language of the Covenanters, though this, being the speech of a movement rather than of a locality does not concern us here. War, faith and fanaticism are the knots which mesh the characters in this historical net, but they represent direct narrative processes for the most part, unmediated by the more evocative exploitation of detail implicit in particular landscapes, particular localities.

By May 1817, Scott had begun *Rob Roy*. For months he had been ill with gall-stones, in frequent severe pain, considerably weakened and very thin. The periodic depression brought about by this condition, and by the laudanum prescribed to relieve it, is remarkably manifested in an unusually personal poem written at this time. Apart from the verse epistles which form the Introductions to each of the six Cantos of *Marmion*, Scott rarely spoke of himself in his verse; but in these lines we see him interpreting the effects of illness through the medium of a familiar landscape:

> The sun upon the Weirdlaw Hill,
>   In Ettrick's vale, is sinking sweet;
> The westland wind is hush and still,
>   The lake lies sleeping at my feet.

H

> Yet not the landscape to mine eye
>   Bears those bright hues that once it bore;
> Though evening, with her richest dye
>   Flames o'er the hills of Ettrick's shore.
>
> With listless look along the plain,
>   I see Tweed's silver current glide,
> And coldly mark the holy fane
>   Of Melrose rise in ruin'd pride.
> The quiet lake, the balmy air,
>   The hill, the stream, the tower, the tree,—
> Are they still such as once they were?
>   Or is the dreary change in me?
>
> Alas, the warp'd and broken board,
>   How can it bear the painter's dye!
> The harp of strain'd and tuneless chord,
>   How to the minstrel's skill reply!
> To aching eyes each landscape lowers,
>   To feverish pulse each gale blows chill;
> And Araby's or Eden's bowers
>   Were barren as this moorland hill.

Here he distinguishes painfully between what his intellect understands is happening, and how differently his senses interpret what they record; a landscape of beauty and pride, rich in association both personal and historic, perceived only as a desolation. It is a moving and melancholy forecast of the note he was to strike in the *Journal* he kept from 1825 until just before his death in 1832.

Nevertheless, *Rob Roy*, in a massive first edition of 10,000 copies, appeared at the end of December; within a fortnight, a second impression of 3000 was issued, though Scott had some reservations as he confided to Morritt the following January:

> I did not much write him *con amore* and I think he smells of the cramp . . . I had too much flax on my distaff and as it did not consist with my patience or my plan to make a fourth volume I was obliged at last to draw a rough, coarse and hasty thread.[5]

The novel provides several characteristic examples of Scott's use of environment as we have seen it in his earlier writing. The hero, Frank Osbaldistone, of Northumbrian descent, is brought up in London by his anti-Scottish father, and fed by his old Northumbrian nurse on northern tales in which the Scots appear as 'a race hostile by nature to the more southern inhabitants of this realm'. Like Waverley, with whom he has clear affinities (as he has with Darsie Latimer in *Redgauntlet*), his real education occurs in a series of 'tours' he makes as a young dreamer, uninterested in his father's world of international commerce. The first of these is from London to Northumberland; 'my native north', he calls it, 'the abode of my fathers', where he is introduced to his uncle's family at Osbaldistone Hall in the Cheviot Hills. Among other things, this is a journey from a prosperous metropolitan world of commercial enterprise which he does not understand and repudiates, to a rural world of dying, violent feudalism where he does not belong. From here, Frank travels to Glasgow, where he finds himself once again on the fringes of commercial society, and finally he journeys to the Highlands, making a further excursion into a world of ancient manners, of poverty and brutality. Inevitably, he becomes for a time the lost hero: he is a Protestant Southron in a Catholic environment, first in Northumberland and then in Scotland; he is a Hanoverian loyalist among Jacobite intriguers; he is an impractical and romantic youth suddenly exposed in a world of unfamiliar traditions and alien allegiances; all this at a time when religious, political and even personal family alliances are, particularly to him, obscure, controversial, equivocal and crucial—the period of the Jacobite rising of 1715.

Rob Roy adds little to what Scott had already achieved in the use of locality as a literary medium; it is in many respects a variation on *Waverley* themes, though less accomplished than that novel. By January 1817, and in much better health, he was at work on a novel 'far superior to Rob Roy in point of interest',[6] whose theme he had been turning over in his mind for almost a year, since he received from Mrs Goldie of Dumfries the story of Helen Walker. She, 'refusing to save her sister's life by an act of perjury, and undertaking a pilgrimage to London to obtain her pardon',[7] gave him his heroine.

Jeanie Deans in *The Heart of Midlothian* is a study in displacement, undergoing in the central chapters of the novel a complete environmental change. In appearance, she is far from conventionally romantic; nearing thirty, she was 'short, and rather too stoutly made for her size, had grey eyes, light-coloured hair, a round good-humoured face, much tanned with the sun'. A homely body, whose mental, moral and material security are seen throughout the tale to depend on the observance of simple domestic virtues in an austere, rural family environment. In itself unenterprising and humble (though her father has farmed with some success), this social and moral milieu, strongly coloured by the severe Presbyterianism of Davie Deans, paradoxically promotes her great adventure: seeking out the Duke of Argyle at the heart of the Hanoverian court in London, to plead for the life of her step-sister, Effie, ten years her junior, and now condemned for infanticide.

The time is September 1736, the ninth year of the reign of George II and Queen Caroline; the scene, when the novel opens, a tumultuous Edinburgh, tense with the fear and anxiety of what came to be known as the Porteous Riots. Indeed, the narrative proper begins in Chapter II with a description of the Grassmarket, the place of execution, 'not ill chosen for such a scene, being of considerable extent, and therefore fit to accommodate a great number of spectators, such as are usually assembled by this melancholy spectacle'.

In April of this year a smuggler, Andrew Wilson, was hanged. Before his death he had become a popular figure by making possible the escape of his partner, Robertson, at the cost of his own continued, and fatal, detention. Their capital crime had been the theft from the customs of smuggled goods of theirs which had been impounded. In the general view, this was no great matter. Smuggling, as we have seen, was not considered a mortal, or even a reprehensible business by the mass of the people, and Wilson's reputation was such that the city authorities feared a rescue attempt at the very gallows. Consequently John Porteous, the severe and unpopular Captain of the Civic Guard, was called in to see that order was maintained. The actual execution was not interrupted, but the Edinburgh crowd attacked the Guard afterwards and were repulsed by gunfire on the orders of Porteous, in the face of which several were killed. Porteous was brought to trial for murder and found guilty and then, on appeal to Queen Caroline (George II was abroad), was reprieved. At this stage the people took the law into their own hands, seized Porteous from prison before the official notice of reprieve reached the city, and hanged him from a dyer's pole near the place of common execution with no more disturbance or violence than was necessary for the accomplishment of their avowed and limited purpose. These incidents form a prologue to the central action of the novel, and though the fiction that follows is not directly concerned with the event, the whole provides an introduction to the novel's themes of moral dilemma, the rule of law, the nature of justice, mercy, compassion and the parameters of a sustaining faith.

During these events, Effie Deans has been arrested on a charge of child-murder, and while Porteous is being taken from the prison in which she is also held, Robertson, the father of her child, disguised as a woman, urges her to escape; she does not respond, lets the riot go by, and with it her opportunity. She is later tried and condemned to death. Jeanie, however, is successful in her quest; Effie is pardoned, though banished from Scotland for fourteen years, and marries Robertson, who is, in fact, Sir George Staunton. Their child, who was not killed but sold by the midwife to a robber, eventually kills his father unknowingly. It is then discovered that since his renunciation of a life of crime, Staunton has worn a penitential hair shirt. Effie ends her days in a convent abroad.

To appreciate the situation in which both Effie and Jeanie are placed, and in which both have to make heartbreaking decisions, it is necessary to understand something of the social and religious pressures that bear on them. Most important of these was the Kirk, which exercised supreme authority over the morals of the Scots community during this period. Its governing body, the Kirk-Session, expected and received from its elders reports and rumours of all ill-doing in the parish; much time was spent hearing witnesses and sifting evidence on even the most trivial matters, and a system of fines, graduated according to the heinousness of the offence, was operated, which had a crushing minimum of £4 Scots, more than a year's wages for most people.[8] This practice was grossly inconsistent in its treatment of rich and poor, where a leniency which allowed the laird to escape with a derisory fine was compensated in the case of the poor by the additional humiliation of the pillory, or stool of repentance. The unfortunate offender, dressed in sackcloth, was compelled to stand before the pulpit on a stool facing the congregation while he or she was publicly rebuked by the minister who was free to repeat the process for as many Sundays as he thought fit; cases of twenty-six repetitions are recorded. For the innocent and the uncaught this became a vicious form of entertainment on an otherwise very bleak sabbath.

Inevitably, rather than endure such an ordeal, some distraught girls killed their illegitimate children, a practice which grew to such a degree that by an Act of 1690 (to which Saddletree refers in Chapter V) even the concealment of pregnancy (the alleged crime on which Effie's fate turns) was made a capital offence.[9] The law was observed; the hangings were carried out, often more than one at a time. As Graham wryly comments, it seems 'rather to have increased the number of executions than to have lessened the number of delinquents . . . It may be that the abolition of congregational censure did not cause fewer hapless children coming undesirably into this world, but at least it prevented so many being untimely despatched to the next'.[10] And Allan Ramsay, who died in 1758, records the common horror in:

> The Fair ane, frighted for her Fame,
> Shall, for her Kindness, bear nae Blame,
>   Or with Kirk-censure grapple;
> Whilk gart some aft, their leev alane,
> Bring to the Warld the luckless Wean,
>   And sneg its Infant Thrapple.[11]

In such a context, Effie is a born victim. Scott spends some time on a realistic appraisal of her physical attractiveness; heads are not slow to turn when she passes, and her presence distracts the local youth from their innocent pursuits of putting the stone, casting the hammer, and playing at bowls; even rigid Presbyterians have been known to sigh after her. She is blithe, bonny, young and spoilt; a singer of popular songs, naïvely wayward, a secret dancer, and in love, none of which qualities could possibly have endeared her to the Kirk.

Much of the story of the two sisters centres on the sanctity of family, hearth and home, with a peculiar Scottish intensity. Scott's own childhood was morally austere and he lived apart from his parents, at Sandyknowe and Bath, for almost six infant, invalid years. In maturity, however, 'Never was a more virtuous or a happier fireside than his . . . A high and pure sense of duty presided over whatever he had to do as a citizen and a magistrate; and as a landlord, he considered his estate as an extension of his hearth . . . However his imagination might expatiate, it was sure to rest over his home. The sanctities of domestic love and social duty were never forgotten'.[12]

Lockhart is partial, but he is not the only witness to say such things of family life at Abbotsford. The theme is explored in many ways in the Waverley novels; in hospitality, for example, in *Redgauntlet,* and family pride in *The Bride of Lammermoor,* but in *The Heart of Midlothian* Scott investigates the psychological aspects of a character's immediate environment to a depth which had not been attempted before, and which he was never to achieve quite so successfully again.

Douce Davie Deans, a relatively prosperous dairy farmer or 'cow feeder', though still subservient to the laird, lives with his daughters in a small, isolated cottage at St Leonard's, under Salisbury Crags, less than a mile south-east of the Grassmarket and the gallows of the West Port. Their life together is simple and hard in 'the quiet, uniform and regular seclusion of their peaceful and monotonous household'. Jeanie and her father manage the farm between them and, because she shows signs of being less amenable to their rigorous régime, Effie is sent as shop-girl and servant to the house of Bartoline Saddletree, the harness-maker, close by the Tolbooth Kirk in the city. Here, it is hoped, Mrs Saddletree, a 'far awa' cousin' of the family, will keep a motherly eye on her. At St Leonard's, the routine continues unvaried, the time occupied largely by work and prayer; father and daughters eat frugally, and end the day, after the cattle have been tended for the night, with 'family exercise', the extempore sermonising by the head of the household on some passage or theme from the Bible. In summer this takes place about eight o'clock and it is part of Effie's backsliding, before she is sent to Saddletree's, that she is absent from home dancing 'on the green down by' at such a late hour. Her father does not know this, but he hears the word 'dancing' in Effie's conversation with Jeanie, and seizes on the theme; it is, he says,

> 'a dissolute and profane pastime, practised by the Israelites only at their base and brutal worship of the Golden Calf at Bethel, and by the unhappy lass wha danced the head aff John the Baptist, upon whilk chapter I will exercise this night for your farther instruction'.
>
> (Ch. XI)

The family unit is a tight one, strained almost to destruction by Effie's plight and the legal, ecclesiastical, social and emotional tensions it imposes upon all three. In the course of the central episode of the novel, Jeanie Deans becomes voluntarily separated from home, family and friends in a process of gradual and intensifying isolation, a series of tours from the known to the unknown, undertaken in no daring spirit of adventure, but with a stern, undeviating humanity, in duty to her family, herself and her God. Her morality is founded on a Calvinistic love, and the dilemmas which arise from domestic distress produce almost irreconcilable tensions between love of kindred, respect for law, and duty to God. The stresses arising from her situation are explicit by the end of Chapter X, when Effie is arrested.

> The stunning weight of a blow so totally unexpected bore down the old man, who had in his early youth resisted the brow of military and civil tyranny, though backed with swords and guns, tortures and gibbets. He fell extended and senseless upon his own hearth; and the men, happy to escape from the scene of his awakening, raised, with rude humanity, the object of their warrant from her bed, and placed her in a coach, which they had brought with them.

In the confusion, Effie's abrupt departure goes almost unnoticed except by Jeanie, and then too late. She runs screaming in vain after the coach, but is stopped by neighbours 'who almost forced her back into her father's house'. The fact that Scott chooses to have Effie arrested at home is important, and the episode is shot through with ironic overtones, especially when the Calvinistic rhetoric and the unrelenting 'tough, true-blue Presbyterian' vigour of Davie Deans proves inadequate in the face of domestic calamity.

Scott's skill in recreating the resounding periods of Presbyterian eloquence appears at its best in Old Mortality, but in The Heart of Midlothian, especially at this point, its function is more subtle than the mere expression of character. With a thundering impotence of language vividly reminiscent of King Lear, Scott ironically reinforces our sense of

Deans's desolation. The juxtaposition of her father falling senseless to the hearth and Effie being raised from a bed not of love but of sickness gives an emphasis both forceful and economical to the initial breaking up of the family under strains which they have not yet learned to tolerate. Thus the chapter ends with a dialogue which leaves us in no doubt of Jeanie's moral, spiritual and material isolation. Dumbiedikes, the simple minded Laird, and her neighbours are alike worse than useless in offering their 'appropriate sources of consolation'; her father is wholly inhibited by his religious pride. Now she must both sustain him in his affliction and act for the reprieve of her sister, alone.

The breaking-up of the family started with Effie's waywardness, but from this point onward the depth of the hurt is expressed through the voluntary detachment of its members one from another, after their formal separation by the action of the law. When Effie is imprisoned, the magistrates forbid Jeanie to see her until the eve of the trial; even at this meeting, they are in the presence of Ratcliffe, the prisoner turned turnkey (like Dougal, in *Rob Roy*). Effie's isolation emerges poignantly here, when she realises she must endure the loss of her father as well as of her child. 'I am his bairn nae langer now . . .' (Ch. XX). At the trial, Jeanie is separated from her father because 'she maun be enclosed' as a witness; Deans himself refuses to sit, as he is invited, beside Effie. 'I cannot own her', he says, and seeks an obscure corner, averting his eyes from the proceedings. All of this intensifies Effie's frail isolation as she enters the court to the raucous turbulence of an unfeeling and curious rabble.

> With inflamed countenances and dishevelled dresses, struggling with, and sometimes tumbling over each other, in rushed the rude multitude, while a few soldiers, forming, as it were, the centre of the tide, could scarce, with all their efforts, clear a passage for the prisoner to the place she was to occupy. By the authority of the Court, and the exertions of its officers, the tumult among the spectators was at length appeased, and the unhappy girl brought forward, and placed betwixt two sentinels with drawn bayonets, as a prisoner at the bar.
>
> (Ch. XXI)

It is worth recalling at this point that Effie is brought into the court after being imprisoned in the Tolbooth, 'The Heart of Midlothian'. This ancient and inhuman jail in the centre of Edinburgh's Old Town was demolished in 1817 (when Scott took some of its stones to embellish Abbotsford), and a few years later, Lord Cockburn remembered it bitterly, and vividly:

A most atrocious jail it was, the very breath of which almost struck

down any stranger who entered its dismal door; and as ill placed as
possible, without one inch of ground beyond its black and horrid walls.
And these walls were very small; the entire hole being filled with little
dark cells; heavy manacles the only security; airless, waterless, drain-
less; a living grave. One week of that dirty, fetid, cruel torture-house
was a severer punishment than a year of our worst modern prison—
more dreadful in its sufferings, more certain in its corruption, overwhelming the innocent with a more tremendous sense of despair,
provoking the guilty to more audacious defiance.[13]

Effie spends several weeks in this place, her trial delayed 'In hopes she
might be induced to speak out on a subject infinitely more interesting to
the magistracy than her own guilt or innocence' because she is invited to
betray her lover who is being pursued for crimes other than seduction.
Scott makes nothing of the social canker of such a place; the theme had to
wait for Dickens's attacks on prisons like Newgate and the Marshalsea;
he was only five when the Tolbooth was pulled down.

The separation within the confined space of the courtroom where, of
all places, the family should be one, is ironically made more acute by the
considerateness of Fairbrother, the defending advocate. He puts what he
believes to be trivial questions at first, to give Jeanie time to compose
herself:

'You are, I think, the sister of the prisoner?'
'Yes, sir.'
'Not the full sister, however?'
'No, sir. We are by different mothers.'
'True; and you are, I think, several years older than your sister?'
'Yes, sir.'   (Ch. XXIII)

The division is cruelly wedged.

Effie's life hangs now on Jeanie's perjury. Her alleged crime of child-
murder is compounded by concealment of her pregnancy which, under
the law of the time as we have seen, implies premeditation. If it can be
shown that she has told anyone of her condition, this charge, at least,
would be removed. But in spite of the encouragement of the court, Jeanie
will not lie: 'She never breathed a word to me about it', she says.

The assembly is audibly shocked by this, and Deans, hitherto shrink-
ing into obscurity, takes the limelight as he collapses 'with his head at
the foot of his terrified daughter'. It is a strange, temporary family re-
union. 'Let me gang to my father', Effie keeps repeating, and Jeanie,
bending to help him, speaks softly, 'He is my father—he is our father'.
The three soon part, however; Jeanie and Davie Deans leave the court
and are accommodated at the house of Bartoline Saddletree, while Effie

remains alone to face her sentence of death by hanging. Soon, Jeanie leaves her father and sets out for London to plead for her sister's pardon, stained, she feels, with vicarious guilt.

So, she begins her lonely journey; a new and unusual kind of tour in fiction though, as we have seen, a technique that Scott appreciated and exploited, having its origins both in the picaresque novel and in the growing popularity of tourism. But Scott saw more clearly than any other novelist of his time the possibilities of using regional characters and manners to explore wider issues of conduct and the problems of moral judgement. Environmental factors do not only mark character, they impose their directives on behaviour; hence a relatively simple conception of character in the figure of Jeanie Deans can be tellingly employed when she is removed to an alien environment. The journeys of Deloraine in *The Lay*, and of Marmion I have already discussed, and Darsie Latimer's in *Redgauntlet* has a similar basis; most of Scott's Scottish novels use the method to some degree, most importantly perhaps in *Waverley* and *Guy Mannering*.

Jeanie's journey is different from these mainly in that she undertakes it not in a mood of relaxed and idle curiosity, but in circumstances which put upon her severe psychological pressures. For example, she makes her journey from Scotland to England, whereas in the other novels they are either to or in Scotland. She makes it, moreover, in 1736, when the Jacobite rising of 1715 was still fresh in the memory and the desultory and protracted preparations for what was to be the Forty-Five were being carefully watched by the British government. It was a time when Scots were still regarded with curiosity and a cautious, condescending hostility, as Smollett recalled in *Humphry Clinker* (1771) where Jerry Melford, travelling from London to Scotland, writes from Morpeth in Northumberland: 'From Doncaster northwards, all the windows of the inns are scrawled with doggrel rhimes, in abuse of the Scotch nation, and what surprised me very much, I did not perceive one line written in way of recrimination.'[14] Jeanie, moreover, is a traveller with a difference, seeing with an innocent eye, and rawly conscious of her foreignness.

After a slight detour to the village of Liberton to take leave of her betrothed, Reuben Butler, whom she fears she may never see again, she travels south at the rate of about twenty miles a day. Her fears are not unfounded. Between this moment and her next sight of Arthur's Seat lie eight hundred miles of ill-marked, unsurfaced track, its direction made and remade by horsemen, carters, and walkers like Jeanie, according to where the driest and least disagreeable way was to be found across land that was as yet largely unenclosed. Scott gives few details of her actual route as far as York. but from his general account it is clear that she follows the line of the Great North Road, probably across the Lammer-muir Hills and into England at Coldstream, though there was another road that followed the coast through Dunbar, Berwick and Alnwick. The two met at Morpeth, in Northumberland. Another fork of the main routes occurred at Darlington. Here Jeanie takes the eastern road to York, but rejoins the other at Ferrybridge where she stays at The Swan, 'the best inn then and since, upon the great northern road', says Scott. She goes on to Tuxford and then to Newark where she stays at the Saracen's Head. It is between here and Grantham that she is set upon and abducted. Thereafter, having escaped with Madge Wildfire and been given asylum at Willingham Rectory, she completes her journey to London by coach from Stamford. Scott must have travelled the route himself many times and indeed Jeanie's loneliness and determination are felt at the outset by Scott's consciousness of the ease of such a journey in his own day, 'a matter', he writes, 'at once safe, brief, and simple, however inexperienced or unprotected the traveller.' But Jeanie travels on her bare feet, sometimes lucky enough to be offered 'a cast in a wagon', or free hospitality.

In spite of the melodramatic abduction and escape to follow, near Grantham, the early stages in England are by far the most stressful part of her journey. It is not until she is south of Durham, with two hundred and sixty miles to go before she reaches London, that she feels in alien territory and becomes acutely conscious of her isolation when her bare feet, dress, speech, and manners call forth sneers, taunts and sarcasm 'couched in a worse *patois* by far than her own'. (The Scotch dialect, Matthew Bramble observed in *Humphry Clinker*, 'certainly gives a clownish air even to sentiments of the greatest dignity and decorum'.) Total environmental change is a severe experience; Jeanie is compelled in these circumstances to adopt some form of protective colouring and behaviour, though she does so unwillingly, feeling even the temporary loss of her true self. She wears shoes and stockings, changes her tartan shawl for a straw bonnet (with some embarrassment; this being worn only by married women in her own land, it lends an ironic sophistication to her person, though only she is aware of it), and she speaks as little as possible. 'She confessed afterwards, that, 'besides the wastrife, it was lang or she could walk sae comfortably with the shoes as without them; but there was often a bit saft heather by the road-side, and that helped her weel on' (Ch. XXVIII). Shoelessness was common in Scotland, and no infallible sign of poverty in a land where very few, whatever their rank, were rich. In Jeanie's day women wore shoes on Sundays, but it was a painful concession to the sabbath, and they usually carried their footwear as far as the church before wearing it.

Scott creates an austere and compassionate journey which he describes, without fancifulness, as a pilgrimage. Indeed, his frequent references to Bunyan, especially in Chapters XXX and XXXI, enrich and deepen the elaborate realism of the novel. 'Did ye never read the Pilgrim's Progress?', Madge Wildfire asks Jeanie during their flight from Meg and her accomplices near Grantham. 'And you shall be the woman Christiana, and I will be the maiden Mercy, for ye ken Mercy was of the fairer countenance, and the more alluring than her companion' (Ch. XXX). During this time, Jeanie's mind is on everyone but herself: 'If they think me weel, and like to do weel', said the poor pilgrim to herself, 'my father will be kinder to Effie, and Butler will be kinder to himself.' As a fictional heroine of 1818, Jeanie is no small achievement.

When she reaches Newark, Scott reminds us of her loneliness by a simple, though possibly faulty topographical reference; she has been warned of highwaymen on Gunnerby Hill, near Grantham.

> 'I'm glad to hear there's a hill', replied Jeanie, 'for baith my sight and my very feet are weary o' sic tracts o' level ground—it looks a' the way between this and York as if a' the land had been trenched and levelled, whilk is very wearisome to my Scotch een. When I lost sight of a muckle blue hill they ca' Ingleboro', I thought I hadna a friend left in this strange land.'   (Ch. XXIX)

(Ingleborough is forty miles from Jeanie's route and not the most noticeable object to a stranger's eyes, even if she is looking for hills. Nevertheless, Scott makes his point.) In the midst of her perilous way, led by Madge, Jeanie, like Darsie Latimer, lights on what is apparently an earthly paradise.

> 'But now we will gang to the Interpreter's house, for I ken a man that will play the Interpreter right weel; for he has eyes lifted up to heaven, the best of books in his hand, the law of truth written on his lips, and he stands as if he pleaded wi' men—Oh, if I had minded what he said to me, I had never been the castaway creature that I am!—But it is all over now.—But we'll knock at the gate, and then the keeper will admit Christiana, but Mercy will be left out.'   (Ch. XXXI)

Willingham Rectory is the counterpart of Mount Sharon in *Redgauntlet*, a peaceful habitation tainted at the heart. The stain in this case spreads from the hero/villain, George Staunton, alias Robertson, tearaway, smuggler, jailbird, Madge Wildfire's seducer, father of Effie's child. After the anxiety and weariness of the road, after the violence of her capture by Meg Murdockson, Jeanie escapes with Madge Wildfire's help to the tranquil and landscaped refuge of the Rectory whose periodically revised architecture, 'a combination of roofs and chimneys of different ages, united to render the front, not indeed beautiful or grand, but intricate, perplexed, or, to use Mr Price's appropriate phrase, picturesque' (Ch. XXXII). With its extensive grounds, the best trouting stream in all Lincolnshire, and a handsome interior, the haven seems complete. But this is not what Jeanie is seeking, and it rouses in her mind uneasy comparisons with the Manses of her own country, 'where a set of penurious heritors, professing all the while the devotion of their lives and fortunes to the Presbyterian establishment strain their inventions to discover what may be nipped, and clipped, and pared from a building which forms but a poor accommodation even for the present incumbent' (Ch. XXXII).[15]

Willingham provides Jeanie with shelter, comfort and relief, but for all its attractions, she does not see in it her ideal of the good life; this she envisages later, when she dreams of accompanying Effie in her banishment:

Jeanie's fancy, though not the most powerful of her faculties, was lively enough to transport her to a wild farm in Northumberland, well stocked with milk-cows, yeald beasts, and sheep; a meeting-house hard by, frequented by serious Presbyterians, who had united in a harmonious call to Reuben Butler to be their spiritual guide; Effie restored, not to gaiety, but to cheerfulness at least;—their father, with his grey hairs smoothed down, and spectacles on his nose;—herself, with the maiden snood exchanged for a matron's curch—all arranged in a pew in the said meeting-house, listening to words of devotion, rendered sweeter and more powerful by the affectionate ties which combined them with the preacher.   (Ch. XXXIX)

Work, piety, a united family, and a familiar, natural landscape, even in exile. Roots.

Later, safely in London, she drives with the Duke of Argyle through a luxuriant, fertile countryside and they pause to look at the view:

A huge sea of verdure, with crossing and intersecting promontories of massive and tufted groves, was tenanted by numberless flocks and herds, which seemed to wander unrestrained and unbounded through the rich pastures. The Thames, here turreted with villas, and there garlanded with forests, moved on slowly and placidly, like the mighty monarch of the scene, to whom all its other beauties were but accessories, and bore on his bosom an hundred barques and skiffs, whose white sails and gaily fluttering pennons gave life to the whole.

(Ch. XXXVI)

For all the implied beauty, Scott's prose is laboured, cliché-ridden and lifeless here. Jeanie's response to the Duke's deliberately provocative, 'We have nothing like it in Scotland,' breathes a different air, its cadences unforced and smooth:

> 'It's braw rich feeding for the cows, and they have a fine breed o' cattle here,' replied Jeanie; 'but I like just as weel to look at the craigs of Arthur's Seat, and the sea coming in ayont them, as at a' thae muckle trees.' (Ch. XXXVI)

Both style and view are equally artificial in the Thames passage; but, though Jeanie's reply is less incisive than most of Scott's dialect writing, her longing is expressed in terms which, while making explicit her love of place, do so in a way that defines the very Scottishness from which she takes her identity, and which she now finds so vulnerable. This is why she and Argyle can speak as they do, nationality in the Scottish context of the times implying less a political allegiance than a personal relationship overriding class and power in common exchanges; a relationship whose virtue and power Scott felt deeply and unsentimentally.

Though Jeanie's moral drive seems at a first reading to grow out of naïve goodness, a closer consideration reveals how Scott has shown the heroine and her father to be products of a particular locality at a particular time; the finger of history has moulded them both.

Deans is first described as a 'tough true-blue Presbyterian' oppressed by the old Laird Dumbiedikes (an unimportant figure except as an example of the petty tyranny of the small landlord in a tight community, yet in his death more memorable than Falstaff). Scott is careful not to pin epithets on Deans as mere labels, and to show how from childhood onwards he had been affected by the more aggressively physical and expansively verbal characteristics of the Covenanting brethren. To understand his reaction to Effie's lapse and to its condemnation under the law we need to observe what Scott tells us of its origins.

These are to be found in the Presbyterian meeting at Talla-Linns in 1682. The place is a remote glen in the wild borderland between Moffatt and Peebles and there, by the Talla,

> men who, in the recollection of the severities to which they had been exposed, had become at once sullen in their tempers, and fantastic in their religious opinions, met with arms in their hands, and by the side of the torrent discussed, with a turbulence which the noise of the stream could not drown, points of controversy as empty and unsubstantial as its foam. (Ch. XVIII)

Here Davie Deans listened as a boy, his brain 'thoroughly heated by the noise, clamour and metaphysical ingenuity of the discussion'; listened to all the severe and fanatical bigotry of an embattled and persecuted sect, persuaded by many arguments, unable to reconcile one with another. He has since followed the cult with a vigorous yet qualified faith, and now it is put to the proof. In his dilemma, 'the voice of nature ... exclaimed loud in his bosom against the dictates of fanaticism'. He resolves that the decision whether or not to bear witness in court shall be Jeanie's, and Jeanie's alone. To give testimony in a court of justice under a government which did not accept the Presbyterian word was seen by the extremists, and indeed by Deans, as an act of defection from the Covenant; this he cannot do himself, nor will he urge it upon his daughter. But Jeanie is not troubled by this scruple of appearing in court: 'She never doubted but she was to be dragged forward into the court of justice, in order to place her in the cruel position of either sacrificing her sister by telling the truth, or committing perjury in order to save her life' (Ch. XIX).

Deans's creed offers him no way through, and he will not yield it to the promptings of paternal love. His dilemma goes back to the testimonies of Talla-Linns, place and time conspiring to produce an effect impossible elsewhere and in another age; his stern upbringing of the responsive but unimaginative Jeanie has nurtured a mind of 'a grave, serious, firm and reflecting cast' (Ch. IX), but without the sound and the fury of the brood of Talla-Linns. Nevertheless locality has shaped her in its own way, sharpening her fearful apprehension of powerful local superstitions, the terror of witchcraft, and the reputed entrance to the interior of the earth under the crags. At Muschat's Cairn, not far from her dwelling, she has met, as a total stranger, one whom she is later to know as Robertson, Effie's lover, though in reality young George Staunton of Willingham. Alone with her in the haunted darkness, he forcefully urges her to perjury:

'You will let your sister, innocent, fair, and guiltless, except in trust-ing a villain, die the death of a murderess, rather than bestow the breath of your mouth and the sound of your voice to save her.'

'I wad ware the best blood in my body to keep her skaithless', said Jeanie, weeping in bitter agony, 'but I canna change right into wrang, or make that true which is false.' (Ch. XV)

Though she rejects his argument, it is with a strength that resists not only the persuasive rhetoric of a stranger, but which also shuts from her mind the traditions of a locality which she believes haunted by the powers of evil; it is an irony of the times that she should feel this way, such superstition being encouraged by the very nature of her Presbyterianism.

The opening of this chapter, in fact, blends imperceptibly but cogently the dominant influences at work both on father and daughter, and from father to daughter. These two are at the same time strained and saved by their lack of imagination, an abridgement of faculties which, though depriving their lives of much that would commonly be thought profitably enjoyable, carries them through difficulties which would have subdued more lively minds. The stolid heroes of Conrad have their psychological forebears in Scott.

After London, Jeanie's going hence, much as her coming hither, is shadowed by hanging and mob violence. The last significant episode in the novel, before it crumbles into a heap of Highland fragments, is Chapter XL, where Scott recounts the execution of Meg Murdockson, and the lynching and subsequent death of her daughter, Madge Wildfire. In these events, Scott draws together all the influences of locality which have played some part in the development of his theme, and we can see Jeanie caught in the strange threads of this intricate web: superstition, national prejudice, history, rootlessness, family. The role in the plot of Meg and her daughter is conventionally mechanical; they appear and vanish with a predictable coincidental conveniency. But their importance as individuals, as women of a particular place and time, is vital in relation to Scott's themes of consicence and moral guilt, and his use of tradition and locality. Meg is a wildly melodramatic character of the same breed as Norna of the Fitful Head in *The Pirate*, and Meg Merrilies in *Guy Mannering*. In spite of the strength of her presence, she remains a shadowy figure throughout, a symbol of evil and poverty, a constant threat to the pure pilgrim. Yet in her sickening death as witch and thief, Scott evokes with a few brief outlines a whole history of Border violence, vengeance, outlawry and scant justice. Meg is one with the past of her race.

Jeanie completes her tour, having followed the eastern route south, by taking the western road north towards the border through Penrith and Carlisle, traversing what had been the most lawless region in the Borders in the old riding days. When the party reach Carlisle and see the gibbet on Haribee, they

could discern plainly the outline of the gallows-tree, relieved against the clear sky, the dark shade formed by the persons of the executioner and the criminal upon the light rounds of the tall aerial ladder, until one of the objects launched into the air, gave unequivocal signs of mortal agony, though appearing in the distance not larger than a spider dependent at the extremity of his invisible thread, while the remaining form descended from its elevated situation, and regained with all speed an undistinguished place among the crowd.   (Ch. XL)

Meg's epitaph is uttered by one of the spectators: 'Shame the country should be harried wi' Scotch witches and Scotch bitches this gate—but I say hang and drown.' 'We hae but tint a Scot of her', says another, 'and that's a thing better lost than found.' The passage is tense with irony.

Meg is one part of the dark underworld of the novel through which the pure Jeanie must move to achieve her ends: nocturnal meetings at Muschat's Cairn, inmates of the Tolbooth, smugglers, footpads and broken men. Her death at Haribee (a place of execution redolent with ballad outlawry) is the macabre end of a grotesque, sordid existence, and its association with what was almost Effie's fate is not coincidental. Jeanie's singleness of purpose and devotion have saved her sister from being hanged by a vicious law (the echoes of *Measure for Measure* are explicit throughout); it has been the means of rescuing her from the underworld into which she has naïvely fallen, with the possibility of ultimately being hanged like Meg. The improbabilities of the third part of the novel should not be allowed to obscure the clear implications of its course so far; George Staunton is a corrupt, vicious, inhumane and plausible charmer, whose strength would inevitably have led Effie to destruction. The main tensions in the moral fable lie between Jeanie and Staunton. Up to this point, Scott has developed his characters consistently and in depth; George's reform in the closing chapters is as irrelevant as it is improbable.

The deranged, beautiful whore, Madge Wildfire, dies a different death. Isolated, like Jeanie, by her nationality as much as by her state of mind, outcast by the nature of her family, she (who discoursed so feelingly of *Pilgrim's Progress*) is exposed to the ignorant rage of the Carlisle mob as they leave the scene of her mother's hanging. Madge clings to the carriage in which Jeanie is travelling with Argyle's agent, Mr Archibald, pitifully seeking help to cut her mother's body down.

There came up, however, a parcel of savage-looking fellows, butchers and graziers chiefly, among whose cattle there had been of late a very general and fatal distemper which their wisdom imputed to witchcraft. They laid violent hands on Madge, and tore her from the carriage, exclaiming—'What, doest stop folk o' king's highway? Hast no done mischief enow already, wi' thy murders and thy witcherings?'

(Ch. XL)

I

The episode is pathetic in its unheroic realism. Mr Archibald, also threatened for being a Scot, makes no superhuman gesture to rescue Madge, but goes for help, while the final dereliction of the poor woman, seduced and abandoned by Staunton, driven out of her mind by a wretched childbirth, is brought vividly and sickeningly before us: 'As they drove off, they heard the hoarse roar with which the mob preface acts of riot or cruelty, yet even above that deep and dire note, they could discern the screams of the unfortunate victim' (Ch. XL). Fatally injured by a rabble which, unlike the Porteous mob, is inflamed by fear, prejudice and superstition, not by a sense of rough justice, she is carried to the workhouse hospital where she lies alone in a ward of empty beds. She speaks little, keeps her secrets, sings intermittently her 'bonny songs', and dies with the words warm on her lips of the finest of Scott's lyrics, a piece of unsurpassed literary balladry:

> Proud Maisie is in the wood,
>   Walking so early;
> Sweet Robin sits on the bush,
>   Singing so rarely.
>
> 'Tell me, thou bonny bird,
>   When shall I marry me?'—
> 'When six braw gentlemen
>   Kirkward shall carry ye.'
>   .   .   .
> 'Who makes the bridal bed,
>   Birdie, say truly?'—
> 'The grey-headed sexton,
>   That delves the grave duly.'
>   .   .   .
> 'The glow-worm o'er grave and stone
>   Shall light thee steady;
> The owl from the steeple sing
>   "Welcome, proud lady".'
>
>   (Ch. XL)

Fragmentary, tragic, haunting in its Ballad echoes her dying song is wholly fitting because her origin is in the folk; she is of the race of Ophelia, not of Rochester's wife.

As in *Rob Roy*, Scott uses a coarse thread at the end, drawing events to a close in 1751 after the deaths of Staunton, Deans and the Duke of Argyle, and with the startling discovery of Meg Murdockson's last confession, which reveals her part in the seduction of Madge by Robertson, and her dealings with Effie's bairn. One feature of the final sequence remains of interest: Scott's moral evaluation of Effie. As I have indicated, his treatment of her has always been sympathetic, affectionate, humorous and realistic; and she is presented as the helpless victim of her own way-ward personality, a spoilt upbringing and a cruel law. Aside from this, however, she is the companion of criminals and the mother of an illegitimate child. So is Madge Wildfire who dies, mad, at the hands of a mob. What are we meant to think of Effie, now Lady Staunton? Scott made his own view of such characters very clear in the early 1820s in an essay on Robert Bage, one of his *Lives of the Novelists*; a view that seems to arise from a rigidity of moral principle apparently at odds with the more generous impulses he exercises in his fiction.

> It is true, we can easily conceive that a female like Miss Ross in *Barham Downs*, may fall under the arts of a seducer, under circumstances so peculiar as to excite great compassion, nor are we so rigid as to say that such a person may not be restored to society, when her sub-sequent conduct shall have effaced recollection of her error. But she must return thither as an humble penitent, and has no title to sue out her pardon as a matter of right, and assume a place as if she had never fallen from her proper sphere. Her disgrace must not be considered as a trivial stain, which may be communicated by a husband, as an exceeding good jest, to his friend and correspondent; there must be, not penitence and reformation alone, but humiliation and abasement, in the recollection of her errors. This the laws of society demand even from the unfortunate; and to compromise farther would open the door to the most unbounded licentiousness.[16]

Effie does suffer for her misdeeds, and for the sorrow she has brought on others, but not by social ostracism, humiliation and abasement. On the contrary, she becomes a bright star in the high social firmament, seen by the Duke of Argyle (who has no reason to associate Lady Staunton with Jeanie's appeal) as 'the toast of the town, the most beautiful creature at court'. Staunton has seen to it that she is educated to take her place in society—another instance of a Scott character assuming a protective camouflage—and she has spent four years in a convent, though it is clear that at this stage the purpose of her sojourn is grooming not penitence. Nevertheless, she endures acute remorse, fear of discovery and, in spite of wealth and the acclaim of her circle, exists in near despair. 'If wealth, and distinction, and an honourable rank, could make a woman happy, I have them all', she writes to her sister, interpreting 'rank' as Scott did himself, as if the holder were thereby rendered automatically virtuous. She feels she is punished in the fact that her two babies die, and childlessness intensifies the enduring repentant melancholy of her husband. Punishment for past deeds seems to exist at a variety of levels here, but not on the harsh plane of social retribution that Scott advocates in writing of Bage. Jeanie, however, seems to speak for him when she reflects with contempt on the 'staggering and unsatisfactory condition of those who have risen to distinction by undue paths' (Ch. XLVIII), but she excuses her, as Scott also appears to do, on the grounds that she is the victim of circumstances. Scott resolves the matter with characteristic equivocation by committing her, 'after blazing ten years in the fashion-able world', to a convent on the Continent. 'She never took the veil, but lived and died in severe seclusion, and in the practice of the Roman Catholic religion, in all its formal observances, vigils and austerities' (Ch. LII). One remembers Glenallan.

Scott's trite moral conclusion that guilt can never confer happiness, and that 'the paths of virtue, though seldom those of worldly greatness, are always those of pleasantness and peace', is disappointing, and, in the light of the superb novel that precedes it, irrelevant. The values from which the novel really draws its strength are less simple and superficial. They are implicit in almost every stage of Jeanie's heroic journey to London and back, representing as it does a moral as well as a topo-graphical pilgrimage. In spite of her apparent single-mindedness, sus-tained by the unassailable religious conviction of a dour and dogged Calvinism, we are well aware that she is guided to safety at Willingham by a mad prostitute, having first been afforded a temporary reprieve from the robbers' violence by showing them the note that Ratton had given her. He is the thief turned Tolbooth jailer; self-interested and unscrupu-lous. The glimmering of conscience which moves him to help Jeanie is bitterly qualified when we recall his earlier conversation with Madge Wildfire:

> 'And I'll tell ye, Ratton, blithe will Nichol Muschat be to see ye, for he says he kens weel there isna sic a villain out o' hell as ye are, and he wad be ravished to hae a crack wi' you—like to like, ye ken—it's a proverb never fails—and ye are baith a pair o' the deevils peats I trow —hard to ken whilk deserves the hettest corner o' his ingle-side.'
>
> Ratcliffe was conscience-struck, and could not forbear making an involuntary protest against this classification. 'I never shed blood', he replied.
>
> 'But ye hae sauld it, Ratton—ye hae sauld blood mony a time. Folk kill wi' the tongue as weel as wi' the hand—wi' the word as weel as wi the gulley!—' (Ch. XVII)

Virtue is not self-sufficient, it appears; the nature of righteousness is as complex as the nature of landscape, and as difficult to interpret; within

the total context of *The Heart of Midlothian* it is nowhere more ener-
getically or more ironically indicated than in Madge's wild words to
Jeanie in Willingham churchyard:

> 'Do ye think, ye ungratefu' wretch, that I am gaun to let you sit doun
> upon my father's grave? The deil settle ye doun;—if ye dinna rise and
> come into the Interpreter's house, that's the house of God, wi' me, but
> I'll rive every dud aff your back!'   (Ch. XXXI)

CHAPTER VII

The Bride of Lammermoor (1819)

The tone of optimistic realism which Scott sustains throughout *The Heart of Midlothian* is most evident in the attitudes and fortunes of Jeanie and Effie Deans and Madge Wildfire. At his best, Scott uses fantasy and reality as mutually supportive, while at the same time presenting them as forces whose abrasive antagonism etches more deeply on the mind of the reader his unshakable belief that somehow good will be the final goal of ill. Whenever in this novel we move in darkness, it is with either the recollection or the promise of light. The world that holds the Tolbooth is the same that sustains Willingham Rectory, and these localities appear not as simple extremes but as comparable habitations where the delicate balancing of duty and desire is scrupulously carried out. In both worlds we are made conscious of the interplay of elements in a moral *chiaroscuro*; in both, humanity appears strong, wayward, cruel, selfish, as well as generous and aspiring; misguided often, but never wholly lost, always redeemable.

Scott's next novel, however, written during months of illness and extreme physical pain, evokes a world of unrelieved darkness and nightmare. In *The Bride of Lammermor* all the characters move blindly in the obscurity of their own selfish passions; all are tainted: the hero, Edgar Ravenswood, by his vengeful pride, his opponent Sir William Ashton by his fearful time-serving, and Lady Ashton by her ruthless and ambitious reverence for family status; the common people are in the main moved by a surly resentment against their former masters whose vices they are now seen to have inherited. Those characters who at first appear to have no share in this sullen rebelliousness turn out to be the inhabitants of an obsolete, illusory realm of feudal vassalage. Pride and self-interest are opposed by a purity so ineffectual in the nature of the doomed Lucy Ashton that we see from the beginning that it cannot survive long in the brutish world symbolised by the Ravenswood estates, inhabited by the deluded and ruled by political adventurers.

The action is set about the year 1710, in the reign of Anne, last of the Stuart monarchs. Three years earlier, as we have seen, the controversial Union of Parliaments had taken place, followed by an abortive Jacobite rising in 1708; five years later the Earl of Mar led his unsuccessful rebellion in the name of James, the Chevalier de St George, the Old Pretender. Slowly and painfully the embryo of modern Scotland was assuming a recognisable form, having been conceived not in mutual concord but in stubborn conflict in the Revolution of 1688. It is to this event that we must turn briefly for an understanding of the political and religious tensions which underlie the loyalties and antagonisms of the novel, as well as for an appreciation of the melancholy dilemma with which Scott confronts us. The world of *Lammermoor* holds only two possibilities, both unattractive: a decadent, old but independent Scotland, and a corrupt, new anglicised one. For Scott, as we know, the problem was still a real one, and he felt it deeply.

In *The Bride*, Lord Ravenswood, father of the hero, Edgar, 'had espoused the sinking side' in the Revolution of 1688, 'his blood had been attainted and his title abolished' (Ch. II). This was the year in which, having antagonised two nations by his Roman Catholic impositions, James II of England and VII of Scotland had been deposed and sought refuge in France. Under his successor, William II, the Scottish Parliament in 1690 restored Presbyterianism as the established religion of Scotland, and abolished episcopalian practices. The old Lord Ravenswood of Scott's tale remains loyal to the old religion, to its Tory politics and Jacobite sympathies, losing all round to the Presbyterian Whig, Sir William Ashton, and in the mid-1690s, having parted with Ravenswood Castle and its lands, he retires to Wolf's Crag, 'a lonely and sea-beaten tower', on the bleak cliffs between Eyemouth and St Abbs Head, surrounded by 'a black domain of wild pastureland'. At the beginning of the novel he dies, having lived for some fifteen years in this eyrie in almost constant litigation against Sir William, the *parvenu* purchaser of his property, and is succeeded by Edgar his son, who vows vengeance on the man he believes responsible for his father's impoverishment and death.

Wealth, political power, and hence Family, had been achieved by Sir William as recently as the seventeenth century, though Lady Ashton is of the ancient and renowned family of Douglas. The distinction is made early in the novel between an old, decaying Scotland, and the new world of the English Union; between a naïve traditionalism and a political and commercial opportunism. Even Lady Ashton's proud name of Douglas becomes only a tool of political intrigue.

The narrative framework is simple, but into it Scott weaves bright threads of Anglo-Scottish political chicanery, a desperate and impotent Jacobitism, superstition and prophecies, all contained by the Lothian landscape of south-eastern Scotland. Edgar Ravenswood inherits what is left of the family property, the tower of Wolf's Crag, when his father dies. The novel opens with the funeral of old Ravenswood, and Edgar's vow of vengeance on Ashton who, he feels, has unfairly succeeded in ruining his father. He and Lucy Ashton fall in love after he shoots a white bull which threatens her while she is out walking with her father. As a result, Sir William and Edgar come close to reconciliation but the possibilities of marriage between the two families are destroyed by the ambitious and heartless Lady Ashton. The lovers are separated; after a forced marriage to another man, Lucy goes mad, murders her husband on their wedding night and soon dies. Edgar, riding to duel with her brother afterwards, is drowned in the quicksands of the Kelpie's Flow.

The tragedy of *The Bride of Lammermoor*, then, is bred in family feud, but it is here a hostility somewhat lacking in the traditionally sanctioned, even honourable quality of blood-feud. Ashton has bought Ravenswood by fair, though severe, means, by the standards of the times; as the Ravenswoods have lost it by their negligence of both men and money: they have ignored the value of their tenants as well as of their patrimony. The new owner is an opportunist, 'a silver-tongued lawyer of the very highest order', a time-server, not an evil man; but the old man remains to his dying day implacably vengeful and his son inherits little else but a gothic turbulence, a hollow cry for vengeance and a pile of crumbling stone. We soon recognise that the real source of the antagonism is selfish pride, not family honour at all, though each side pretends that honour is at stake. Scott mercilessly exposes Edgar's false view (with which the reader may at first be inclined to sympathise) by producing a ruthless parody of it in the old family retainer, Caleb Balderstone, 'the only male domestic', Ravenswood tells Bucklaw, 'that remains to the house of Ravenswood'. This ancient and irrepressibly loyal seneschal is commonly criticised as an extravagant caricature to whom Scott has given too much space; the author did later admit that 'he might have sprinkled rather too much parsley on his chicken'.[1] Yet Balderstone's unwavering and hilarious concern that he should 'never let the honour o' the house suffer', ironically does but skin and film the ulcerous place where we soon see that the family has no credit and little honour except in the atra-bilious imagination of its heir. Scott's pessimistic irony is fully revealed at the end of the tale when the Ravenswood estates are restored to Edgar: he recovers them neither by direct legal means, nor by the time-honoured exercise of his own strong arm, but fortuitously as a result of the sudden political ascendency of the Tory party, the influence of his relative, the Marquis of A——, and the simultaneous decline of Ashton's place and fortune.[2]

At this stage, we see quite clearly that the Master of Ravenswood has no serious commitment beyond that of being a romantic hero. He is caught up in the political schemes of both Ashton and the Marquis of A——, because he is for them a useful counter in the games they play. Neither of these men, moreover, has any greater dedication than Edgar to causes outside themselves: Ashton sails with all currents, and the Marquis is suspected of Jacobitism. Edgar's mission to Europe on the Marquis's behalf is, to say the least, unconvincingly introduced, being concerned with his scheming

> related to a secret and highly important commission beyond sea, which could only be intrusted to a person of rank, talent, and perfect confidence, and which, as it required great trust and reliance on the envoy employed, could not but prove honourable and advantageous to him.
>
> (Ch. XXV)

In its abstract woolliness, the passage is no more than a clumsy device for removing young Ravenswood for a twelvemonth and giving us the illusion that he is a man of consequence.

However, Edgar Ravenswood appears in a different and more significant light in the context of his own locality. In the novel as a whole, two main functions of landscape are apparent, though it must be acknowledged that these are, at times, cut across by passages of sententious and vacuous eloquence that simply interfere with their function. Scott's more telling use of landscape in this novel is to be found in his presentation of parallel worlds: Lucy Ashton lives subdued on the fringes of her parents' world of politics, law, administration and social advancement; but she inhabits even more vividly a literary dream world, where she moves along the paths of Spenser's *Faerie Queene*, or becomes Miranda on Prospero's magic island. Here she dwells in the same ideal world as the young Waverley, a realm in which she builds palaces of 'a delusive though delightful architecture', and in which he 'like a child among his toys, culled and arranged, from the splendid yet useless imagery and emblems with which his imagination was stored, visions as brilliant and as fading as those of an evening sky'. Waverley, however, eventually enters the real world and survives; for Lucy, it is death.

The other is closely linked to it, a land evoked in local tradition and legend, mediated largely through Blind Alice to the eager imagination of Lucy. This is a less literary context, full of dark terrors and prophecies, echoing in its violence and tragedy the actual events in the lives of the main characters. Lucy lives in both worlds, and is a victim of both.

It is in his exploitation of a more intimate environment, however, that Scott has deployed his themes and characters with both skill and insight. The estates of the antagonists are symbolised by their family residences, but their condition is revealed in depth not through the romance of the star-crossed Lucy and Edgar, nor through the political and religious framework, but through the folk: Blind Alice, the villagers of Wolf's-hope, Mortsheugh the sexton, and the three old hags who traffic in life and death, marriage and funeral, this world and another.

Though of ancient foundation, Ravenswood Castle is seen in the novel always as a modernised dwelling, adapted over the centuries both in architecture and landscaping to the taste of varying periods; it is clearly representative of the fluctuating allegiances of its present owner, who 'had sailed long enough amid the contending tides and currents of time to be sensible of their peril, and of the necessity of trimming his vessel to the prevailing wind' (Ch. XV). The original is probably Crichton Castle in Midlothian, of which Scott was so fond, but the similarities between the real and the fictional buildings are much less important in this case than they are with the Master of Ravenswood's remaining tower, Wolf's Crag.

The Castle of Ravenswood exists virtually in a historical vacuum; its strongest associations in the novel are legendary and supernatural, not historical and political. Wolf's Crag, however, is firmly linked with change and personality in historic time. 'This, then', Ashton rather clumsily exclaims when he first sees it, 'is the ancient castle of Wolf's Crag, often mentioned in the Scottish records' (Ch. IX). It is repeatedly referred to in terms which call attention not only to its age and decrepitude, but to its associations with historical events of the past two hundred years. Men have gone out from Wolf's Crag to die at Flodden; the secret chamber in which Bucklaw and, later, Ashton are accommodated has sheltered the fugitive Earl of Angus, and played its part in the mysterious Gowrie Conspiracy: all, occasions of secrecy, darkness, rebellion and death.

In his Introduction to the novel Scott writes,

> The imaginary castle of Wolf's Crag has been identified by some lover of locality with that of Fast Castle. The author is not competent to judge of the resemblance betwixt the real and imaginary scene, having never seen Fast Castle except from the sea. But fortalices of this description are found occupying, like ospreys' nests, projecting rocks, or promontories, in many parts of the eastern coast of Scotland, and the position of Fast Castle seems certainly to resemble that of Wolf's Crag as much as any other, while its vicinity to the mountain ridge of Lammermoor renders the assimilation a probable one,

but later, introducing *Chronicles of the Canongate*, after denying that in any of his fictional localities he had any purpose of describing particular places, he adds a note that 'I would particularly intimate the Kaim of

Uric, on the eastern coast of Scotland, as having suggested an idea for the tower called Wolf's Crag, which the public more generally identified with the ancient tower of Fast Castle'.

It may be true that, in Scott's words, 'the iron-bound coast of Scotland affords upon its headlands and promontories fifty such castles as Wolf's Hope' [sic].³ It would be pointless to attempt to identify Wolf's Crag too closely with Fast Castle but the three incidents mentioned above do have possible or particular associations with Fast Castle and are consequently of some interest in the environmental structure of the tale, allowing a life to the tower which makes it much more than a picturesque item in the landscape. It stands, too, as a symbol both of the tottered fortunes of the family, and of the obsolete and isolated mind of Edgar, pitched nervously at the edge of a precipice beneath which, between the castle and the village he is to perish in the quicksand of the Kelpie's Flow. This landscape image, in fact, parallels that which Scott applies to Lucy's quiet life, whose present 'smoothness of current resembled that of the stream as it glides downward to the waterfall'.

The tower of Fast lies not between St Abbs Head and Eyemouth as Wolf's Crag does but a few miles north of St Abbs, some twenty miles north-east of Flodden Field. The Marquis of A—— recalls that his ancestor 'had been feasted there, when he went forward with the then Lord Ravenswood to the fatal battle of Flodden, in which they both fell' (Ch. XXV). In 1513, the castle was in the hands of Sir Patrick Home, who fought at Flodden, where his son Cuthbert fell to the sword of Dacre.

In 1600 the place belonged to one Logan of Restalrig, 'a deboshed drunken man', who was said to have conspired with the Laird of Gowrie to assassinate James VI. His 'doer' or agent, an Eyemouth notary called Sprot, confessed in 1608 that the King was to have been taken to Fast Castle, after which Logan would be rewarded by the gift of the castle of Dirleton, near North Berwick. He produced letters supposed to have been written by Logan to Gowrie, though these are believed to be forgeries. Whatever the truth of the matter, Logan's bones were dug up in 1609, three years after his death, and brought with gothic solemnity into court, where sentence was duly pronounced on them. This is what lies behind the passing reference at the end of Chapter VII, where Caleb Balderstone is seeking accommodation for Bucklaw in a castle where there is so little in the way of furniture and bedding. The secret chamber offers him a way out, 'For wha', said he, 'would have thought of the secret chaumer being needed? it has not been used since the time of the Gowrie Conspiracy, and I durst never let a woman ken of the entrance to it, or your honour will allow that it wad not hae been a secret chaumer lang'.

It is significant, too, that the Master of the King's Household, implicated in the Gowrie affair, was called Craigengelt, the name Scott gave to his shadowy Jacobite agent in the novel.

Young Ravenswood belongs to both houses; he can live only with the ruin and decay of Wolf's Crag and the absurd loyalties of Balderstone; yet Lucy provides a tenuous but graspable lifeline by which he may be restored to the present. At one point, while she and her father are accommodated at Wolf's Crag, Sir William speaks explicitly of restoration: 'means might be found, *ad re-aedificandum antiquam domum*' (Ch. IX). The words are part of the strained courtesies exchanged by host and guest at the old tower and their conversation has a pointed counterpart when the roles are reversed and Edgar becomes a guest in his former home, the now opulently modernised Ravenswood Castle. He notices the changes with increasingly depressed spirits. This is not simply a house that has been re-edified, redecorated, brought up to date; these would be positive changes; improvements. For Edgar, however, what has been done signifies the shearing away of his own childhood, even the wiping out of his ancestry. Shown into the lavishly renovated withdrawing room, he is stunned by the unfamiliarity of what once had been home, but assuming indifference says:

> 'You will not be surprised, Sir William, that I am interested in the changes you have made for the better in this apartment.
> ... 'We were obliged to leave', he said, 'some armour and portraits in this apartment—may I ask where they have been removed to?'
> 'Why', answered the Keeper, with some hesitation, 'the room was fitted up in our absence—and *cedant arma togae*, is the maxim of lawyers, you know—I am afraid it has here been somewhat too literally complied with. I hope—I believe they are safe—I am sure I gave orders—may I hope that when they are recovered and put in proper order, you will do me the honour to accept them at my hand, as an atonement for their accidental derangement?' (Ch. XVIII)

It is unlikely that a family so keen on its history would leave behind its ancestral portraits, but the point is made and the Keeper's sly fumbling to cover his momentary confusion betrays his true outlook. He takes no pride and no part in the history of Ravenswood. The present is all to him, the castle no more than a substantial material acquisition, the complacent testimony to his worldly success. In a different but no less deadly way the new man is as hollow as the old.

Shortly after Lord Ravenswood's death, Sir William and Lucy walk through the extensive and well-tended park surrounding the castle, and Scott's irony is at once apparent: 'they paced slowly on, admiring the different points of view for which Sir William Ashton, notwithstanding the nature of his usual avocations, had considerable taste and feeling.' They meet Norman, the forester, a tenant who regrets, almost resents, Ashton's indifference to hunting and country life. ' "It was not so, he had heard, in Lord Ravenswood's time...', and as for Edgar, 'There hasna been a better hunter since Tristrem's time ... We hae lost a' sense of woodcraft on this side of the hill" ' (Ch. III). Ashton attempts to conceal his discomfiture by tipping the forester, who equivocally accepts the dollar 'with a smile in which pleasure at the gift is mingled with contempt for the ignorance of the donor' (Ch. III).

Sir William has taste, but, knowing neither the topography nor the tenants of his estate, shows no interest in either. A subdued irony lies in the fact that though he is the owner, he is never called by the territorial name 'Ravenswood', a form of address which would have been a natural acknowledgement of his identification with both people and locality. On this brief tour, he needs to be conducted by his more knowledgeable and sympathetic daughter, whom he mocks because she makes it 'a point of conscience to record the history of every boor about the castle'. The irony is blunt as the next chapter opens: 'Lucy acted as her father's guide, for he was too much engrossed with his political labours, or with society, to be perfectly acquainted with his own extensive domains, and, moreover, was generally an inhabitant of the city of Edinburgh' (Ch. IV). Their purpose in continuing the walk is, at Lucy's suggestion, to see Old Alice, who has for long lived on the Ravenswood estate, and knows all about the family. Her father is at once both curious and hostile: 'And what should I have to do with them, pray, Lucy ... or with their history or accomplishments?' When they meet, he notices her English accent, and in the brief dialogue that follows Scott emphasises Sir William's alien spirit by dwelling on Alice's success in putting down roots.

> 'It is here', said the blind woman, 'that I have drank the cup of joy and of sorrow which heaven destined for me. I was here the wife of an upright and affectionate husband for more than twenty years—I was here the mother of six promising children—it was here that God deprived me of all these blessings—it was here they died, and yonder, by yon ruined chapel, they lie all buried—I had no country but theirs while they lived—I have none but theirs now they are no more.'
>
> (Ch. IV)

This is both the language and the sentiment we have already heard from Meg Merrilies at Derncleugh. For Alice, as for Meg, it is locality that counts; her land is defined by her family; where they lived and died, she belongs; for Ashton and his like, nationality is a political counter, a label without which the individual, whatever his ties, cannot really be said to exist. For minds like his, statelessness means annihilation, not the close life of family and community. Ashton did not know even of Alice's existence, much less of her ruined cottage and extreme destitution. With courteous condescension, having promised to help, he adds, 'I hope you will continue to reside on this property of mine rent-free for your life'. Alice's reply is devastating, though equally courteous. 'I hope I shall,' said the old dame composedly, 'I believe that was made an article of the sale of Ravenswood to your lordship, though such a trifling circumstance may have escaped your recollection' (Ch. IV).

The bitterness of this again lies in an equivocal irony. We have already seen how inextricably bonded she is with the oneness of her family and the estate. She remains now a mere fragment of property; the humanity of the rent-free provision was Ravenswood work; Ashton never knew it was there. Unlike Scott's, his estate is no extension of his hearth.

Alice's last words to him are cautionary: 'Take care what you do; you are on the brink of a precipice.' He first mistakes this for the warning of a political *coup,* but once again the truth is more local: 'You have driven matters hard with the house of Ravenswood. Believe a true tale—they are a fierce house . . .' Blind Alice points out what Ashton has failed to see; her concern is with people, not with ciphers.

By the end of the chapter, the Lord Keeper's place in the community is left in no doubt; he does not belong; he does not speak, think or behave as a man in his place should, and he is not wanted.

One might be forgiven for seeing at first the house of Ravenswood as the very reverse: an indigenous family, ancient in tradition and renown, powerfully connected with Border names of equal repute: Douglas, Home, Swinton, Hay and others. But as these bonds of locality are strong, so is the consequence of their slackening overwhelming. Our sympathies are at first engaged by Scott's impressive, gloomy evocation of the traditional (and proscribed) Scottish solemnities of old Ravenswood's funeral. He is buried with the rites of the Scottish episcopal communion, in defiance both of the law and of the Lord Keeper who is responsible for administering it. His agent attempts to stop the service but withdraws under threat from the assembled guests, while the clergyman, 'affrighted at the scene, and trembling for his own safety, hastily and unwillingly rehearsed the solemn service of the church, and spoke dust to dust, and ashes to ashes, over ruined pride and decayed prosperity' (Ch. II).

Edgar swears vengeance, and the mourners return to the tower for the traditional obsequious carouse, an expensive observance of the old ways which is sufficient to complete the young Master of Ravenswood's impoverishment. At this point our hearts may well go out to this youthful, isolated, romantic remnant of a house of tarnished honour and degraded fortunes. But Scott does not leave the matter here. He indulges us temporarily but soon with the voice of the people and in so doing outlines more clearly and without sentiment exactly in what this tarnishing and degradation consist.

Edgar's poverty pushes Balderstone to ingenious shifts 'for the credit o' the house', and one of his first tasks is to seek food in the neighbouring village of Wolf's-hope, where not long before he had exacted tribute as of right. But times and manners have changed; the villagers have gradually emancipated themselves from the old feudal ties with Wolf's Crag and are no longer amenable to Ravenswood demands. They are so far organised as to have employed an attorney, Davie Dingwall, to look over their affairs, and to him Caleb is compelled to plead where once he commanded. But he finds a dusty answer. The villagers agree 'That their hens had caickled mony a day for the Lords of Ravenswood, and it was time they suld caickle for those that gave them roosts and barley' (Ch. XII). And Dingwall, unmoved by Caleb's eloquent urgency, his arguments from antique custom and hereditary respect, remains immovably opposed to the old ways. 'His clients', he said, 'had determined to do the best they could for their own town, and he thought Lord Ravenswood, since he was a lord, might have enough to do to look after his own castle . . . New times were not as old times . . .' (Ch. XII).

Scott's counterpointing is ingenious; in Ashton's interview with Alice we see how the new landlord has no real involvement with his estate and its people, who remain loyal to the idealised myth of master and man. Caleb's interview with the villagers and with Dingwall, however, show another part of the estate which realistically rejects the old bonds, achieves independence, and scorns the notion of Family superiority. This view is made explicit in another context, when Edgar speaks to Mortsheugh the sexton about Alice's burial. Like Alice, the gravedigger lives in pathetic destitution, in 'a solitary cottage adjacent to the ruined wall of the cemetery, but so low that, with its thatch, which nearly reached the ground, covered with a thick crop of grass, fog, and houseleeks, it resembled an overgrown grave' (Ch. XXIII). Mortsheugh is bitter in his poverty, and remorseless in his condemnation of the house of Ravenswood whose ruin he sees as retribution, not as misfortune.

'I kenna wha should favour them', said the gravedigger; 'when they had lands and power, they were ill guides of them baith, and now their head's down, there's few care how lang they may be of lifting it again.'

'Indeed', said Ravenswood; 'I never heard that this unhappy family deserved ill-will at the hands of their country. I grant their poverty— if that renders them contemptible.'

'It will gang a far way till't', said the sexton of Hermitage, 'ye may tak my word for that—at least, I ken naething else that suld mak myself contemptible, and folk are far frae respecting me as they wad do if I lived in a twa-lofted sclated house. But as for the Ravenswoods I hae seen three generations of them, and deil ane to mend other.'

(Ch. XXIV)

Mortsheugh's vassalage to the family has scarred him indelibly and literally. His revolt is deeply embedded in Scottish history, forced as he was to follow his master to the battle of Bothwell Brig in 1679. He is not concerned with the battle (being on the winning side) but indignant at the misuse of his talents as trumpeter to Lord Ravenswood, which function, he insists, 'was to blaw folk to their warm dinner, or at warst to a decent kirkyard, and no to skirl them awa to a bluidy brae side, where there was deal a bedral but the hooded craw'. The scene is mildly comic but Mortsheugh's pithy eloquence forces to the surface a yet shadowy notion of unnecessary humiliation, and the exploitation of 'huz puir dependent creatures' for the honour of the family.

In their failure to observe the traditional laws of family and feudal relationships, Scott makes it clear that both houses are corrupt and we find in the last paragraph of the novel that canker, the great leveller, has done its work: 'The family of Ashton did not long survive that of Ravenswood'. But by this time Scott has made equally, if perhaps regretfully clear, that the old feudalism is dead, and the newer one too.

The old hags prepare us for this end when they present themselves at Lucy's funeral, 'snuffing the carrion like vultures', viciously rejoicing in the fall of the house of Ashton:

'Did I not say', said Dame Gourlay, 'that the braw bridal would be followed by as braw a funeral?'

'I think', answered Dame Winnie, 'there's little bravery at it; neither meat nor drink, and just a wheen silver tippences to the poor folk; it was little worth while to come sae far a road for sae sma' profit, and us sae frail.'

'Out, wretch!' replied Dame Gourlay, 'can a' the dainties they could gie us be half sae sweet as this hour's vengeance?'   (Ch. XXXV)

Despite their prophesyings and their close but superficial resemblance to the Weird Sisters in *Macbeth*, the true function of these old women is social, not supernatural.

Lucy is buried with maimed rites, in a coffin that bears neither name nor date, and in circumstances which vividly recall Madge Wildfire's 'Proud Maisie':

> 'Tell me, thou bonny bird,
>   When shall I marry me?—'
> 'When six braw gentlemen
>   Kirkward shall carry ye.'

Indeed, after the violence and vituperation of most of the characters, rich, poor, good and bad, we may be glad for a moment to dwell on the brief life of the adolescent maid, a pale and passive figure, indifferent as a character, yet by no means insignificant in the structure of the novel. We first find her singing to an ancient air words which 'seemed particularly adapted to her character':

> Look not thou on beauty's charming,—
> Sit thou still when kings are arming,—
> Taste not when the wine-cup glistens,—
> Speak not when the people listens,—
> Stop thine ear against the singer,—
> From the red gold keep thy finger,—
> Vacant heart and hand and eye,—
> Easy live and quiet die.   (Ch. III)

Caught between the empty rant of the two families, derided by her ambitious and worldly mother as 'the Lammermoor shepherdess', she leads a quiet, solitary and isolated existence; yet of these families she is the only member who cares about people, who troubles to learn the characters and history of her father's tenants, who attempts to make Ravenswood Castle, and not Edinburgh, her home. Her affinity with Old Alice is much more than the easy condescension of mistress to servant; both sense the domestic importance of place. Lucy is also imaginative and where, in *The Heart of Midlothian*, Jeanie Deans's stolid strength carries her through all her trials, Lucy's imagination renders her the fearful inhabitant of two worlds; in one she is the victim of the ambition and political scheming of her parents, in the other, she moves through local legend and superstition to madness and death. In this world, 'her secret delight was in the old legendary tales of ardent devotion and unalterable affection, chequered as they so often are with strange adventures and supernatural horrors' (Ch. III). Ironically, the real world is superficially the same for her at first, but it lies outside the manipulation of the mind; there she finds that ardour cools, affection alters, adventures

K

and horrors, far from being the subjects of a safely self-indulgent romantic introspection, are in the end powerful and evil enough to break both her mind and her heart, reducing all that she represents of tenderness, loyalty and beauty to dust in a nameless kist, croaked over by three old hags.

CHAPTER VIII
The Pirate (1821)

Grimly, even humorously at times, defiant of his continuing illness, pain and debility, Scott began *A Legend of Montrose* as soon as he had completed *The Bride of Lammermoor*. 'It was written', he explained in his 1829 Introduction, 'chiefly with a view to place before the reader the melancholy fate of John Lord Kilpont, eldest son of William Earl of Airth and Menteith, and the singular circumstances attending the birth and history of James Stewart of Ardvoirlich, by whose hand the unfortunate nobleman fell.' Set in the Highlands in 1644–5, it is a tale of deadly clan feud interlocked with the history of the Civil War; but of locality, environment and the formative influences on men of their habitations Scott has little to say, and nothing to enrich the colours of these skeins as he had woven them in *Waverley*.

The two novels were published together in June 1819, as the third series of *Tales of My Landlord*. In the two years that followed, Scott completed and published no fewer than five substantial novels,[1] though it is not until *The Pirate* appears in 1821 that we once more come across new approaches to the interaction of place and people.

He was still very ill. In July, he wrote to Maria Edgeworth:

> I have had dreadful bad health for many months past, and have endured more pain than I thought was consistent with life. But the thread, though frail in some respects is tough in others; and here I am with renewed health, and a fair prospect of regaining my strength, much exhausted by such a train of suffering.[2]

Too weak to write much, he started dictating *Ivanhoe* to John Ballantyne as the long recovery began. When it was published the following December it sold 10,000 copies in less than a fortnight, even at the high price of thirty shillings. It is a curious work, this first 'English' novel of Scott's, but not entirely foreign to my theme.

The medieval period and the Yorkshire location were a new departure as Scott explained in his 1830 Introduction, where (referring to the continuing fiction of his anonymity) he wrote: 'The present author felt that in confining himself to subjects purely Scottish, he was not only likely to weary out the indulgence of his readers, but also greatly to limit his power of affording them pleasure.' He regarded it as 'a tale of chivalry, not of character'[3] and wrote to Lady Louisa Stuart (who had called it 'an odd new kind of book')

> I . . . am glad you found anything to entertain you in *Ivanhoe*. Novelty is what this giddy-paced time demands imperiously, and I certainly studied as much as I could to get out of the old beaten track, leaving those who like to keep the road, which I have rutted pretty well.[4]

His immense industry, however, was, and continued for the rest of his life to be, an inadequate substitute for an ideal of the novel as a work of art; his sole avowed claim both as poet and novelist was to please his public, and he succeeded, but we can hardly doubt now that his genius was diminished by the ends he dictated for it. *Ivanhoe*, says Lockhart, was 'received throughout England with a more clamorous delight than any of the Scotch novels had been'.[5] But such an appeal to English taste of the period could be said to have destroyed Scott, professionally tempting though it obviously was. Like his poetic predecessors, Robert Fergusson and Robert Burns, his distinctive achievement was the brilliant use of his own language to lay open place and history as a literary medium, yet after this time the only powerful Scottish work to come from his pen was *Redgauntlet*, four years later. No doubt English readers were relieved at not having to struggle once more with passages of Scottish dialogue, and one result was the novel's success in maintaining a conventional rather than a critical popularity for over a century. Of course, it embodies serious themes of national and racial conflict, moral obligation, and the pressure on individual loyalties of a changing social order and it has its defenders, but considering it entire, I find it difficult to deny the justice of Walter Bagehot's observation that

> the charm of *Ivanhoe* is addressed to a simpler sort of imagination,— to that kind of boyish fancy which idolises medieval society as 'the fighting time' . . . A martial society, where men fought hand to hand on good horses with large lances, in peace for pleasure, and in war for business, seems the very ideal of perfection to a bold and simply fanciful boy.[6]

Now, it remains for us little more than a chauvinistic cliché, 'a novel', as R. C. Gordon says, 'of gusto and confusion'.[7] The Yorkshire location is precisely delineated in the opening paragraph but thereafter we are offered little more than vigorously narrated adventures in the greenwood, combat in the lists, and the destruction, not without its symbolic value, of a Norman stronghold. The Jew Isaac and his beautiful daughter

Rebecca appear like a literary gold mine discovered by Scott and virtually passed over. Not that Scott's basic interest has altered with his change of place, period and costume; it has merely become obscured and blunted. As in the Scottish novels, we are involved in a conflict between an occupying power and an indigenous people.

By the time *Ivanhoe* appeared, on 18 December 1819, Scott already had further plans. He was discussing with his publishers another English novel, to be set this time in the reign of Elizabeth I, but working hard also on a Scottish story of the sixteenth century, *The Monastery*, which came out early in March 1820. Scott virtually acknowledges the compulsiveness for him of Scottish themes in the 1830 Introduction:

> It would be difficult to assign any good reason why the author of *Ivanhoe*, after using, in that work, all the art he possessed to remove the personages, action and manners of the tale to a distance from his own country, should choose for the scene of his next attempt the celebrated ruins of Melrose, in the immediate neighbourhood of his own residence.

It is, of course, in the light of what I have so far written, not difficult at all. Scott himself, in the paragraphs that follow this remark, admits that the whole region acts like a romantic magnet, exerting on him the irresistible power of its traditions, history, superstitions and scenery. In *Ivanhoe,* all of these were applied from without; in *The Monastery,* as in the earlier novels, they are embedded. Unfortunately, this alone is not a sufficient recipe for a work of art and in overdoing the ingredients Scott ruins the dish.

The events, which take place between 1547 and 1557, follow the fortunes of two brothers who engage opposing causes in the religious conflicts of the age, Halbert Glendinning supporting the Protestants under Lord James Stewart and Edward taking monastic vows which eventually bring him to be Abbot of St Mary's at Kennaquhair (Melrose). The novel is not uninteresting but it is overrich, one flavour subduing another, leaving the palate confused and the appetite unfulfilled. The narrative is generous in its exposition of Border landscape and character, but overall these rarely rise above the level of information and anecdote; one feels that they are only being used, not truly animated. Involvement is absent, and Scott knew it. The book met with general critical coolness, and Scott's hurt drew from him an acknowledgement that it was

> not very interesting; but it was written with as much care as the others that is with no care at all and
> 'If it isna weel bobbit we'll bobb it again'
> On these points I am Atlas.[8]

The acknowledgement not only confirms once more the carelessness with which he wrote, but an underlying contempt for his readers. Even Lockhart was driven to admit that it was a failure.

Scott's conscience, as well as his practical sense, did indeed decide him to 'bobb it again', and he set *Kenilworth* aside to concentrate on a redemptive sequel to *The Monastery*. The resulting novel, *The Abbot*, shares and extends the locality and traditions of its predecessor and purges some of the earlier work's weaknesses such as the absurd White Lady of Avenel and the anachronistic euphuist, Sir Piercie Shafton; but it makes no substantial use of locality as an interpretative medium. The events take place ten years after the conclusion of *The Monastery* and concentrate largely on the captivity of Queen Mary in Lochleven Castle, and her escape.

Kenilworth, a tragic story of the love of Amy Robsart and the Earl of Leicester in the reign of Elizabeth I, was published in January 1821. Like many of Scott's tales, its origins go far back in his own life, to a favourite poem of his childhood, William Mickle's *Cumnor Hall*. One of his schoolfellows, John Irving, recalled:

> After the labours of the day were over ... we often walked in *the Meadows*,—(a large field intersected by formal alleys of old trees, adjoining George's Square)—especially in the moonlight nights; and he seemed never weary of repeating the first stanza—

> > The dews of summer nighte did falle
> > The moone (sweete regente of the skye)
> > Silver'd the walles of Cumnor Halle,
> > And manye an oake that grewe therebye.[9]

It was greeted with unqualified acclaim and appears to have done for its locality, temporarily at least, what *The Lady of the Lake* had done for the Trossachs a decade earlier, though this was clearly a result of the writer's reputation rather than of any evocation of the fiction; Scott had no direct acquaintance with the locality and it forms no powerful influence within the novel. He had, indeed, written to Archibald Constable in September of the previous year for information about Amy Robsart (whose name he had forgotten) and Cumnor. 'I like', he said, 'to be as minutely local as I can.' In terms of giving his action a clearly localised pattern of movement he is successful; further exploitation of the region he does not attempt.

By August 9 of the same year he had handed to James Ballantyne the first volume of *The Pirate* (originally called *The Buccaneer*), a novel drawn from his voyage to the Orkney and Shetland Islands with William

Erskine, then Sheriff of Orkney and Shetland, in the summer of 1814. It was completed and published early in December to be met by cool, largely adverse reviews.

Like most of Scott's novels of Scottish life, *The Pirate*, set about the year 1700, has at its heart a cultural duality and conflict; unlike them, the friction arises not from an uneasy Anglo-Scottish relationship but from a confrontation of Scandinavian and Scottish elements in the Shetland Islands. *The Pirate*, moreover, has no hero morally perplexed by twin allegiances like Edward Waverley, or Darsie Latimer, or Jeanie Deans; the battle between the two opposing cultures is direct, unsubtle, and frequently facetious. Ancient Shetland, or Hjaltland, is represented by the Nordic laird, or Udaller, Magnus Troil, implacably antagonistic until the last chapter to all innovation, and especially to Triptolemus Yellowley, the recently arrived factor, sent as an 'improver' to Shetland by its aristocratic Scottish overlord.

The basis of their opposition, however, is real enough, rooted in history, commemorated in tradition and saga. The islands of the Shetland group lie two hundred miles west of Bergen, and about the same distance north of Aberdeen. Until 1472, when they became Scottish, they were Norwegian territory, and by the time the transfer took place the language, folklore and legal system were entirely Norse, a condition which the mere change of ownership did little to alter for centuries. The Scandinavian heydey is commemorated in the *Orkneyinga Saga*, celebrating the life of the islands and the Earls of Orkney. As late as 1567, an Act of the Scottish Parliament confirmed the validity of ancient Norse laws in both Orkney (fifty miles to the south) and Shetland. Elements of the old language survived into the eighteenth century before they were completely absorbed into the dialect, and are still strongly evident in the place-names. Norse domestic and farm implements continued in use for centuries; the single-stilted plough, for instance, which Troil and Yellowley argue over in Chapter XIV, was not replaced by a more efficient tool until the reign of Victoria.

Scott's own contact with the area was slight, but penetrating. In 1814, shortly after the publication of *Waverley*, he accepted an invitation from the gloriously titled Commissioners for the Northern Lights to accompany them on an inspection of the Scottish lighthouses. The excursion came at a fortunate time. He was busy with *The Lord of the Isles* and seeking scenic stimulus for descriptive passages; more important in relation to *The Pirate*, however, was his recent association with the publication of *Illustrations of Northern Antiquities*, by his friends Henry Weber and Robert Jameson. According to Lockhart, Scott had a considerable share in Weber's contribution, giving, among other things, an account of the *Eyrbyggia Saga*, a work he considered to be the most interesting record of Icelandic history and literature. The Saga's most recent editors point to the affinity between the world of this narrative and that of Scott's romantic imagination, with its antiquarian elements, hauntings, the 'unquiet graves of the malevolent dead', violence and heroism. 'But the author of the Waverley Novels must have been still more powerfully fascinated by the elaborate structure of a narrative in which the lives of many remarkable and varied individuals are set against a background of historical events to produce an imaginative view of history.'[10]

Scott's historical imagination is certainly at work in *The Pirate* but the novel is not located in time by the defining framework of historical action, and it is worth noting that here, as well as in *St Ronan's Well*, or *The Antiquary*, the absence of any substantial historical context leaves us with only filleted fiction. Most of the novels I discuss have their action fixed in time and place by the determining movement of specific historical events. *Waverley* and *Redgauntlet*, very different in both locale and plot, derive from the philosophies, myths and events which grew out of the Stuart cause in the eighteenth century; *The Bride of Lammermoor* springs from the Revolution of 1688 and the beginning of that gradual withering of ancient and traditional Scottish life which by Scott's time was almost complete; *The Heart of Midlothian* begins with the Porteous Riots of 1736 (an event which is much more than just a spectacular opening to the more domestic narrative) and has its moral heart in the growth of Presbyterianism; *Guy Mannering* is in its main plot almost without this scaffolding but is held in time as well as place by the Border environment of Dandie Dinmont, and the eighteenth-century Edinburgh of the lawyer Pleydell.

The life and literature of old Scandinavia had long interested Scott. In 1790, as a student in Edinburgh, he had given a paper to the Literary Society 'On the Manners and Customs of the Northern Nations', and in 1792 he addressed the Speculative Society 'On the Origin of the Scandinavian Mythology'.[11]

This early interest never lost its hold and was introduced into Scott's fictional world seven years after his lighthouse tour when he came to write *The Pirate*. During the voyage, he kept a careful journal,[12] recording closely observed and considered features of landscape, people and manners. Much of what he saw of terrain, tradition and domestic economy he was to embody in the novel.

In contradistinction to the social and ethical issues which are revealed through the interaction of Troil and Yellowley, the romantic plot is little better than pantomime, especially in its piratical sections; the incident here lacks the fundamental seriousness of comedy or satire and so fails to make any substantial statement. Scott, in this part of the work, may have a tale to tell, but he has nothing very much to say. The hollowness of the romance sounds through the empty dialogue and the reverberating woodenness of its main characters: the Mertouns, father and son, inhabit their own shallow worlds of naïve convention; Clement Cleveland, with the giveaway forename, is an apparently ruthless pirate who turns out to have a heart as well as a shipload of gold; Minna and Brenda Troil, the Udaller's daughters, are puppet heroines who have neither cause nor conviction, and, lacking the fire of Jeanie Deans or Flora MacIvor, manifest through the tale little more than the polite bewilderment of anglicised gentility quite foreign to Scott's realistic portrayal of the Nordic chauvinism of Magnus Troil and his dependants.

Along with a number of other, less central, characters, these are presented without the kind of social and historical frame which would confer upon them a credible dimension; they exist without any specific environmental defining features other than the most superficial. The pirates lack even a hint of realism and find no literary niche in either satire or farce; the Shetlanders almost emerge from the shadows into the brilliant landscape but never really become part of it. Mertoun senior, an Englishman in his forties and a repentant pirate self-exiled to Shetland, is the former seducer of Ulla Troil and by her the father of Cleveland; he rejects human society, even in the small Shetland community, and lives a secluded life of moody misanthropy. But it is an attitude without depth, a protracted moodiness, not a considered philosophical detachment from 'the current of human passions'. It is no surprise to learn that in the end 'he was generally believed to have retired into a foreign convent', which as we have seen is Scott's usual way of disposing of his more gloomy or reflective characters, such as Redgauntlet and Flora MacIvor. His son, Mordaunt, described as being absorbed into the life of the island, acts the part only of the conventional hero; though brought up in the community, he gives the impression always of being a visitor from beyond the Shetland world, and his eventual marriage to Brenda Troil is a mere piece of fictional manipulation. Though superficially contrived, the Mertouns are tolerably credible; though the alter-hero, Cleveland, appearing first as the vicious and bloodstained pirate, turns out in the end to be no more than a reluctant villain and dies fighting for his king in a 'gallant and honourable enterprise'. His crew, with the voluble ex-actor as their spokesman, remain at the level of Gilbert and Sullivan buccaneers, so uncertain is Scott's havering between comedy and villainy. Indeed, passages of pure Gilbert and Sullivan are not hard to find:

'You must settle it somehow, gentlemen', said Captain Cleveland, 'it is time we were under weigh. Mr Triptolemus Yellowley, are we to be honoured with your company?'

'I am sure, Captain Cleveland', stammered the factor, 'I would have no objection to go anywhere with you, only—.'

'He has no objection', said the provost, catching at the first limb of the sentence, without awaiting the conclusion.

'He has no objection', cried the treasurer.

'He has no objection', sung out the whole four bailies together, and the fifteen councillors, all catching up the same phrase of assent, repeated it in chorus.   (Ch. XXXV)

Such operatic facetiousness is representative of a number of jarring incidents where one level of fiction does not key easily to another, and it almost always occurs when the control of a sustaining, convincing environment, a felt history, is missing. In spite, for example, of ample circumstantial reference to the Restoration stage, Jack Bunce, the actor whom Cleveland seduced from the theatre to the Spanish Main, is as unacceptable a figure as his former acquaintance on the boards, Claud Halcro, now minstrel in the Troil household. The conversation of the one is larded with dramatic references, of the other with reminiscences of 'glorious John' Dryden; but in both, the circumstance of time remains unquickened by the inspiration of history.

Even the unfortunate Norna of the Fitful Head (formerly Ulla Troil, driven close to insanity by Mertoun's seducing her, and the erroneous belief that she is a parricide) has little of the moving realism that raises Meg Merrilies and Madge Wildfire above the empty rant of melodrama. On several occasions Scott makes it clear that she is not to be understood as having genuine commerce with the supernatural; that she is no more than a poor, half-mad woman, with the cunning of her kind and a knack of forecasting the weather. Yet his emphasis on her wild attire, waving arms and staring eyes destroys the balance. 'Lay aside this useless affectation of mystery', Basil Mertoun tells her. 'With the vulgar and ignorant it has its effect, but upon me it is thrown away' (Ch. XXV). He speaks the reader's sentiments. In fact, Norna has all the elements of locality which should make her a credible figure, but in portraying her Scott never reaches the height of his own conception. A mixture of Shakespearean witch and Scandinavian Norn from one point of view, from another she is no more than a superstitious villager distracted by grief and guilt, her occult powers existing more in the minds of her credulous neighbours than in any charms she possesses. These images blur together like superimposed rubbings and her role in the novel remains uncertain and erratic. Her whole mentality is one of unrealised potential, but this country of the mind was one landscape Scott's optimistic eyes turned away from and he sets barely a foot in it, though his awareness of Norna's condition appears explicitly at the end of the tale when she has resumed the name of Ulla Troil, has recovered some of her earlier self, and is beginning to lead a normal life in the community:

Formerly, from the dreadful dictates of spiritual despair arising out of the circumstances of her father's death, she seemed to have considered herself as an outcast from Divine grace; beside that, enveloped in the vain occult sciences which she pretended to practise, her study, like that of Chaucer's physician, had been 'but little in the Bible'. Now the sacred volume was seldom laid aside; and to the poor ignorant people who came as formerly to invoke her power over the elements she only replied—'The winds are in the hollow of His hand.' (Ch. XLII)

Here, as so often happens in Scott, one finds in a relatively minor character formidable potential for literary, usually tragic development. Alongside Norna's spiritual desolation one might place, for example, the cowardice of Conachar in *The Fair Maid of Perth*, the despairing scholarly wit and alcoholic violence of Nanty Ewart in *Redgauntlet*, or the melancholy isolation of Lord Glenallan in *The Antiquary*, doing a lifetime penance for what he mistakenly believes has been his incestuous marriage. The weakness or error which drives Norna to the verge of sanity, Conachar to suicide, Nanty Ewart to drink and murder, Glenallan to an obsessional penance, has about it in each case (and there are more) a touch of Greek tragedy. But for the detailed examination of such conditions as major preoccupations of the novelist, the time was not yet. The agonies of the sinful spirit so cogently perceived in this one paragraph lay beyond a border Scott dared not cross, though his friend, James Hogg did;[13] and possibly not before Emily Brontë did any other novelist set foot in that dark country of strange gods and fallen idols. Scott is well aware of it both from personal experience and from travellers' tales but it finds no place in his fiction.

This side of *The Pirate*, conventional in its gothic supernaturalism and lifeless romance, is unsatisfactory. Edgar Johnson's conclusion that the novel 'hardly falters in skill' seems simply perverse, yet in his next breath he reveals the importance of the work. 'Nowhere', he writes, 'has Scott shown more clearly his profound understanding of the organic role of tradition in a culture.'[14] *The Pirate* is flawed right across but it would be foolish for this reason to refuse to listen when Scott reflects on social history, human relationships, moral man in a changing landscape. It is here that the vitalising depth of Scott's theme lies. Alongside the romance, the characters of Magnus Troil and Triptolemus Yellowley are seen to function, not merely to exist or move, within the terms of the landscape they occupy. John Buchan describes Troil as 'not only a vividly realised human being, but the lawful product of his environment'.[15] He is quite differently imagined from, say, Mordaunt, Bunce or Cleveland, and the more serious and substantial issues of the novel are to be found in his relationship with Yellowley.

Magnus Troil, Shetland Udaller, Norse by nature and tradition, has a worse threat to face than the impositions of a Scottish government on an old Norwegian culture. The persistent purchase of land by the Scots, through fair means or foul, threatened to reduce the status of the islanders from that of independent, if small, landowners, to that of mere tenants. The Udaller's pride, though it often appears as an unthinking, parochial prejudice against all change, has also for its motivation the threatened loss of independence. Troil's response is to assert both his rights and his identity by an extravagant observance of all the traditional richness of his Scandinavian forebears. The simple device of a party allows Scott to provide an opportunity for the provision at Burgh Westra, Troil's house, of lavish hospitality, heavy eating and drinking, family feud, and folk-customs such as the guising, the elaborate sword-dance, and the less happily executed imitation of saga minstrelsy.

'The ancient days and the genuine manners of these islands are no more', says Troil at the beginning of the novel, taking up a stance we have already seen reflected in Scott's own feelings towards Scotland. With typical fairness, Scott here makes his own countrymen the alien intruders upon Scandinavian tradition, conducting his management of the conflict in conditions where his own paradoxical anglophobia is temporarily neutralised. (The figures in the romantic plot, who offer so little, are all strongly anglicised.) What Scott chooses to present of the ancient days and the genuine manners is a mixture of heroic generosity and hospitality, tribal welfare, a jealous family pride, and an intensely primitive, superstitious outlook. Troil, the exponent of all this, sees in Yellowley only the parsimonious, narrow pedantry of an unsympathetic and interfering foreigner, the 'new Scotch tacksman, who is to teach all us Zetland savages new ways' (Ch. IV). The factor, on the other hand, prim, sober and unimaginative, has gone to Shetland 'determined to honour the name he bore by his exertions, in precept and example, to civilise the Zetlanders, and improve their very confined knowledge in the primary arts of human life' (Ch. IV).

This is the theme that holds together, and in some tension, the disparate elements of a loosely conceived romance. The factor appears as the apostle of environmental change, the gospel of which he reads narrowly. Scott so balances the discussion that we recognise both the attractiveness

and the backwardness of Troil's life as well as the desirability of Yellowley's plans, reluctant though we may feel to follow the lead of such a
man. In the course of the novel, both learn their lessons, though Scott
produces their mutual illumination somewhat abruptly, and not clearly
as the result of a growing enlightenment. Troil in the end recognises that
inevitable changes must be accommodated, directed and used, not
irrationally rejected, if his people are to survive; while Yellowley discovers that one cannot impose upon an ancient culture even small
improvements in agricultural technology without damaging some facets
of community life which need to be appreciated in depth, so that change
is a guided and controlled process, not an alien imposition. The reconciliation is symbolised by generous hospitality offered, accepted and
enjoyed; in the end, Yellowley is 'never so happy as when he could escape
from the spare commons of his sister Barbara to the genial table of the
Udaller' (Ch. XLII). Yellowley is not yet the prodigal host but he has
moved some warm distance from the character which his house earlier
merited of 'a threshold which, on all ordinary occasions, abhorred the
passage of a guest' (Ch. XI). In their disputes Troil and Yellowley simply
demonstrate the opposition of sentiment and logic. There is no gainsaying
the practicality of Yellowley's proposals, or the emptiness of Troil's
defence, but both approach the issue of improved agriculture and fishing
with narrow, almost closed minds.

'What on earth', says Yellowley, 'can you or any other man say in
defence of that thing you call a plough, in this blinded country?
Why, even the savage Highlandmen, in Caithness and Sutherland, can
make more work, and better, with their gascromh, or whatever they
call it.'
    'But what ails you at it, sir?' said the Udaller: 'let me hear your
objections to it. It tills our land, and what would ye more?'
    'It hath but one handle, or stilt', replied Triptolemus.
    'And who the devil', said the poet, aiming at something smart,
'would wish to need a pair of stilts if he can manage to walk with a
single one?'
    'Or tell me', said Magnus Troil, 'how it were possible for Neil of
Lupness, that lost one arm from his fall from the crag of Nekbreckan,
to manage a plough with two handles?'
    'The harness is of raw seal-skin', said Triptolemus.
    'It will save dressed leather', answered Magnus Troil.
    'It is drawn by four wretched bullocks', said the agriculturist, 'that
are yoked breast-fashion; and two women must follow this unhappy
instrument, and complete the furrows with a couple of shovels.'

'Drink about', Master Yellowley,' said the Udaller; 'and as you say in Scotland, "never fash your thumb".' (Ch. XIV)

The passage is one of a number in which Scott shows the old ways of the island to be primitive and inefficient, the obsolete relics of an outdated culture. A little earlier, however, he has symbolised the threat to old freedoms in a very different way. Young Mordaunt is accompanied to Troil's house at Burgh Westra (where the dispute over the plough design occurs) by Yellowley and his sister Barbara. In order to go on horseback, they must catch their ponies, which graze freely on the moorland

> where shelties, geese, swine, goats, sheep, and little Zetland cows are turned out promiscuously, and often in numbers which can obtain but precarious subsistence from the niggard vegetation. There is, indeed, a right of individual property in all these animals, which are branded or tattooed by each owner with his own peculiar mark; but when any passenger has occasional use for a pony, he never scruples to lay hold of the first which he can catch, puts on a halter, and, having rode him as far as he finds convenient, turns the animal loose to find his way back again as he best can—a matter in which the ponies are sufficiently sagacious.   (Ch. XI)

This is one of the many practices which Yellowley proposes to abolish, though he is temporarily prepared to make use of the custom. On the journey to Troil's, Yellowley talks endlessly of improvements he intends to make, but his enthusiasm as a planner has not embraced the practical art of riding a sheltie and he is ignominiously pitched into a stream by his mount, an indignity which only intensifies his passion for improvement:

> 'I will have cussers from Lanarkshire, brood mares from Ayrshire: I will not have one of these cursed abortions left on the islands, to break honest folks' necks. I say, Baby, I will rid the land of them.'
> 'Ye had better wring your ain cloak, Triptolemus', answered Baby.
> (Ch. XI)

And so the generosity and liberal trust of island life is vindicated against a blind environmental, well-intentioned officialdom.

Eventually the two sides are clumsily reconciled, not only in the friendship of Troil and Yellowley, but in Troil so far swallowing his Nordic pride as to allow Brenda and Mordaunt to marry, comforting himself with the thought that it was as well 'his daughter married the son of an English pirate as of a Scottish thief'.

Much of Scott's Tour, his reading, and his conversations with his friend

William Erskine, Sheriff of Orkney and Shetland, provide firm documentary substance for *The Pirate*, but this remains on the whole an assemblage of information whose significance is rather dimmed than enhanced by its fictional form. It is as if the strength of Scott's inspiration diminished in proportion to the distance from the Borders of the locality with which he deals.

CHAPTER IX
Redgauntlet (1824)

After *The Pirate*, Scott once more turned his mind southward beyond Scotland and drove himself relentlessly, not without detriment both to his health and to the quality of his fiction, to write *The Fortunes of Nigel*, set in London about 1616, *Peveril of the Peak*, set mainly in Derbyshire and the Isle of Man in the late seventeenth century, and *Quentin Durward*, a romance of fifteenth-century France.[1] In none of these is the environmental matrix particularly influential on character, action or philosophy; places remain locations rather than media. They were followed, however, in December 1823, by a work in which Scott returned to Scotland, though not entirely to Scottish themes and people.

St Ronan's Well, which Scott places 'on the southern side of the Forth, and not above thirty miles distant from the English frontier' (Ch. I), is probably drawn mainly from his own locality, especially from Inner-leithen and Peebles, with some recollection of Gilsland in east Cumberland, where he had met Charlotte Carpenter whom he married in December 1797. This novel is the only one of Scott's to be set in his own time; a reference to the death of the poet John Leyden places the action after 1811.

The promise of its opening chapter, alas, remains unfulfilled. Here hopes are raised by a vivid and energetic description of social and environmental change in and around St Ronan's, the old village (the Aultoun) having fallen into decay and now being thrust even further into obscurity by the popularity of the new 'spaw' which has developed a mile and a half away. Ironically, the decadence of the old village is represented by the vigorous and outspoken landlady of the Cleikum Inn, Meg Dodds, who

> ruled all matters with a high hand, not only over her men-servants and maid-servants, but over the stranger within her gates, who, if he ventured to oppose Meg's sovereign will and pleasure, or desire to have either fare or accommodation different from that which she chose to provide for him, was instantly ejected with that answer which Erasmus tells us silenced all complaints in the German inns of his time,

Quaere aliud hospitium, or, as Meg expressed it, 'Troop aff wi' ye to another public.' As this amounted to a banishment in extent equal to sixteen miles from Meg's residence, the unhappy party on whom it was passed had no other refuge save by deprecating the wrath of his landlady, and resigning himself to her will.   (Ch. I)

Meg's hospitable despotism allows her to operate in traditional fashion at the heart of village life; by contrast, the 'Wellers', inhabitants of the new village and frequenters of The Fox Hotel, govern themselves by a committee of management whose task is rendered even more burdensome by the fact that

their subjects were divided into two jarring and contending factions who every day ate, drank, danced, and made merry together, hating each other all the while with all the animosity of political party, endeavouring by every art to secure the adherence of each guest who arrived, and ridiculing the absurdities and follies of each other, with all the wit and bitterness of which they were masters.   (Ch. III)

The characters of the spa are indeed guests, not inhabitants; in this place they have neither home nor occupation.

The plot of the novel is needlessly confusing, multi-directional, and unprofitably complicated; no satisfactory balance is achieved between an indigenous nostalgia for the bypassed Aultoun, sharp satire on the Wellers, and the melodramatic adventures of Clara Mowbray, her brother, and young Tyrrel, the dashing hero who, on the death of Clara whom he has loved, renounces the world and, with tired predictability, enters into a Moravian mission.

The book's reception was mixed, though once again crowds descended on the supposed locality of its incidents. Scott indeed acknowledged the strain of its composition and in March 1824, discussing *Redgauntlet* in a letter to Ballantyne, remarked, 'I never liked *St Ronan's*—this I think better of'.[2] Three years after its publication he wrote of it in his *Journal*: 'The fashionable portraits are not the true thing.'[3] John Buchan argued that Scott here was unaware of the extent of his achievement: 'The romancer has become a realist, and the fribbles and bucks of the Well are drawn with a cruel fidelity. The key is kept low, and no glamour is allowed to veil the ugliness.'[4] To a degree this is so, but these qualities do not dominate; realism in Scott tends to take its verity from a variable but balanced blend of history, culture and environment, none of which have much of a showing in *St Ronan's Well*.

By their nature as visitors, the Wellers are dispossessed of locality, each living in a self-centred world of his own invention, a state which

L

makes real communication both fearful and improbable beyond the level of diurnal trivialities. Locality, in their case, diminishes until it disappears within their own heads. The New Town of St Ronan's is consequently a non-place with neither history nor future, its ephemeral occupants detached in speech, manner and uselessness from the organic community of the Aultoun; they have nowhere either to be or to go. Not that the Aultoun triumphs; it remains a shadowy construct, held together by a few crumbling customs and the brilliant dominion of Meg Dods. When the New Town is demolished on Mowbray's orders, old St Ronan's merely continues to exist, almost deprived of life. Such a pessimistic conclusion arises not from observation, or from philosophy, or from a logical development of forces in the plot, but from exhaustion; as a result, *St Ronan's Well* remains a novel not of action and reflection, but of manipulation; a novel that might have been.

Happily, the same cannot be said of *Redgauntlet*. Begun as soon as *St Ronan's* was finished, it was in the hands of the printer by June 2, Scott's only novel to be published in 1824, though he began work immediately on the first of the *Tales of the Crusaders, The Betrothed*.

Redgauntlet signals a remarkable recovery from the vagaries of its blemished predecessor and though its reception was less than effusive it can be seen now as an unqualified success, a great novel. Scott is once more in a literary and historical context where he can move with ease and familiarity: the western borders of Scotland in the late eighteenth century. His foot never falters.

In some respects the theme, though superficially familiar, was more unusual than that of *St Ronan's*, since one of its major characters has dedicated himself entirely to the now discredited cause of Prince Charles Edward, twenty years after Culloden. With her usual perceptiveness, Lady Louisa Stuart wrote of it to Scott:

> It has taken my fancy very particularly, though (not to flatter you) I could almost wonder why: for there is no story in it, no love, no hero —unless Redgauntlet himself, who would be such as the Devil in Milton; yet in spite of all these wants, the interest is so strong one cannot lay it down, and I prophesy for it a great deal of mauling and abuse, and a second edition before the maulers know where they are.[5]

At the heart of the novel lie both the reality of Jacobitism and its attendant myths. The cause of the Stuart succession after the exile of James II in 1688 developed into an increasingly obsolescent form of nationalism which held the minds and lives of a diminishing number of Scotsmen, largely Highlanders, long after it had ceased to be a credible political force. The events take place in the Borders between Edinburgh,

Dumfriesshire and Cumberland, their main action fixed about the Solway Firth, that broad and often treacherous reach of water which separates England from Scotland in the west. Much of Scott's own younger life informs the tale as if, after more than a quarter of a century of study, writing, law and estate management, he sets out to re-examine as well as recreate certain aspects of his earlier self and of an earlier Scotland. The personal significance to Scott of many of the places and characters in this novel shows his intense involvement with its themes; it is a feature which has not lacked commentators, from the time of Lockhart onwards:[6]

> *Redgauntlet* is, in part, a memory of first love, first friendship, and of filial affection. In the industrious Alan, so scant of pocket money, so piously obedient and energetic, to please his sire, in uncongenial labour, we have Sir Walter in his youth, and in his neat, precise, economical parent, so contemptuous of literary or military or any but legal success, we have the father who feared that the son would prove 'but a gangrel scrapegut'.[7]

For any reader acquainted with the principal occasions of Scott's youth, it is not difficult to see in Alan Fairford a portrait of the artist as a young man, and in Darsie Latimer the young manhood of his friend, William Clerk, though Latimer can also be seen as Fairford/Scott's *alter ego*. Similarly apparent is the resemblance between the mysterious, romantic and superfluous Green Mantle, and Scott's lost, youthful love, Williamina Belsches. The identifications are interesting but in no way add to our understanding of the novel; we may, however, go further and find in the way these characters interlock and interact with Redgauntlet an exploration of Scott's own state of mind at a period when much that he valued in Scottish life was dying, when much that he feared in English culture was taking its place. Nothing could have been chosen to demonstrate this more suitably than what Burns called 'sentimental Jacobitism', that is, the faith of those whose sympathy with the lost Stuart cause after the 1745 rising became a mere emotional peg for their national loyalties now that the old, feudal, heroic but primitive Scotland was being transformed by a new English dynamic in politics, technology, economics and social progress. Scott, as we have seen, had already considered the problem in fiction, in *Waverley*, for example, and most particularly in *The Bride of Lammermoor*, but now in *Redgauntlet* he concentrates wholly on Jacobitism at its least attractive, as it appeared in the mid 1760s. At this period (very recent for Scott, within a decade before he was born) there is no longer a place for the dispersed and sentimental remnant of an almost forgotten cause. Redgauntlet must lose; new ways of life must be seen to supersede the old; but he must lose appropriately, sorrowing with dignity and resignation not for the loss, but for what is lost. At the end, Redgauntlet leaves for France, and bids farewell to his nephew, Darsie:

> 'Nephew, come hither. In presence of General Campbell, I tell you that, though to breed you up in my own political opinions has been for many years my anxious wish, I am now glad that it could not be accomplished. You pass under the service of the reigning monarch without the necessity of changing your allegiance—a change, however,' he added, looking around him, 'which sits more easily on honourable men than I could have anticipated; but some wear the badge of their loyalty on the sleeve, and others in the heart.'
>
> (Ch. XXIII)

In the terms of the novel as a whole, Redgauntlet's attiude is understandable; his total commitment to the house of Stuart, moreover ('I had set my whole desires on one point—God knows, with no selfish purpose—') is enhanced and made more intelligible when one understands what such loyalty meant in eighteenth-century Scotland, and especially what it came to mean after the bitterness of Culloden.

The earlier part of Charles Edward's career I sketched in Chapter III, on *Waverley*; after 1746 the scene changes, and with it the characters, action and ethos. Highland dress and arms were proscribed and their resumption half a century later was as much a piece of nostalgic exhibitionism as a gesture of ethnic pride, and in fact owed a great deal to Scott's gifts as impresario, in arranging the visit to Edinburgh in 1822 of a kilted George IV. Historically, Jacobitism is largely a Highland story and though Scott occupies himself with this aspect of it in *Waverley* he virtually ignores it in the west Lowland context of *Redgauntlet*. By this time, 1767, Charles has become the romantic fugitive, his charisma even taking strength from defeat and isolation. But the paths of legend and of history are fast diverging; Charles, as the years go by, becomes a sordid, intriguing royal exile, growing more parsimonious, alcoholic, selfish and arrogant, and behaving violently to those close to him. It is in relation to this ultimate caroline shabbiness that the irony lies of Redgauntlet's selfless and unscrupulous devotion; from his Prince, as from his Scotland, the glory has departed.

By far the most effective environmental features in *Redgauntlet* occur in the opening epistolary section where Darsie Latimer recounts at some length the details of his tour in Dumfriesshire. Here is a young man of twenty-one, rich, idle and alone, kicking his heels in the expectation of plenty, an inheritance not to be realised before he is twenty-five, until when he is mysteriously forbidden to enter England. What, in the mid-1760s, should such a person do but make a Tour? Scott provides similar opportunities for environmental exploration, it will be remembered, in other works, notably in *Waverley*, *Guy Mannering*, and in *Rob Roy*.

On the announcement of his good fortune, Latimer has renounced the study of law in Edinburgh, and has temporarily forsaken the society of his only friend, Alan Fairford, in whose house he has lived for the past four years. It might be the young Guy Mannering come again:

> It was the beginning of the month of November 17—, when a young English gentleman, who had just left the university of Oxford, made use of the liberty afforded him, to visit some parts of the north of England; and curiosity extended his tour into the adjacent frontier of the sister country. He had visited, on the day that opens our history, some monastic ruins in the county of Dumfries, and spent much of the day making drawings of them from different points . . .
>
> (*Guy Mannering*, Ch. I)

A similar freedom from study blesses Latimer and rouses the amicable envy of his friend Fairford, whose melancholy farewell he refers to in almost the first words of his first letter from Dumfries: ' "It seemed to say, 'Happy dog! you can ramble at pleasure over hill and dale, pursue every object of curiosity that presents itself, and relinquish the chase when it loses interest" '.' Fortunately, the chase never loses interest; Darsie becomes involved, through a chance meeting on Solway Sands, with his uncle, Sir Hugh Redgauntlet, in preparations for a (wholly fictitious) *coup* to restore the decayed Charles Edward twenty years after his defeat at Culloden and his flight to France in 1746. Scott concentrates on Latimer's isolation. He may be rich and idle; he is also irresolute, lacking direction and, most of all, ignorant of his own identity, knowing neither father nor mother, nor the source of his inheritance. He sees himself as a solitary individual 'in a country where all the world have a circle of consanguinity extending to sixth cousins at least' (Letter I). He is, moreover, a double man of confused loyalties: born of a Scottish father and an English mother, he is now an orphan; English by early upbringing, yet educated in the Scottish capital as an English boy. Now, forbidden to cross the border his nature, like the Solway itself, flows uncertainly and treacherously between the two nations. And the Solway, which significantly is fed by both Scottish and English waters (there is no River Solway), ebbs and flows through the novel between the bleak shores of Scotland and the glinting, inviting English hills, like a gilded mirror of Darsie's fortunes. He is the son of Sir Henry Darsie Redgauntlet, born in 1746, the year in which his father was executed at Carlisle for supporting Charles Edward's 1745 insurrection. Afraid that her brother-in-law, Hugh Redgauntlet (whose Jacobite enthusiasm she blames for her husband's death) will exercise powers of legal guardianship over the child, Darsie's mother removes him from Scotland, and imposes on his early years an English stamp of Hanoverian loyalties.

Scott's initial presentation of Darsie's isolation and lack of identity, in spite of the arch and elaborate idiom in which the hero writes, is poignant and real. The boy knows he is rich in money but his experience of life is bitter, 'brought from the solitude of my mother's dwelling into the tumult of the Gytes' class at the High School; when I was mocked for my English accent, salted with snow as a Southern pig, rolled in the gutter for a Saxon pock-pudding' (Letter I). Writing of his own unhappy early schooldays at the Edinburgh High School between 1787 and 1793, Lord Cockburn recalls a similar experience: 'Among the boys, coarseness of language and manners was the only fashion. An English boy was so rare, that his accent was openly laughed at.'[8] Now that Darsie is come to his majority, Solway, as well as being an image of himself, is both an isolating and a seducing power, a barrier that, like most prohibitions, forbids and tempts at the same time. At the beginning of his tour, he spends a night at Shepherd's Bush, near Dumfries on the northern shore of the Firth and the following day, after he has watched horsemen spearing salmon stranded in the pools by the receding tide,

> I lingered on the sands, with my looks turned to the shores of England, still gilded by the sun's last rays, and, as it seemed, scarce distant a mile from me. The anxious thoughts which haunt me began to muster in my bosom, and my feet slowly and insensibly approached the river which divided me from the forbidden precincts, though without any formed intention.   (Letter IV)

At this point he is roused by Redgauntlet and the struggle begins between the idle, disorientated dreamer and the furious Jacobite whose direction is all too clear, and all too obviously hopeless. During the course of the novel with the slow, inevitable rhythm of tidal movement, Darsie's fortunes flow as those of his uncle ebb. The next day, having spent the night uneasily in Redgauntlet's house in the hamlet of Brokenburn, he resumes his journey back to the inn at Shepherd's Bush, and looks south across the Firth at dawn where the rising sun 'already began to peer above the eastern horizon, and gild the distant mountains of Cumberland and Liddesdale'. He looks across the estuary, dreaming of golden prospects, from the wilderness of the northern shore:

> 'Advancing about a hundred yards from the brink of the glen, we gained a still more extensive command of this desolate prospect, which

seemed even more dreary as contrasted with the opposite shores of Cumberland, crossed and intersected by ten thousand lines of trees growing in hedgerows, shaded with groves and woods of considerable extent, animated by hamlets and villas, from which thin clouds of smoke already gave sign of human life and human industry'.

(Letter VI)

The primary symbolism in these passages is clear in the contrast between the almost pathless waste of the Scottish side, where Latimer is astray, and all the evidence of growth, purpose and work on the other, where he is to find himself. More deeply, however, lies a poignant parallel with a prosperous and powerful Hanoverian England, and a defeated, wasted Scotland. The memory of Culloden and Cumberland's atrocities died hard. Again, the division is more than nationalistic; as we have seen for Scott, Jacobitism represented not so much a political allegiance as a way of life, a complex historical entity, the life of old Scotland which died in 1746 stripped ignominiously of its regalia when dirk, kilt and bagpipes were proscribed. With these overtones, Redgauntlet's fanaticism, though it has all the trappings of lively melodrama, is fundamentally tragic.

The episode of Darsie's departure from Brokenburn ends dramatically with a further contrast: 'My conductor had extended his arm, and was pointing the road . . .' when another way forward obliquely presents itself with the arrival of the Quaker Joshua Geddes from Mount Sharon. In Redgauntlet and Geddes we find polarised the conflicting forces in Latimer's mind, a tension which Scott achieves by making the Solway as a source of fish the link between them. The events reflect a time when the old, wild inefficient spearing methods are overtaken by more modern tidal nets, of disputed legality but indisputable effectiveness. Redgauntlet's fish-spearing, boisterous, wasteful, spectacular and slow is as demoded as his support of a decadent prince. Joshua Geddes's nets are unobtrusive and commercially profitable; they represent the new men whose appetite for fish is limited only by methods of communication and distribution, and who will replace the solitary, indigenous subsistence fisher who catches for his own needs only, or for those of the immediate and organic community. We have already met the latter in the Mucklebackits of *The Antiquary*.

The violent attack on the Tide-Net Fishing Company's station made by Redgauntlet and his men is an exciting episode, if an elaborate way of abducting Darsie; in its way it reflects the excessive reaction of a dying culture to the smooth new practices that are to administer the final blow. ('Kill the young spy!' one of the fishermen shouts as Darsie is taken, offering another isolating legacy of his English upbringing, the adult version of his kindergarten persecutions.) The raiders take him, barely conscious, over the Solway, and it is in England that he learns who he is in the full terms of time, place, family and history. The whole process is like a rebirth:

> A deep sound, which, in the confusion of my senses, I identified with the cries of the rioters, was the first thing of which I was sensible; next, I became conscious that I was carried forward in some conveyance, with an unequal motion, which gave me much pain. My position was horizontal, and when I attempted to stretch my hands in order to find some mode of securing myself against this species of suffering, I found I was bound as before . . .

His delivery is accomplished to the roar of the incoming tide and the bogging-down of the wheels in the quicksand. In the face of imminent death he struggles to look out of the cart:

> There lay my native land—my own England—the land where I was born, and to which my wishes since my earliest age had turned with all the prejudices of national feeling—there it lay, within a furlong of the place where I yet was; that furlong, which an infant would have raced over in a minute, was yet a barrier effectual to divide me for ever from England and from life.

His deliverer is Redgauntlet:

> My eyes began to swim—my head grew giddy and mad with fear— I chattered and howled to the howling and roaring sea. One or two great waves already reached the cart, when the conductor of the party whom I have mentioned so often was, as if by magic, at my side. He sprang from his horse into the vehicle, cut the ligatures which restrained me, and bade me get up and mount in the fiend's name.
> Seeing I was incapable of obeying, he seized me as if I had been a child . . .   (Ch. IV)

And so Darsie Latimer comes anew into the world, in England, to learn that he is after all a Scot, yet, again, loyal to George.

Six years earlier, Scott had used a similar image, much more explicitly, in The Heart of Midlothian, when a coach overturns:

> The 'exertions of the guard and coachman', both of whom were gratefully commemorated in the newspapers, having succeeded in disentangling the horses by cutting the harness, were now proceeding to extricate the insides by a sort of summary and Caesarian process of delivery, forcing the hinges from the doors which they could not open

otherwise. In this manner were two disconsolate damsels set at liberty from the womb of the leathern conveniency.   (Ch. I)

Solway is also smugglers' territory, a little to the east of the *Guy Mannering* locality, and much of the transport and communication in *Redgauntlet* are carried on by means both of smugglers' boats and smugglers' local knowledge. Their role seems to emphasise the ambiguity as well as the hopelessness of the Jacobite cause; both this smuggling and this loyalism take life from a philosophy in which robbery and national pride are curiously blended. The movements of Charles Edward, especially in being exiled, returning, making surreptitious landings in remote inlets, are not very unlike those of the alcoholic Nanty Ewart, declined gentleman and smuggler extraordinary. The ambiguity is neatly pointed at the end of the tale when Ewart overhears Redgauntlet refer to him contemptuously as 'the smuggling fellow', and soliloquises:

'Smuggling fellow—ay, smuggler—and, start your cargo into the sea—and be ready to start for the Hebrides, or Sweden—or the devil, I suppose. Well, and what if I said in answer—Rebel, Jacobite—traitor —I'll make you and your d—d confederates walk the plank—I have seen better men do it . . .'   (Ch. XXIII)

The matter is clinched a few moments later when Nanty the smuggler and Nixon, the hypocritical Jacobite supporter kill each other.

But to return to the meeting of Latimer and Geddes: Redgauntlet, seeing Darsie's helplessness and ignorance of the country, describes him as 'a moping boy in a dark night', and the restlessness of occupation and wandering in these opening letters drives home the rootlessness and anonymity of his being, his underlying fear of freedom, his unheroic and unromantic desire for hearth, home and guidance:

Once more the idea of thy father's fireside came across me; and I could have been well contented to have swopped the romance of my situation, together with the glorious independence of control which I possessed at the moment, for the comforts of the chimney corner.
                                                                        (Letter IV)

'My situation' forms a sad contrast with 'thy father's fireside', and though Darsie's homesickness in these circumstances is understandable as well as conventional, the emotion is in Scott rather more than mere nostalgia. In the Waverley Novels, the domestic hearth is an environment nearly always heavy with overtones of domestic virtue and the whole moral ambience of idealised home and family; it is one of the centres of meaning in *The Heart of Midlothian*, for example, as we have already seen.

For a brief time, Latimer finds rest, shelter and quietude at Mount Sharon, the home of Joshua Geddes, much as Jeanie Deans does in Willingham Rectory, but even this tranquillity is deceptive. Scott employs here one of his favourite gauges of individual quality—the hospitality test.

It is basic to Scott's code of good breeding that the enduring demands of hospitable entertainment override the ephemeral emotions of personal relationships. The requirement that you offer unstinted hospitality to your guests, even if they are your enemies, even if you are to do battle with them, is a Nordic quality, strongly emphasised in the Norse sagas (another local literature in which environment, history and character, place and manners are closely interrelated), and Scott observed it throughout his life. It makes an early appearance in the poems: Marmion's entertainment at Tantallon, for example, or, in *The Lady of the Lake*, the meeting of Roderick Dhu and Fitzjames, of rebel and king, where, though he knows his companion is an enemy, Roderick nevertheless remains the honourable host:

> 'It rests with me to wind my horn,—
> Thou art with numbers overborne;
> It rests with me, here, brand to brand,
> Worn as thou art, to bid thee stand;
> But, not for clan, nor kindred's cause,
> Will I depart from honour's laws;
> To assail a wearied man were shame,
> And stranger is a holy name;
> Guidance and rest, and food and fire,
> In vain he never must require.'
>
> (IV, xxxi)

In *Redgauntlet*, the benevolence of Redgauntlet himself, of Saunders Fairford and of Joshua Geddes are so closely placed as to make comparison inevitable, and even intentional. The Catholic Redgauntlet's entertainment is offered roughly, but it is none the less complete in its masculine austerity, even to the extent of saying a Protestant grace before meat. Scott subtly qualifies Redgauntlet's manner as a host, using the conduct of the meal from beginning to end not only as a pointer to his character but as a way of assessing Latimer's priggish propriety. During supper

little passed between me and my entertainer, unless that he did the usual honours of the table with courtesy, indeed, but without even the affectation of hearty hospitality which those in his (apparent) condition generally affect on such occasions, even when they do not actually feel it. On the contrary, his manner seemed that of a polished landlord towards an unexpected and unwelcome guest, whom, for the sake of his own credit, he receives with civility, but without either goodwill or cheerfulness.   (Letter IV)

At this stage, neither knows the identity of the other. Darsie fills an awkward pause with an apology, observing that ' "I feared my intrusion upon his hospitality had put his family to some inconvenience." ' ' "I hope you see no appearance of it, sir," he replied with cold civility.'

The meal is a common enough piece of fictional machinery but Scott consistently takes the opportunity of naturalistic description to establish the nuances as well as the broad outlines of character. In his reply to Darsie's Letter IV, Alan Fairford writes:

> You have often remarked that my father, though a scrupulous observer of the rites of hospitality, seems to exercise them rather as a duty than as a pleasure; indeed, but for a conscientious wish to feed the hungry and receive the stranger, his doors would open to guests much seldomer than is the case.

Such a forced hospitality, Fairford goes on, has just been offered to one, Herries of Birrenswork (really, Darsie's entertainer, Redgauntlet) who is seeking advice. His whole manner seemed to say, 'It is my pleasure to dine with you, and I care not whether I am welcome or no' (Letter V). What is interesting about this whole episode is the way it counterpoints Darsie's entertainment at Brokenburn, putting Redgauntlet, Jacobite and Catholic, in the formally cool and hospitable hands of Fairford senior, his opponent both in politics and religion.

This game of convivial brinkmanship, where hospitality and hostility are uneasily yet traditionally interwoven, is in strong contrast to the welcome Latimer finds at Mount Sharon (Letter VII) where he goes from Brokenburn after witnessing a prickly encounter between Redgauntlet and Geddes. Having all the characteristics of an earthly paradise, Mount Sharon is to all appearances the very refuge Latimer has longed for from the bleak exposure of his mind and body during the previous twenty-four hours.

> The wilderness and the solitary place shall be glad for them; and the desert shall rejoice, and blossom as the rose. It shall blossom abundantly, and rejoice even with joy and singing; the glory of Lebanon shall be given unto it, the excellency of Carmel and Sharon, they shall see the glory of the Lord, and the excellency of our God.
>
> (Isaiah, 35, i–ii)

But Darsie does not find what he is seeking, even here, and soon longs for the wilderness again.

The whole Mount Sharon episode, delightful in its order, calm and gentleness after the roughness of Redgauntlet's household, is qualified by overtones of hard commercial dealing. 'Young gentleman,' Redgauntlet warns as Darsie leaves with his new host, 'this pious pattern of primitive simplicity will teach thee the right way to Shepherd's Bush; ay, and will himself shear thee like a sheep, if you come to buying and selling with him' (Letter VI). This is something more than a Catholic opposition to another religious persuasion and more than a Scottish laird's hostility to trade. Geddes has inherited from his father a wealth gained from 'various branches of commerce', as well as Mount Sharon. But this modern mansion was built over the site of a Border pele, Sharing Knowe, which his father demolished, ruthlessly discarding the past in favour of material interests. Scott here forces Geddes into an ambiguous position where, for all his disapproval of worldliness, he lives off the profits of successful trade, uninvolved in the business of making money because he is 'satisfied with the portion of worldly substance which he already possessed'. Out of the ruins of the old pele his father had kept the original huge fireplace: 'he reserved the hearth of his ancestors in memory of their hospitality, as also the pious motto they had chanced to assume', but it looks out of place in the new house, and though the motto *Trust in God* remains, 'the worldly and military emblems displayed on the shield and helmet, together with all their blazonry' have been chiselled away. 'Chanced to assume' is a most telling phrase, pointing to a kind of lawless piety common in the Borders during the reiving days when, as the Scottish historian Lesley wrote, the Borderers 'never count their beads with such earnestness as when they set out upon a predatory expedition'. So Geddes's identity is a bastard sort of selected heredity, after all.

In contrast to the sumptuousness of this place, Redgauntlet's austerity seems truly virtuous. At Brokenburn, Darsie had breakfasted on milk and unbuttered bread; Geddes feels that this has not adequately broken his fast and, after a lengthy extempore prayer, treats his guest to a meal of 'tea and chocolate, eggs, ham and pastry, not forgetting the broiled fish'. Scott then gives Darsie his head in a detailed description of the prosperous, modernised farm and the elaborately landscaped grounds, leaving what looks like an apologetic loophole: 'I know that you, Alan, will condemn all this as bad and antiquated; for ever since Dodsley has described Leasowes, and talked of Brown's imitations of nature and Horace Walpole's late Essay on Gardening, you are all for simple nature —condemn walking up and down stairs in the open air, and declare for wood and wilderness' (Letter VII). The description of the willow walk that follows is a pleasant piece of picturesque writing, well suited to Darsie's interlude with Geddes's sister, 'the fair Quaker':

The brook, restrained at the ultimate boundary of the grounds by a natural dam-like or ledge of rocks, seemed, even in its present swoln state, scarcely to glide along; and the pale willow-trees, dropping their long branches into the stream, gathered round them little coronals of foam that floated down from the more rapid stream above. The high rock which formed the opposite bank of the brook, was seen dimly through the branches, and its pale and splintered front, garlanded with long streamers of briers and other creeping plants, seemed a barrier between the quiet path which we trode and the toiling and bustling world beyond. The path itself, following the sweep of the stream, made a very gentle curve; enough, however, served by its inflection completely to hide the end of the walk, until you arrived at it. (Letter VII)

Like the lilies of the field, Geddes toils not, neither does he spin, and, beautifully arrayed, he is as unconscious as the lilies of any moral equivocation. His sister has more scruples but contrives to subdue them: she is not prepared to accept fishing profits at the cost of bloodshed and she is unhappy about the rearing and killing of domestic fowl. She soothes, without convincing, herself, by trying to believe that 'it was according to the law of their being. They must die, but they knew not when death was approaching; and in making them comfortable while they lived, we contributed to their happiness as much as the conditions of their existence permitted to us'. Darsie is not persuaded by this piece of self-deception but the argument reinforces the equivocal nature of life at Mount Sharon.

So far, Latimer's tour has offered him two modes of life, their principles mediated through landscape and the home. One is the dedicated and savage sincerity of Redgauntlet, a man possessed by a lost cause; the other is the bland ease of Geddes, whose superficially plausible principles are uncomfortably belied by his practice; he lacks a demon, and even poor Peter Peebles, who almost makes Saunders Fairford contravene the laws of hospitality, has that (Letter XIII). Both men have possessions: Redgauntlet gives all to his cause, while Geddes gives what is convenient. In association with Darsie, Geddes is in many ways seen to be a good man, but this is the Dickensian goodness of easy benevolence such as we find in Mr Brownlow's concern for Oliver Twist, or the Cheeryble Brothers' care for Nicholas Nickleby. The reader is less scathed by Joshua's humiliations than by Redgauntlet's doomed pride.

Each of these two we first meet in a landscape, and then at home; a third character, who has only landscape to live in, is Wandering Willie. Stifled after a few days by the insipidity of life at Mount Sharon, Darsie seeks interest beyond its secure, well-trimmed bounds, escaping, as he says, from art to nature. He emerges into what had formerly seemed to him a dreary wilderness, and 'the air I breathed felt purer and more bracing. The clouds, riding high upon a summer breeze, drove, in gay succession, over my head, now obscuring the sun, now letting its rays stream in transient flashes upon the broad mirror of the distant Firth of Solway' (Letter X). Here, on the open heath, he meets 'Willie Steenson —Wandering Willie—the best fiddler that ever kittled thairm with horsehair'.

Latimer asks the classical question, Is he of this country? and is answered by a man whose roots are unmistakable and whose blindness is hardly loss of sight. 'This country!' replied the blind man. 'I am of every country in broad Scotland, and a wee bit of England to the boot. But yet I am, in some sense, of this country, for I was born within hearing of the roar of Solway.' For the first time since leaving Edinburgh Darsie finds someone who, paradoxically homeless, nevertheless *belongs*; he is part of his country, not merely a peripatetic attachment, and in this embodies some of the qualities of the Last Minstrel, which I discussed earlier, and of Edie Ochiltree. No wonder, then, that Darsie temporarily identifies with him, disguising himself as a tramping fiddler and playing at the Brokenburn dance. It is Willie who feels Darsie's emptiness, in spite of appearances: 'Ye maun learn to put the heart into it, man—to put the heart into it'; and who, sightless and sage, proves, like Hobbie Noble in the Ballad, 'a guide worth any twa' to the lost Latimer. 'How the deuce', says Darsie, 'am I to guide the blind man where he is going? I know little or nothing of the country.'

'And ye ken mickle less of my hinny, sir', replied Maggie, 'that ye think he needs ony guiding; he's the best guide himsel' that ye'll find between Criffel and Carlisle. Horse-road and footpath, parish-road and kirk-road, high-road and cross-road, he kens ilka foot of ground in Nithsdale.' (Letter X)

This comprehensive sense of locality can arise only from a condition of being and belonging in an intimate context of specific place, with all this implies of family, tradition and community with a total and commonly understood history. Eventually, when Latimer is held prisoner by Redgauntlet, he hears Willie singing below, and they communicate sufficiently to raise the prisoner's spirits by singing and playing snatches of old Ballads as a crude kind of code. It is, of course, finely appropriate that Willie should be a 'blind crowder', in Sidney's phrase, and it is both gracious and fitting that when all the adventuring is done, both share the same place, where Wandering Willie ends his days 'unco beinly in Sir Arthur Redgauntlet's ha' neuk'.

Darsie has found his chimney corner at last; the hospitable place, with its teller of tales.

What conclusions may we draw from such an ending?

Unlike the uneasy equivocation I argued Scott leaves us to ponder at the end of *Waverley*, there is no paltering here. Jacobitism is seen to be no longer a force in anyone's life and there is no need for compromise. As the Prince and Redgauntlet leave for France, General Campbell speaks: 'It is now all over', he said, 'and Jacobite will be henceforward no longer a party name.' Its demise is all the more crushing in the light of George III's permission, conveyed by Campbell, for all rebels, including Charles Edward himself (on whose head there is a high price), to depart peacefully to their homes without fear of arrest or punishment. The quiet gesture, coolly administered, is a sharp sign of the slightness of their threat in a larger world.

This end is prepared for and qualified by some neat counterpointing a litle earlier. The Jacobites have been betrayed to the English authorities by Cristal Nixon, Redgauntlet's servant. In the hopes of enlisting the help of Nanty Ewart and the use of his brig to capture the Prince, Nixon shows his hand, and tempts Ewart with the reward for Charles's capture. His offer is fatally refused. Nixon, Hanoverian spy and treacherous Jacobite is in the end killed by Ewart, an outlawed but, on his own terms, loyal Hanoverian. 'I like King George', he admits, 'but I can't afford to pay duties.' Scott does not allow this romantic integrity to save him, however; Nixon shoots him to stop his mouth, but he lives just long enough to slay the spy with a sword blow. Nanty is an attractive rogue on the pattern of the educated and gentlemanly derelict; Nixon a shifty double-dealer. The fact that neither is allowed to survive and indeed the fact that each is the agent of the other's death is representative of the novel's uncompromising conclusion.

This is to be seen also in the situation of the Prince. He has come at the invitation of his 'subjects', but will have no dealings with conditional support; and their condition is that he will put from him his mistress (in life, Clementina Walkinshaw, whose sister was a person of some influence at the English court). Virtue, in this work, must be seen to triumph, and it is not alone the Nixons and the Ewarts who are vulnerable. Moreover, in this instance, the arrogant Stuart is not defeated by his opponents but rejected by his supporters. His answer is indeed, in this exigent, feebly Falstaffian: that he has already considered dismissing the lady but will never do so upon compulsion. The Jacobite gentlemen are confused, embarrassed and disappointed; Darsie alone sees in this 'a fair period to a most perilous enterprise'.

When Charles Edward takes his leave, his parting words sustain the paradox: 'I bid you farewell, unfriendly friends', he says to his followers. 'I bid you farewell,' (bowing to the General) 'my friendly foe.' As they move towards the brig

> the last heir of the Stuarts leant on Redgauntlet's arm as they walked towards the beach; for the ground was rough, and he no longer possessed the elasticity of limb and spirit which had, twenty years before, carried him over many a Highland hill, as light as one of their native deer. (Ch. XVII)

He was at this time in his middle forties, a prime age for a leader, but the symbolism of his degeneration, though delicately and even nostalgically managed, is inescapable.

Within three years of their departure, Redgauntlet has entered a monastery.

Of the major characters (Fairford and Lilias having been disposed of in marriage) only Darsie remains and, as we have seen, he finds his true place. All his life England has, in one way or another, been a temporary refuge where the threatened Scot may find shelter and by means of which he may eventually establish himself in his patrimony when the time is right. It is thus that Scott represents all that he desired for his two countries.

CHAPTER X

Conclusion

The eight years that remained to Scott after *Redgauntlet* were for him a period of domestic distress, financial misfortune and deteriorating health, though during the whole time he continued to create with apparently undiminished vigour. His massive *Life of Napoleon Buonaparte* was published in 1827, the same year as that in which his *Tales of a Grandfather* appeared, a history of Scotland written for Lockhart's son which he followed in 1831 by a history of France. He supplied Prefaces for a collected edition of the Waverley Novels, meticulously revised his nineteen-volume *Swift's Life and Works* (1814) for a second edition, completed a number of short stories, contributed many occasional essays and reviews to various journals, and published eight novels.[1] It is a noble achievement of prodigious industry, barely credible when one recalls the circumstances of his life at the time: Lady Scott died in 1826 after long suffering asthma and dropsy; Constable, his publisher, failed in the same year and Scott, who was financially deeply committed in the firm, was made bankrupt; local people to whom he had always felt close proved violently hostile to his reactionary political views; and after 1826 he endured pain and debility from rheumatism, and a number of increasingly grave paralytic strokes. The melancholy decline of the Great Unknown is recorded movingly and without self-pity in the *Journal* he began in 1825 and continued to within a few months of his death in 1832. The year before, he wrote with defiant weariness

> *May* 8—I have suffered terribly, that is the truth, rather in body than in mind, and I often wish I could lie down and sleep without waking. But I will fight it out if I can. It would argue too great an attachment of consequence to my literary labours to sink under.... My bodily strength is terribly gone; perhaps my mental too?

Of his huge output during this time, it is his fiction that suffers most; his hand simply could not rest, but his imagination dimmed under the shadow of financial anxiety and domestic sorrow and was almost extinguished by what he felt to be the necessity of writing merely to clear off his debts, placing his faith not in any artistic ideal but in the uncritical

M

pockets of his admirers. Of the novels he wrote from *The Betrothed* to *Castle Dangerous* only *Woodstock* and *The Fair Maid of Perth* remain memorable, and even they have their *longueurs*; the rest, though substantial in size and weight, diminish rather than increase Scott's literary stature.

Woodstock, a Civil War tale of 1651, is something of a *tour de force* of historical characterisation, but *place* has no importance in it beyond the simple function of locating, as distinct from localising, events. In the following year, 1827, Scott published the first volume of *Chronicles of the Canongate*, a collection of short tales presented by the imaginary editor, Chrystal Croftangry. It contains two Scottish stories of distinction, *The Two Drovers* and *The Highland Widow*. In the latter, a tale of the fundamental antagonism of Saxon and Gael, the landscape provides a rich setting for the action, but beyond this has little literary significance in relation to those combined elements of history, locality and occasion which have formed the substance of my theme. 'The framework', Scott wrote in his *Journal*, 'may be a Highland tour, under the guardianship of the sort of postilion whom Mrs Murray Keith described to me—a species of conductor who regulated the motions of his company, made their halts, and was their cicerone.'[2] In fact his narrator takes what she calls the fashionable 'short Highland tour' in the 1780s, but after an introductory chapter descriptive of her journey through the Highlands the locale plays little part in the central narrative of the Highland Widow's story.

In *The Two Drovers*, set at the end of the eighteenth century, we find a similar basic antagonism less crudely fashioned. Robin Oig M'Combich, Highlander, and Harry Wakefield, Yorkshireman, are bound in friendship and mutual respect by their work and their skill as drovers, though divided by an imperfect acquaintance with each other's language and hence, essentially, of each other's way of life.

The two friends meet at Falkirk and drive their herds south together into Cumberland, a journey of some hundred miles which constitutes a kind of professional Tour, where we intermittently see landscape through the drover's rather than the tourist's eye. Their fatal quarrel, in the event arises over the renting of land in Cumberland for the temporary feeding of their cattle, a necessity imposed by the differences in land use in the two countries. As far south as Bewcastle Waste (where, it will be remembered, Dandie Dinmont was attacked)

the cattle under the charge of our drovers derived their subsistence chiefly by picking their food as they went along the drove road or sometimes by the tempting opportunity of a *start and owerloup*, or invasion of the neighbouring pasture, where an occasion presented itself. But now the scene changed before them; they were descending towards a fertile and enclosed country, where no such liberties could be taken with impunity, or without a previous arrangement and bargain with the possessor of the ground. This was more especially the case, as a great northern fair was upon the eve of taking place, where both the Scotch and English drover expected to dispose of part of their cattle, which it was desirable to produce in the market rested and in good order. Fields were therefore difficult to be obtained, and only upon high terms. This necessity occasioned a temporary separation betwixt the two friends, who went to bargain, each as he could, for the separate accommodation of his herd.   (Ch. II)

While Wakefield bargains with the bailiff, Robin Oig comes to an agreement with the squire, and they find they have both rented the same pasture. Wakefield is offended by what he believes to be the Highlander's deceit, refuses Oig's offer to share the land, and finds poorer ground elsewhere. They later meet at the inn; Wakefield remains obdurate and in the end is killed by Oig, who is subsequently executed. He has taken private vengeance in defiance of the law, and is stoically prepared for the inevitable consequence. 'I give a life for the life I took', he said, 'and what can I do more?'

Throughout the tale Scott keeps us reminded of the latent antagonism of the societies these two men represent; it does not prevent friendship but it inhibits true understanding. We have already seen examples of this kind of relationship, especially in *Waverley* and *Rob Roy*, but it is never so closely and sympathetically treated as here, where a simple *contretemps* exposes the sensitive rawness of the bond between the two men. Though specifically functional local elements are slight in the tale, one cannot mistake the seriousness of Scott's presentation of the clash of cultures. The dispute and its sequel arise from honourable anger, honourable retaliation, honourable sorrow on both sides; but both men draw their sense of what is due to a particular occasion from wholly different traditions and beliefs. One cannot escape the conclusion that this friendship, with its underlying tensions, between Wakefield and M'Combich, is symbolic of Scott's deeply pessimistic view of the Anglo-Scottish union, however superficially hopeful he may appear to be.

The second volume of *Chronicles of the Canongate* which appeared in 1828 consists of a single, Scottish, fourteenth-century tale, *The Fair Maid of Perth*. It is Scott's last novel of any consequence, an uneven work which makes no use of environment in depth, though it contains a profoundly sympathetic study of Conachar, the young chieftain 'whose nerves, supported by feelings of honour, or say by the spur of jealousy, support him against constitutional timidity to a certain point, then suddenly give way'.[3] His secret motive in this delineation, as he confessed to Lockhart, 'was to perform a sort of expiation to my poor brother's manes. I have now learnt to have more tolerance and compassion than I had in those days.' His refusal to attend the funeral of his brother Daniel, or even to wear mourning for him, because he had been killed in the West Indies under suspicion of cowardice, had long lain on his mind; now he made amends. It is here, but too late, that Scott begins to touch the theme of true tragedy; he is too ill to dig deep and the novel remains, like all those others removed from his own time, an adventurous romance whose sources are books rather than his own experience or the anecdotes of the living.

Scott's historical fiction is generated from the interfusion of locality with occasion at specific periods, with a central figure whose birth, family and education render him a victim, or at least a very vulnerable traveller in an alien, rapidly changing world. This is particularly true of Waverley, of Jeanie Deans, and of Darsie Latimer, as well as of Frank Osbaldistone, though in his case the result is less successful. In all of these the author, a Scot of uneasy allegiance, attempts the impossible though often-tried feat of seeing the future in the past. Historically in Scotland personal relationships were established on the basis of intimate ties of kinship and the possession of land, ties that only grew stronger under increasing pressure to change from an alien southern culture; in the circumstances it was natural that many of Scott's contemporaries should see their future largely in terms of a benevolent feudalism. The tradition is encapsulated in the old Scots phrase 'of that Ilk', which indicates that the person named has the same surname as his property or title. Chrystal Croftangry, for example, the fictional collector of Chronicles of the Canongate, settles in Edinburgh at a place called Littlecroft; 'we have dubbed it Little Croftangry, and the men of letters belonging to the Post Office have sanctioned the change, and deliver letters so addressed. Thus I am to all intents and purposes Chrystal Croftangry of that Ilk'.[5] The close connection of surname, land and dwelling permeates Scottish history and can be most clearly seen in such Border Ballads as Jock o' the Side and Kinmont Willie.

But the cultural dilemma in which the members of Scott's generation found themselves was a genuine one and the cleaving to an obsolete feudalism, though tenable by an individual landlord in the management of his own estate, as with Scott and Abbotsford, can in no way be regarded as the basis of a categorical imperative by means of which the security and future happiness of Scotland would be ensured. Scott was shy of commerce, and the world of hard trading and the financial reward or failure that may come of buying and selling take on only a shadowy existence, often presented in equivocal terms, in his novels; this is the world of Frank Osbaldistone's father which the romantic hero despises, the world of Joshua Geddes's modern fisheries, the world of Sir William Ashton. It is a world, moreover, shared by the Mucklebackits, by Douce Davie Deans and by Triptolemus Yellowley in their different ways. When Scott himself ventured outside the virtually self-contained social frameworks of paternalistic Abbotsford or legal Edinburgh he stepped into the world of commercial publishing with its own structures, economic constraints and business morality; there he fell into a financial maelstrom for which his romantic view of life left him wholly unprepared. His noble solution to bankruptcy was to pay his creditors honourably and fully by working himself to death—'my own right hand shall do it'[6]—in a pathetically quixotic gesture 'for the credit o' the hoose', worthy, were it not so melancholy, of Caleb Balderstone himself.

What Scott discovered in practice was what he had always known in theory: that in a certain type of man, in a certain type of society, strong, well-nourished roots are essential to survival. These one can find only in the history and traditions of an organic community and in such societies Scott was at home. Commercial society is by its nature rootless, shifting, trading allegiance as well as goods for cash as part of its accepted ethic. It was in this absence of community and tradition from the new English power now dominating Scotland that Scott felt so deeply deprived. The social asphyxia that runs through the major novels I have discussed is inescapable; as for Scott, so for Scotland.

The bewildering experience of looking both before and after simultaneously is a theme on which Scott composes many variations. Characters 'of rank and status', whom he always sees as a race apart and gifted by heredity both intellectually and morally, keep their eyes firmly averted from the British present and see only Scotland's past; their loyalty is owed to family and chieftain not to nation and king, and the ensuing dilemma as in *Waverley* (an appropriate, vacillating name) and *Rob Roy*, is sometimes resolved by a conventional marriage which overrides or conveniently ignores the cultural incompatibility of the two nations as they have been presented in the narrative of events before such a Gordian *dénouement*. This is really a throwing up of the difficulty unsolved, though Scott indirectly but certainly admits its intractability in the conclusion of *The Bride of Lammermoor*, with an ending of total despair for Scotland and an incipient but undesired hope for the new English ways.

Only the common folk have developed methods of survival which do not depend for their success on a retrospective submissiveness. For the

Mucklebackits this consists in the daily performance of a task, the fulfilment of hardly acquired skills through the dual agencies of family and locality. 'Folk maun live', says Steenie's father simply, as he clouts his damaged boat on the day of his drowned son's funeral. The villagers of Wolf's Hope survive through their acquisition, by means of the law rather than of the strong arm, of land; this is simultaneously the acquisition of a freedom hitherto denied them by their lords as being unnecessary, and the means are made possible by Davie Dingwall ('the breaker down of walls'), Ashton's agent and therefore indirectly representative of English policies. As we have heard from the lips of Mortsheugh the sexton, the common folk of Wolf's-hope have little respect for a system in which they see in their social superiors only an oppressive selfishness. On this occasion the world of trade is not presented as a possible alternative way of life, but a remarkably similar conversation occurs in the seven chapters of lengthy Introductory matter to the first series of *Chronicles of the Canongate*. Chrystal Croftangry, having wasted his substance, returns to his patrimonial estate hoping to repurchase it from its recent owner. He finds that the old house has been demolished and replaced by a modern building, now itself neglected and decaying. He finds too that his mother's old servant, Christie Steele, now keeps an inn on the estate and, unrecognised as he believes, he questions her about what has happened during his long absence while the place was in the hands of Mr Treddles, a business man who, boldly speculating, ultimately became insolvent. Croftangry leads her on as they sit at tea in the Treddles Arms, once his mother's jointure-house.

'That picture is painted on the wood, madam', said I.

'Ay, sir, or it's like it would not have been left there;—they took a' they could.'

'Mr Treddles's creditors, you mean?' said I.

'Na', replied she drily, 'the creditors of another family, that sweep it cleaner than this poor man's, because I fancy there was less to gather.'

'An older family, perhaps, and probably more remembered and regretted than later possessors?'....

...'Mair regretted—mair missed?—I liked ane o' the auld family very weel, but I winna say that for them a'. How should they be mair missed than the Treddleses? The cotton mill was such a thing for the country! The mair bairns a cottar body had the better; they would make their awn keep frae the time they were five years auld; and a widow wi' three or four bairns was a wealthy woman in the time of the Treddleses.'

'But the health of these poor children, my good friend—their education and religious instruction'—

'For health', said Christie, looking gloomily at me, 'ye maun ken
little of the warld, sir, if ye dinna ken that the health of the poor
man's body, as weel as his youth and his strength, are all at the
command of the rich man's purse. There never was a trade so un-
healthy yet, but men would fight to get wark at it for twa pennies a
day aboon the common wage. But the bairns were reasonably well
cared for in the way of air and exercise, and a very responsible youth
heard them in their carritch, and gied them lessons in Reediemadeasy.
Now what did they ever get before? Maybe on a winter day they wad
be called out to beat the wood for cocks or siclike, and then the
starving weans would maybe get a bite of broken bread, and maybe no,
just as the butler was in humour—that was a' they got.'   (Ch. IV)

Scott can see the future clearly enough, even through the back of his
head; he simply wishes not to look at a large part of it. The psychological
insights embodied in the character of Conachar, the social awareness in
The Antiquary, *The Heart of Midlothian*, *The Bride of Lammermoor*,
even the political melancholy of *Waverley* and *Redgauntlet*, all point a
finger ahead, like the Ghost of Christmas Yet to Come: ' "Men's courses
will foreshadow certain ends, to which, if persevered in, they must lead,'
said Scrooge. 'But if the courses be departed from, the ends will change.
Say it is thus with what you show me!" ' It might have been Scott.

The themes are never developed after 1824; Scott's fictional history
even with Scottish subject matter grows bookish and laboured. 'The great
effort of *Redgauntlet*', John Buchan observed, 'seems to have impoverished his imagination.'[7] In this he was kinder than Coleridge but
Coleridge was the more grieved; in his *Table Talk* he records 'When I am
very ill indeed, I can read Scott's novels, and they are almost the only
books I can then *read*.'[8] But he wrote to his nephew, the Rev. Edward
Coleridge:

My judgement is in perfect coincidence with your remarks on Sir
Walter; and when I think of the wretched trash, that the Lust of Gain
enduced him to publish for the last three or four years, which must
have been manufactured for the greater part, even my feelings assist
in hardening me. I should indeed be sorry if any ultimate success had
attended the attempt to unite the Poet and the Worldling. Heaven
knows! I have enough to feel for without wasting my Sympathy on a
Scotchman suffering the penalty of his Scotchery. In whatever remote
corner of recluse life a man may hide himself, and however unworldly
and 'unpartaking in the evil thing' he and all his pursuits may be, the

calamity of the World's frenzies will hunt him out! I am at this moment heart-sick with fruitless anguish from the ruin of a man who loved me as a Father; but whom I had in vain sought to defascinate.[9]

Scott laid strong foundations, not only for the future of the historical novel but in the use of total landscape as a medium of literary communication, enriching and deepening rather than merely embellishing his themes.

In these things he was a true makar.

Notes

Reference is made to the following editions of standard works:

LOCKHART, J. G. *Narrative of the Life of Sir Walter Scott, Bart.* (London 1900), 5 vols.
SCOTT, SIR W. *Minstrelsy of the Scottish Border*, ed. T. Henderson (London 1931)
SCOTT, SIR W. *The Letters of Sir Walter Scott*, ed. H. J. C. Grierson (London 1932–7), 12 vols.
SCOTT, SIR W. *The Journal of Sir Walter Scott*, ed. W. E. K. Anderson (Oxford 1972)

For Scott's *Introductions*, and Andrew Lang's comments, I have used The Border Edition of *The Waverley Novels*, edited by Andrew Lang (London 1894), 48 vols.

INTRODUCTION

1 J. H. Raleigh, 'What Scott meant to the Victorians'.
2 *Literary Studies*, ii, 147.
3 Lockhart, i, 14, 20, 67.
4 *Yarrow Revisited, and other Poems*, 1831.
5 *The Speaker*, 12 November 1904.
6 *After Strange Gods*, 1934. See T. S. Eliot, *Selected Prose*, ed. J. Hayward (London 1953), p. 196.
7 *Edinburgh: Picturesque Notes*, iv. 1878.

CHAPTER I

1 *The Early Letters of William and Dorothy Wordsworth, 1787–1805*, p. 493.
2 'Lines composed a few miles above Tintern Abbey, on revisiting the banks of the Wye during a tour, July 13, 1798.'
3 *The Lady of the Lake*, London, 1904. Notes by Andrew Lang. Topographical notes by Sir G. C. Airy, K.C.B., Astronomer Royal.
4 *Lives of the Novelists*, p. 175. See also I. Williams (ed.), *Sir Walter Scott on Novelists and Fiction*, p. 83
5 Lockhart, i, 39.
6 *Table Talk*, 4 August 1833.
7 *Sir Tristrem*, Introduction.
8 Lockhart, v. 421.
9 *Letters*, i, 18.
10 Lockhart, i, 34.
11 *Letters*, i, 24. The term 'effect piece' has no fixed technical meaning, and here refers simply to a landscape view incorporating dramatic effects of climate, such as rainbows, storm-clouds, rain and wind, in conjunction with 'savagely romantic' scenery. I am indebted for this information to Mr Andrew Wilton of the British Museum Department of Prints and Drawings.
12 See John Butt, *The Augustan Age*, p. 79.
13 William Gilpin, *Three Essays on Picturesque Beauty*, p. 46.
14 *Letters*, vii, 97. Sydney Smith quoted by Scott in a letter to Lord Montagu.
15 See Manwaring, p. 186.

N

16 Ibid., p. 186.
17 Lockhart, iv, 211.
18 One of the roads constructed by General Wade after the Jacobite rebellion of 1745.
19 *Three Essays on Picturesque Beauty*, p. 55.
20 *Amwell, a Descriptive Poem*, 1776.
21 *The Prelude* (1805) XI, 146ff.
22 *Letters*, i, 120.
23 *Letters*, i, 146. The quotation is from Coleridge's 'Love', 1799.
24 *A Philosophical Inquiry into the Origin of Our Ideas of the Sublime and Beautiful*, iv.ii.
25 See Scott, 'On Landscape Gardening', *Quarterly Review*, March, 1828. *Miscellaneous Prose Works*, vol. xxi.
26 *Letters*, iii, 239.
27 See Scott's Introductory Memoir to his edition of Dryden.
28 William Mason, *The English Garden*, 1772.
29 *Recollections*, p. 89.
30 Ibid., p. 97.
31 'Some Notes on Sir Walter Scott', p. 9.
32 W. H. Auden, *New Year Letter*, 1941.

CHAPTER II

1 Byron, *Journal*, 24 November 1813.
2 *Letters*, viii, 59.
3 *Letters*, ii, 406–8.
4 *Minstrelsy of the Scottish Border*, Introduction, p. 70.
5 *Letters*, iii, 457.
6 Sir Richard Maitland, 'Complaynt Aganis the Theivis of Liddisdaill'.
7 See Scott's 1830 Introduction.
8. Ibid.
9 Lockhart, i, 352.
10 *The Early Letters of William and Dorothy Wordsworth*, pp. 533–4.
11 *Letters*, i, 240.
12 Carey, *Memoirs*, pp. 52–3.
13 *Calendar of Border Papers*, ii, p. 391. Perhaps by Robert Carey.
14 'The Pleasures of Melancholy', 1747.
15 *Letters*, viii, 387.
16 An error. The Borthwick of IV.xxvii refers to the man who cast the guns, not to the castle.
17 Lockhart, i, 470.
18 See also Scott: 'A general account of Edinburgh', *Provincial Antiquities* in *Miscellaneous Prose*, vii, 250.
19 To Wordsworth, 1810. *Collected Letters of S. T. Coleridge*, ed. E. L. Griggs, p. 292.
20 See T. C. Smout, *A History of the Scottish People*, p. 39.
21 See H. G. Graham, *Social Life of Scotland in the Eighteenth Century*, i, 119–20 vi.
22 *Jeffrey's Essays from the Edinburgh Review*, p. 162.
23 *Preface to Lyrical Ballads*, 2nd edn. 1801.

CHAPTER III

1 These are the novels, with date of publication and, in parenthesis, period of action:
1814 *Waverley* (1745–6)
1815 *Guy Mannering* (1760–82)

1816 *The Antiquary* (1790s)
1817 *Rob Roy* (1715–16)
1818 *The Heart of Midlothian* (1736–7)
1819 *The Bride of Lammermoor* (1700–11)
1821 *The Pirate* (c. 1700)
1824 *Redgauntlet* (1766)
1827 *The Highland Widow* (c. 1766)

2 Lockhart, i, 112.
3 *Tales of a Grandfather*, ii, 73.
4 *The Historical Novel*, p. 53.
5 Lockhart, i, 460.
6 *Letters*, iii, 302.
7 *The Jacobite Movement: The First Phase*, p. 160.
8 *Letters*, iii, 454.
9 *Letters*, iii, 465.
10 *Letters*, iii, 477.

CHAPTER IV

1 *Letters*, iv, 12–13.
2 Lockhart, ii, 502.
3 Lockhart, ii, 491.
4 Lockhart, ii, Appendix prints the entire ballad, as it was 'taken down from the recitation of Mrs Young of Castle-Douglas, who, as her family informed Mr Train, had long been in the habit of repeating it over to them once in the year, in order that it might not escape from her memory'.
5 *Letters*, iii, 225–6, 275–8.
6 Crockett, *The Scott Originals*, p. 107.
7 *Journal*, 4 November 1827. Lockhart, v, 156.
8 Jacques Callot (1592–1635). Scott has in mind here a set of etchings of 1621, *Les Bohémiens*.
9 Introduction to *Guy Mannering*.
10 Lord Gardenstone to his tenants at Laurencekirk, Kincardineshire, 1779. See T. C. Smout, *A History of the Scottish People*, p. 263.
11 Lockhart, iii, 62.
12 Lockhart, iv, 295.
13 Quoted by J. H. Raleigh, 'What Scott Meant to the Victorians'.
14 R. C. Gordon, *Under Which King?*, p. 34.
15 Smout, op. cit., pp. 344–5. His quotation is from E. Burt, *Letters from a Gentleman in the North of Scotland*.
16 *Memorials of his Time*, p. 13.
17 Lockhart, iii, 495.

CHAPTER V

1 *Sir Walter Scott*, p. 140.
2 Lockhart, iii, 63. The title refers to the uncompleted catalogue of Scott's Abbotsford collection, which he began in 1830. A *trotcosie* is a kind of hooded cape, usually of wool, it is the garment Ebenezer Cruickshanks wears when he conducts Waverley towards Perth (*Waverley*, Ch. XXIX).
3 *Letters*, iv, 145.
4 *Letters*, iv, 233.
5 Lockhart, iii, 64. See also Scott's Introduction to *Chronicles of the Canongate*, and his letter to Constable, 28 May 1822, *Letters*, vii, 178.
6 Incest as a theme dear to the Romantics is discussed by Mario Praz in *The Romantic Agony* (London 1933).

7 *Boswell's Life of Johnson*, ii, 211 (London 1904). Text of 1799.
8 Lockhart, i, 126.
9 R. Bage, *Hermsprong* (London 1951), Ch. VI.
10 *Letters*, ii, 287.
11 *Journal*, 18 December 1825.
12 Advertisement 1829.

CHAPTER VI

1 Lockhart, v, 187–8.
2 *Letters*, iv, 291–2.
3 *Letters*, iv, 293.
4 Virginia Woolf, *A Writer's Diary* (London 1954), p. 42.
5 *Letters*, v, 50.
6 Ibid.
7 Introduction to *Chronicles of the Canongate*.
8 In 1730, in Stirlingshire, the best ploughman, living with the farmer, had 35s. a year; female servants had 13/4. In 1740, house servants at Gordonston were paid: 'Two gentlemen, £10; five maids, £5.6.4; two cooks, £5; two porters, £3; groom, £5.5s.' See H. G. Graham, *Social Life of Scotland in the Eighteenth Century*, i, 60, 183n.
9 Ibid. ii, 223n. The theme is taken up in John Galt's *The Provost* (1822) Ch. IX, where Jeanie Gaisling is executed for such an offence. The period is 1778.
10 Ibid. ii, 223–4.
11 'An Address of Thanks from the Society of Rakes ...' *The Works of Allan Ramsay*, ed. A. M. Kinghorn and Alexander Law. vol. iii (Scottish Text Society 1961).
12 Lockhart, v, 443, 445, 447.
13 Lord Cockburn, *Memorials of His Time*, Ch. IV.
14 See M. C. Randolph, 'Diamond-Satires in the Eighteenth Century', *Notes and Queries*, 31 July 1943.
15 The manse of a country minister in the early eighteenth century was a poor place; small, low-roofed, sometimes thatched with heather, 'with brew-house on one side and stable and byre on the other, facing a dunghill which stood amongst the rubbish and nettles'. H. G. Graham, op. cit., ii, 14–15.
16 *Lives of the Novelists*, p. 270; See also I. Williams (ed.) *Sir Walter Scott on Novelists and Fiction*, pp. 141–2.

CHAPTER VII

1 Lockhart, iii, 294.
2 See Ch. XXVII.
3 Introduction to *Chronicles of the Canongate*.

CHAPTER VIII

1 *Ivanhoe* (December 1819).
 The Monastery (March 1820).
 The Abbot (September 1820).
 Kenilworth (January 1821).
 The Pirate (December 1821).
2 *Letters*, v, 420.
3 Lockhart, iii, 306.
4 *Letters*, vi, 115. A note gives Lady Stuart's comments.
5 Lockhart, iii, 353.
6 *Literary Studies*, 'The Waverley Novels'.

7 *Under Which King?*, p. 120.
8 *Letters*, vi, 160.
9 Lockhart, i, 113. The poem was first published in Evans's *Old Ballads*, iv, 1784, with this spelling which I have restored from Lockhart's regularisation. The ballad style obviously appealed to Scott.
10 Pálsson and Edwards, p. 11.
11 Lockhart, i, 129, 150.
12 Lockhart, iv (Chs. 28–33).
13 In his *Confessions of a Justified Sinner*, 1824.
14 *Sir Walter Scott*, ii, 821.
15 *Sir Walter Scott*, p. 245.

CHAPTER IX

1 Published respectively May 1822; January 1823; June 1823.
2 *Letters*, viii, 203.
3 28 July 1826.
4 *Sir Walter Scott*, p. 261.
5 David Douglas, *Familiar Letters of Sir Walter Scott*, ii, 208.
6 See for example Lockhart, iv, 144; David Daiches, 'Scott's *Redgauntlet*'.
7 Andrew Lang, Introduction to *Redgauntlet* in the Border Edition of the Waverley Novels.
8 Cockburn, *Memorials of his Time*, Ch. I.

CHAPTER X

1 *The Betrothed*; *The Talisman* (1825)
Woodstock (1826)
The Surgeon's Daughter (1827)
The Fair Maid of Perth (1828)
Anne of Geierstein (1829)
Count Robert of Paris; *Castle Dangerous* (1832).
2 27 May 1826.
3 Preface, 1831.
4 Lockhart, v, 187–8.
5 Introductory, Ch. V.
6 *Journal*, 22 January 1826.
7 *Sir Walter Scott*, p. 269.
8 1 November 1833.
9 E. L. Griggs (ed.), *Unpublished Letters of S. T. Coleridge*, ii, 402. The phrase quoted is from Coleridge's 'Ode on the Departing Year'.

Select Bibliography

Abbreviations:

E.A.P.	English Association Pamphlet
E.C.	*Essays in Criticism*
H.A.S.	Proceedings of the Hawick Archaeological Society
M.L.R.	*Modern Language Review*
P.S.A.S.	Proceedings of the Scottish Antiquarian Society
R.E.L.	*Review of English Literature*
R.E.S.	*Review of English Studies*
S.H.R.	*Scottish Historical Review*

ALLEN, W. *The English Novel* (London 1954)

ANDERSON, J. (ed.) *The Orkneyinga Saga* (Edinburgh 1873)

ARBUCKLE, W. F. 'The Gowrie Conspiracy' (S.H.R. xxxvi 1957)

BAGEHOT, W. 'The Waverley Novels' in *Literary Studies* (London 1911), 2 vols.

BAIN, J. (ed.) *Calendar of Border Papers* (Edinburgh 1894–6), 2 vols.

BALL, M. *Sir Walter Scott as a Critic of Literature* (New York 1907)

BARKER, P. *Journal of a Traveller in Scotland 1795–1796* (S.H.R. xxxvi 1957)

BARRELL, J. *The Idea of Landscape and the Sense of Place* (Cambridge 1972)

BATHO, E. 'Scott and the Sagas' (M.L.R. xxiv 1929)

BELL, A. (ed.) *Scott Bicentenary Essays* (Edinburgh 1973)

BIGGINS, D. ' "Measure for Measure" and *The Heart of Midlothian*' (*Etudes Anglaises* xiv 1961)

BOSWELL, J. *Boswell's Life of Johnson* (London 1904)

—. *Journal of a Tour to the Hebrides*, ed. R. W. Chapman (Oxford 1930)

BRAND, J. *Observations on Popular Antiquities* (London 1913)

BROWN, P. H. *Early Travellers in Scotland* (Edinburgh 1891)

BUCHAN, J. *Sir Walter Scott* (London 1932)

—. 'Some Notes on Sir Walter Scott' (E.A.P. No. 58 1924)

BURKE, E. *A Philosophical Inquiry into the Origin of Our Ideas On the Sublime and Beautiful 1756* (Oxford 1906)

BURRELL, S. A. 'The Apocalyptic Vision of the Early Covenanters' (S.H.R. xliii 1964)

BURT, E. *Letters from a Gentleman in the North of Scotland* (London 1754)

BUTT, J. *The Augustan Age* (London 1950)

BYRON, Lord. *The Works of Lord Byron: Letters and Journals*, ed R. E. Prothero (London 1898–1901

CAREY, R. *The Memoirs of Robert Carey*, ed. F. H. Mares (Oxford 1972)

CARLYLE, A. *Anecdotes and Characters of the Times* (Oxford 1973)

CARLYLE, T. 'Sir Walter Scott' in *Miscellaneous Essays*, vol. vi (London 1869)

CARSWELL, D. *Sir Walter* (London 1930)

COCKBURN, Lord. *Memorials of his Time*, ed. W. Forbes Gray (Edinburgh 1945)

COCKSHUT, A. O. J. *The Achievement of Walter Scott* (London 1969)

COHEN, R. *The Art of Discrimination* (London 1964)

COLERIDGE, S. T. *Collected Letters of S. T. Coleridge*, ed. E. L. Griggs (Oxford 1956–71), 6 vols.

—. *Unpublished Letters of S. T. Coleridge*, ed. E. L. Griggs (London 1962), 2 vols.

COMBE, W. *Dr Syntax's Three Tours* (London 1876)

CORSON, J. C. *A Bibliography of Sir Walter Scott* (New York 1968)

CRAIG, D. *Scottish Literature and the Scottish People* (London 1961)

—. '*Heart of Midlothian*: Its Religious Basis' (E.C. viii 1958)

CRAWFORD, T. *Scott* (London 1965)

—. 'Scott as a Poet" (*Etudes Anglaises* xxiv 1971)

CROCKETT, W. S. *The Scott Country* (London 1905)

—. *In the Border Country* (London 1906)

—. *The Scott Originals* (London 1912)

DAICHES, D. *Sir Walter Scott and his World* (London 1971)

—. *Charles Edward Stuart* (London 1974)

—. 'Scott's Achievement as a Novelist' in *Literary Essays* (Edinburgh 1956)

—. 'Scott's *Redgauntlet*' in *From Jane Austen to Joseph Conrad* (Minneapolis 1958)

DAVIE, D. 'Scott as a Poet' (Proceedings of the British Academy 1961)

—. *The Heyday of Sir Walter Scott* (London 1961)

DEANE, C. V. *Aspects of Eighteenth-Century Nature Poetry* (Oxford 1935)

DEVLIN, D. D. *The Author of Waverley* (London 1971)

DONALDSON, G. *The Scottish Reformation* (Cambridge 1960)

—. *Scotland: Church and Nation through Sixteen Centuries* (London 1960)

—. *Scotland: James V to James VII* (Edinburgh 1965)

DONOVAN, R. A. *The Shaping Vision* (New York 1966)

DOUGLAS, F. *Gold at Wolf's Crag* (Edinburgh 1971)

DOUGLAS, W. 'Fast Castle and its Owners' (P.S.A.S. IV 5th ser. vii)

FERGUSON, W. *Scotland, 1689 to the Present* (Edinburgh 1968)

FISHER, P. F. 'Providence, Fate, and the Historical Imagination in *Heart of Midlothian*' (*Nineteenth Century Fiction* x 1955)

FLEISHMAN, A. *The English Historical Novel* (Baltimore 1971)

FORDUN, J. *Scotichronicon* (Oxford 1722)

FORSTER, E. M. *Aspects of the Novel* (London 1927)

FRANKLIN, T. B. *A History of Scottish Farming* (Edinburgh 1952)

GILPIN, W. *Three Essays on Picturesque Beauty* (London 1792)

GORDON, K. 'The Illustration of Sir Walter Scott' (*Journal of the Warburg and Courtauld Institute* xxxiv 1971)

GORDON, R. C. *Under Which King?* (Edinburgh 1969)

GRAHAM, H. G. *The Social Life of Scotland in the Eighteenth Century* (London 1899), 2 vols.

GRIERSON, H. J. C. *Sir Walter Scott Bart.* (London 1938)

HALDANE, A. R. B. *The Drove Roads of Scotland* (Newton Abbot 1973)

HAZLITT, W. *Lectures on the English Poets* (Oxford 1924)

HIBBERT, S. *A Description of the Zetland Islands* (Edinburgh 1822)

HILLHOUSE, J. T. *The Waverley Novels and their Critics* (London 1936)

HOGG, J. *Familiar Anecdotes of Sir Walter Scott*, ed. D. S. Mack (Edinburgh 1972)

HOLCOMB, A. M. 'Turner and Scott' (*Journal of the Warburg and Courtauld Institute* xxxiv 1971)

JACK, I. *English Literature 1815–1832* (London 1963)

JEFFARES, A. N. (ed.) *Scott's Mind and Art* (Edinburgh 1969)

JEFFREY, F. *Jeffrey's Literary Criticism*, ed. D. Nicol Smith (London 1910)

—. *Jeffrey's Essays from the Edinburgh Review, i, English Poets and Poetry* (London n.d.)

JERNINGHAM, H. E. H. *Norham Castle* (Edinburgh 1883)

JOHNSON, E. *Sir Walter Scott: The Great Unknown* (London 1970), 2 vols.

JOHNSON, S. *A Journey to the Western Islands*, ed. R. W. Chapman (Oxford 1930)

KETTLE, A. C. *An Introduction to the English Novel* (London 1951), 2 vols.

KIELY, R. *The Romantic Novel in England* (Cambridge, Mass. 1972)

LAIDLAW, W. 'Recollections of Sir Walter Scott' (H.A.S. December 1871)

LANG, A. *Pickle the Spy* (London 1897)

LASCELLES, M. 'Scott and the Art of Revision' in *Imagined Worlds* (ed. I. Gregor and M. Mack) (London 1968)

LOCKHART, J. G. *Narrative of the Life of Sir Walter Scott, Bart.* (London 1900), 5 vols.

LUKÁCS, G. *The Historical Novel*, Trans. H. and S. Mitchell (London 1962)

MANWARING, E. W. *Italian Landscape in Eighteenth Century England* (reprinted London 1965)

MAYHEAD, R. *Walter Scott* (Cambridge 1973)

MCCOMBIE, F. 'Scott, Hamlet and The Bride of Lammermoor' (E.C. xxv 1975)

MCLUHAN, H. M. 'Tennyson and Picturesque Poetry' (E.C. i 1951)

MITCHELL, A. and CASH, G. *A Bibliography of Scottish Topography* (Edinburgh 1917), 2 vols.

MUIR, E. *Scott and Scotland* (London 1936)

NICOLSON, J. R. *Shetland* (Newton Abbot 1972)

OLCOTT, C. S. *The Country of Sir Walter Scott* (London 1913)

OMAN, C. *The Wizard of the North* (London 1973)

PAGE, N. *Speech in the English Novel* (London 1973)

PALGRAVE, F. T. *Landscape in Poetry from Homer to Tennyson* (London 1897)

PÁLSSON, H. and EDWARDS, P. (eds.) *The Eyrbyggia Saga* (Edinburgh 1973)

PARSONS, C. O. 'The Dalrymple Legend in The Bride of Lammermoor' (R.E.S. xix 1943)

PEARSON, H. *Walter Scott* (London 1954)

PENNANT, T. *A Tour in Scotland in 1769* (London 1771)

PETRIE, SIR C. *The Jacobite Movement: The First Phase* (London 1948)

PIKE, B. A. 'Scott as a Pessimist: A View of St Ronan's Well' (R.E.L. vii 1966)

POPE-HENNESSY, U. Sir Walter Scott (London 1948)

PRITCHETT, V. S. The Living Novel (London 1946)

QUAYLE, E. The Ruin of Sir Walter Scott (London 1968)

RALEIGH, J. H. 'What Scott Meant to the Victorians' (Victorian Studies vii 1963)

RENWICK, W. L. English Literature 1789–1815 (Oxford 1963)

RUBENSTEIN, J. Sir Walter Scott: A Reference Guide (London 1978)

SCOTT, SIR WALTER. The Letters of Sir Walter Scott 1787–1832 (ed. H. J. C. Grierson) (London 1932–37), 12 vols.

—. The Journal of Sir Walter Scott, ed. W. E. K. Anderson (Oxford 1972)

—. Provincial Antiquities and Picturesque Scenery of Scotland (Edinburgh 1825–6), 2 vols. Text reprinted in Miscellaneous Prose Works, vol. vii.

—. Border Antiquities (London 1889)

—. Tales of a Grandfather, ed. F. W. Farrar (Edinburgh 1888), 2 vols.

—. Lives of the Novelists (Oxford 1906)

—. Poetical Works (Oxford 1906)

—. Minstrelsy of the Scottish Border, ed. T. Henderson (London 1931)

—. (ed.). Sir Tristrem (Edinburgh 1848)

—. The Miscellaneous Prose Works (Edinburgh 1851–7), 28 vols.

—. The Private Letter Books of Sir Walter Scott, ed. W. Partington (London 1930)

—. Sir Walter's Postbag, ed. W. Partington (London 1932)

SMITH, D. NICOL. 'The Poetry of Sir Walter Scott' (University of Edinburgh Journal 1949–51)

SMOUT, T. C. A History of the Scottish People (1560–1830 (London 1969)

SOUTHEY, R. Journal of a Tour in Scotland in 1879 (Edinburgh 1972)

STEVENSON, R. L. Edinburgh: Picturesque Notes (London 1879)

STUART, D. M. 'Sir Walter Scott, some centenary reflections' (E.A.P. No. 39. 1934)

TAYLOR, A. B. (ed.) The Orkneyinga Saga (Edinburgh 1938)

TREVELYAN, G. M. A Layman's Love of Letters (Cambridge 1953)

TREVOR-ROPER, H. R. The Romantic Movement and the Study of History (London 1969)

WATSON, S. R. Picturesque Landscape and English Romantic Poetry (London 1970)

WELSH, A. The Hero of the Waverley Novels (New Haven, Conn. 1963)

WILLIAMS, I. (ed.) Sir Walter Scott on Novelists and Fiction (London 1968)

WILLIAMS, R. The Country and the City (London 1973)

WITTIG, K. The Scottish Tradition in Literature (Edinburgh 1958)

WORDSWORTH, D. Recollections of a Tour Made in Scotland, 1803 (Edinburgh 1974)

WORDSWORTH, W. Guide to the Lakes, ed. E. de Selincourt (Oxford 1970)

—. The Early Letters of William and Dorothy Wordsworth, 1787–1805, ed. E. de Selincourt (Oxford 1935)

YOUNGSON, A. J. The Making of Classical Edinburgh (Edinburgh 1966)

Glossary

augurale: part of Roman camp where a General took auguries
auld: old
awmous: alms
ayont: beyond
baith: both
bale: blaze, bonfire
bannock-fluke: turbot
bedral: sexton
beerys: biers
beinly: happily, comfortably
bield: shelter
big(g): build
birkie: lively lad
blaw: blow
blithe: cheerful
boddle: two pence Scots; one sixth of an English penny
brae: hillside
braw: fine, handsome
brod: offertory plate at church door
buirdly: stalwart
busk: dress flies for fishing
ca': call
carle: old man
carritch: catechism
cateran: Highland robber, freebooter
chaumer: chamber
chumlay: chimney
clarty: dirty, muddy
cleikum: a shepherd's crook
clout: mend
cock-padle: lump-fish
corbie: carrion crow, raven
coronach: lament, dirge
cracks: tales, talk
craig: crag
craw: crow
creagh: Highland raid
cuif: simple
curch: kerchief
cusser: stallion
daud: piece
decuman: main gate of Roman camp
deil ane: not one
ding: dash down
div: do

dollar: five shilling piece
douce: kind, respectable
dour: hard
een: eyes
fail: turf
fame: reputation
fash: trouble
fend: support, provision
fette: brought
flaughter-spade: two-handed spade for cutting peat
flees: flies
fog: moss
frae: from
gabion: a curiosity of small value
gae: go
gangrel: vagrant
gars: makes
gascromh: a semi-circular trenching spade, with a crooked handle in the middle
gate: way, road
gay: tolerably, reasonably
gie: give
glaiket: senseless, thoughtless
gowden: golden
grieve: farm overseer
gulley: large knife
gytes: brats, kids
ha': room, farm kitchen
hae: have
haill: whole
happed: covered
hastati: spearmen, front line of battle
hause-bane: neck-bone
heugh: deep glen, crag
hinny: honey, dear
hope: hill, sheltered slope, small bay
howf(f): popular inn
ilka: every
kaim: low ridge, fortress
kale: greens
ken: know
kenna: don't know
killogie: open space in front of a kiln fire
kilt: upset

kind-gallows: traditional name of Crieff gallows
kist: chest, coffin
kittle: tickle
kye: cattle
landlouper: vagabond
leev alane: quite alone
mair: more
make: mate
mane: complaint
maud: shepherd's plaid
maun: must
mend: improve on
mind: remember
moss-trooper: Border freebooter
muckle: big, much
muir: moor
neuk: corner seat by the fire
nolt: cattle
ohon: alas
or: before
peer: poor
pele: Border tower
pibroch: bagpipe music
pike: pick
pit: put
plack: four pence Scots, the third part of an English penny
praetorium: commander's quarters
reek: smoke
reft: seized, stole
reifis: plunder
rickle: a loose heap
rive: tear
sae: so
sair: sore, severe
sair failed: sadly deteriorated; cf. the old Northumbrian song, 'Sair Fyeld Hinny'
saugh-tree: willow
scale-stair: straight staircase in contrast to a spiral
sclated: slated
screed: strip
shealing: hut
Sheltie: Shetland pony

sic: such
siller: silver, money
skaithless: unhurt
sneg: cut
snood: headband
soupled: loosened up
spence: larder
stirk: steer, bullock
strath: river valley
suld: should
sunkets: delicacies, food of any kind
tacksman: tenant farmer
tane: one
target: small round shield
thack, theek: thatch
thae: those
thairm: catgut
thegither: together
thrapple: throat
tint: lost
tippence: twopence
tod: fox
triarii: veterans, third line of battle
trock: dealing
udaller: freeholder
unco: extremely, very
usquebaugh: whisky
volites: light, mobile troops
wad: would
ware: give
warstle: wrestle
wastrife: extravagance
water: river; often used in the Borders to denote those who lived along its banks
waur: worse
weans: children
wha: who
wheen; whin: a few
whiles: now and then
whilk: which
winna: will not
yauld: agile
yeald: barren
yestreen: last night

Index

Titles of Scott's novels and poems are to be found in their appropriate alphabetical places; his non-fiction is listed under 'Scott'.